90

3570478000

THE LAWS OF THE
KINGS OF ENGLAND
FROM EDMUND
TO HENRY I

CAMBRIDGE
UNIVERSITY PRESS
LONDON: FETTER LANE

NEW YORK
The Macmillan Co.

BOMBAY, CALCUTTA and
MADRAS
Macmillan and Co., Ltd.

TORONTO
The   Macmillan   Co.   of
Canada, Ltd.

TOKYO
Maruzen-Kabushiki-Kaisha

THE LAWS OF THE KINGS OF ENGLAND FROM EDMUND TO HENRY I

Edited and Translated

by

A. J. ROBERTSON, M.A.

CAMBRIDGE

AT THE UNIVERSITY PRESS

1925

PREFACE

THIS edition of *The Laws of the Kings of England from Edmund to Henry I* has been prepared on the same plan as the preceding volume, *The Laws of the Earliest English Kings*, edited and translated by F. L. Attenborough, Cambridge, 1922. It was at first intended to include in it only the laws of the later Anglo-Saxon period, but it was afterwards thought advisable to add those of William I and Henry I (including the compilation known as the *Leis Willelme*) because of their intimate connection with the period immediately preceding.

In the preparation of this edition much assistance has been derived from Professor Liebermann's monumental work, *Die Gesetze der Angelsachsen*, Halle, 1903–16, and I take this opportunity of expressing my indebtedness to it. In the division and numbering of the sections I have almost invariably followed his example, and I have seldom had occasion to correct his readings; in only one case (I Edgar 2; see Notes) is the interpretation of a passage affected thereby. His work has superseded all previous editions. I have, however, made considerable use of Schmid's second edition, *Die Gesetze der Angelsachsen*, Leipzig, 1858, and have occasionally preferred his interpretation of a passage to that given by Liebermann.

It has been impossible within the limits of a small volume such as this to enter into a detailed discussion of disputed points, and in many cases I have been unable to do more than give references to the work of Liebermann and other authorities on the period. Readers who desire to make a more detailed study are referred to Liebermann's edition which is indispensable for such questions as the history of the texts and their relationship with one another, as well as for the terminology of the laws and Anglo-Saxon legal antiquities in general.

As the preparation of this edition was begun in Cambridge I decided to take as much of my text as possible from the manuscripts most easily accessible, namely those in Corpus Christi College. In addition I have collated the manuscripts in the

British Museum; and in all cases I have examined the originals of the texts given here except those derived from MSS Christina Regina 946 in the Vatican, Rome, and Holkham 228. For the latter, which was unfortunately inaccessible to me, I am indebted to Liebermann's edition and to Matzke, *Les Lois de Guillaume le Conquérant en français et en latin*, 1899; for the former to Liebermann's edition alone.

My thanks are due to all those who have kindly allowed me to consult the manuscripts required at Corpus Christi College, Cambridge, the Bodleian Library and Corpus Christi College, Oxford, Rochester Cathedral, York Minster, St Paul's Cathedral, the John Rylands Library, Manchester, and Keswick Hall, Norwich.

I desire likewise to express my thanks to the Carnegie Trust for their award of a Research Scholarship which I held at Girton College, Cambridge; also to the Syndics of the University Press for undertaking the publication of the book and to the staff for the care with which both the printing and the corrections have been carried out. I am also under great obligations to Mr Attenborough and all those who have helped me in the preparation of this edition. I wish most particularly to express my gratitude to Professor and Mrs Chadwick for their generous assistance; without their inspiration and help it would have been impossible for me to complete such a piece of work.

A. J. R.

February, 1925.

CONTENTS

LIST OF ABBREVIATIONS

1. Anglo-Saxon Manuscripts. (See Liebermann, I. p. xviii ff.)

A......British Museum, Harley 55.

    f. 3 b. II, III Edg.; f. 5. I, II Cn.

B......Corpus Christi College, Cambridge, 383.

    p. 2. I Edg.; p. 3. I Atr.; p. 43. I, II Cn. (beginning at I 14, 2);
    p. 78. I, II Edm.; p. 88. II Atr.

C......Corpus Christi College, Cambridge, 265.

    p. 222. IV Edg.

Cp ...British Museum, Cotton Cleopatra B XIII.

    f. 56. Cor. Oath.

D......Corpus Christi College, Cambridge, 201.

    p. 30. VII Atr.; p. 46. II, III Edg.; p. 48. V Atr.; p. 93. VIII Atr.;
    p. 96. I Edm.; p. 126. Fragments of I, II Cn.; p. 128. VI Atr.
    16–49.

F......British Museum, Cotton Nero E I.

    f. 185 b. IV Edg.

G......British Museum, Cotton Nero A I.

    f. 1. I, II Cn.; f. 41. II, III Edg.; f. 87 b. I Edm. Pre.; f. 88.
    III Edg. (G₂); f. 89. V Atr.; f. 95 b. VIII Atr., 1–5; f. 116 b.
    V Atr. (G₂).

H......Textus Roffensis, Rochester Cathedral.

    f. 44. I, II Edm.; f. 46. 1 Atr.; f. 47. Wl. lad; f. 48. III Atr.

Ju ...Oxford Bodley, Junius 60.

    Cor. Oath copied from British Museum, Cotton Vitellius A VII.

K......British Museum, Cotton Claudius A III.

    f. 33 b. VI Atr.

Vr. ...Vatican, Rome, Christina regina 946.

    f. 75 b. X Atr.

York..Minster Library, Eleventh Century Gospels and other documents.

    f. 152. Cn. 1020.

2. Latin Manuscripts.

    (a)   Containing the Quadripartitus.

        Rs......John Rylands Library, Manchester, 155 (formerly 174).

        K ......British Museum, Cotton Claudius D II.

        Co ......Corpus Christi College, Cambridge, 70.

        Or ......Oriel College, Oxford, 46.

    These four compose the 'London' group (see Liebermann, I. p. xxxiv
    s.v. *Lond.*) and represent the earliest form of the Quadripartitus (see
    ibid. pp. xxxviii, 529).

2. Latin Manuscripts, *continued.*

(a) Containing the Quadripartitus, *continued.*

Dm　...British Museum, Cotton Domitian VIII.

R　......British Museum, Regius 11, B II.

T　......British Museum, Cotton Titus A XXVII.

These three form a group.

Br　......'Johannis Brompton Jorevallensis Chronicon' (see Lieber-mann, I. p. xix), preserved in two fifteenth century MSS—Corpus Christi College, Cambridge, 96 and British Museum, Tiberius C XIII.

Hk......Holkham 228, the property of the Earl of Leicester.

M　......Macro, the property of the Gurney family at Keswick Hall, near Norwich.

These three also form a group.

(b) Containing the Tripartita (see Liebermann, I. p. xli).

Ba......The property of the Marquess of Bath.

Cb......Bibliothèque Nationale, Paris, Lat. 4771.

Gr......Gray's Inn, London, 9.

Hv　...Chronica Rogeri de Hoveden.

Hy　...British Museum, Harley 1348.

La......London Lambeth, 179.

Lb......London Lambeth, 118.

Pe......Swaffham's Register, Peterborough Cathedral.

Ph......Phillipps MS 8079, now Cambridge University, 3392.

Ra......British Museum, Regius 13 A XVIII.

Rc......British Museum, Regius 13 C II.

Va......Vatican, Rome, Christina regina 587.

Vi　......British Museum, Cotton Vitellius A XIII.

A later version is found in Rs, K$_2$ (Cotton Claudius D II), Co, Or.

(c) Miscellaneous.

Ce ....Corpus Christi College, Cambridge, 476.

f. 160. Hn. Lond.

Cust ......Liber Custumarum, Guildhall, London.

f. 13 b. Hn. cor.; f. 14 b. and f. 187. Hn. Lond.

El ....Liber Albus, Guildhall, London.

f. 40. Excerptum from Hn. Lond.

E IV......Patent roll of a. 2 Edward IV, pt 5, Public Record Office, London.

Inspeximus of Hn. Lond.

Gl ....Registrum episcopatus Glasguensis.

f. 25. Hn. cor.

H ....See above.

f. 80. Wl. art.; f. 96. Hn. cor.

2. Latin Manuscripts, *continued.*

   (c) Miscellaneous, *continued.*

       Hg.........British Museum, Hargrave 313.

           f. 99. Wl. art. retr.; Wl. lad; Hn. cor.; f. 100. Hn. mon.;
           Hn. com.

       Hl.........British Museum, Harley 458.

           f. 1. Hn. cor.

       Horn......Liber Horn, Guildhall, London.

           f. 205 b and 362. Wl. Lond.; f. 362 b. Hn. Lond.

       Insp.......Rot. Inspeximus Chartarum, Public Record Office,
           London.

           Ann. 1378. Wl. ep.

       Lc.........Registrum Antiquissimum Remigii, Lincoln Cathedral.

           f. 1 and 9. Wl. ep.

       Lp.........Liber pilosus S. Pauli cathedralis Londoniensis.

           f. 1. Wl. ep.

       Ox.........Corpus Christi College, Oxford, 157.

           p. 329. Cn. 1027.

       Rl.........Oxford Bodley, Rawlinson C 641.

           f. 43. Hn. cor.; f. 44. Wl. art.

       S ....British Museum, Harley 746.

           f. 55 b. Leis Wl.; f. 59. Hn. cor.

       Sc ....Scaccarii Liber Rubeus, Public Record Office, London.

           f. 162 b. Wl. art. retr.; f. 163. Wl. lad; f. 163 b. Hn. cor.,
           Hn. mon.; f. 164. Hn. com.

3. Anglo-French Manuscripts.

      Cu ......Cambridge University Ee I. 1.

          f. 3. Wl. art. (French version).

      Hk......See above.

          f. 141. Leis Wl. (incomplete).

4. Editions (see Liebermann, I. p. xlv f.)

      Ld...............William Lambarde Αρχαιονομια (London, 1568) re-
           published with additions by A. Wheelock (Cambridge,
           1644).

      Wilkins ......*Leges Anglo-Saxonicae,* edited by D. Wilkins (London,
           1721).

      Price   }
           ......An edition of the Laws prepared for the Commissioners
      Thorpe}
           of the Public Records by Richard Price but left un-
           finished at his death and completed by B. Thorpe;
           published under the title of *Ancient Laws and Institutes
           of England* (London, 1840). The references are to the
           octavo edition.

4. Editions, *continued*.

Schmid.........*Die Gesetze der Angelsachsen* by R. Schmid, 1st Edition, Leipzig, 1832; 2nd Edition, 1858. The references are to the second edition.

Liebermann...*Die Gesetze der Angelsachsen* by F. Liebermann (Halle, 1903–1916).

5. Names of Kings.

A. & G....Alfred and Guthrum.

Abt. ....Æthelbert.

Af. ...... Alfred.

As..........Æthelstan.

Atr. ....Æthelred.

Cn. ......Canute.

   Cn. 1020... Canute's Proclamation of 1020.

   Cn. 1027... Canute's Proclamation of 1027.

   Cons. ......Consiliatio Cnuti.

   Inst..........Instituta Cnuti.

E. & G....Edward and Guthrum.

Edg. ......Edgar.

Edm.......Edmund.

Edw.......Edward.

ECf. ......Edward the Confessor.

Hl..........Hlothhere and Eadric.

Hn. ......Henry I.

   Hn. com. ...Decree of Henry I concerning the County and Hundred Courts.

   Hn. cor. ...Coronation Charter of Henry I.

   Hn. Lond....London Charter of Henry I.

   Hn. mon. ...Decree of Henry I concerning the Coinage.

In. ...Ine.

Wi....Wihtred.

Wl....William I.

   Wl. art. ....The Ten Articles of Wm I.

   Wl. art. retr....Willelmi articuli retractati.

   Wl. ep. ....The Episcopal Laws of Wm I.

   Wl. lad ....Regulations regarding Exculpation.

   Wl. Lond. ......The London Charter of Wm I.

   Leis Wl..........The Laws of Wm I.

6. Legal Documents.

Að............*Be Mirciscan Aðe.*

Be Blas......*Be Blaserum and be Morðslihtum.*

Be Griðe ...*Be Griðe and be Munde.*

Be Wer. ...*Be Wergilde.*

6. Legal Documents, *continued.*

    Duns. ......Ordinance with regard to the *Dunsæte.*

    Episcopus...De Officio Episcopi.

    Gepync̆o ...Be Leode Geþinc̆um.

    Had. ....*Hadbot.*

    Jud. Dei ...*Judicium Dei.*

    Lib. Lond....Libertas Londoniensis.

    N.P.L. ......*Norðhymbra Preosta Lagu.*

7. Miscellaneous.

    Birch ....Birch, *Cartularium Saxonicum.*

    Brunner ....Brunner, *Deutsche Rechtsgeschichte.*

    BT. ....Bosworth and Toller, *Anglo-Saxon Dictionary.*

    Davis, *Reg. Agnorm.* ....Davis, *Regesta Regum Anglo-Normannorum.*

    DB ....Domesday Book.

    Du Cange........................Du Cange, *Glossarium.*

    E.H.R. ....English Historical Review.

    H.L.R. ....Harvard Law Review.

    Kemble ....Kemble, *Codex Diplomaticus Aevi Saxonici.*

    P. and M........................Pollock and Maitland, *History of English Law.*

    Stubbs, *Reg. Sacr. Anglic....*Stubbs, *Registrum Sacrum Anglicanum,* Second Edition.

    Thorpe, *Dipl.* ....Thorpe, *Diplomatarium Aevi Saxonici.*

THE LAWS OF EDMUND
AND OF EDGAR

THE LAWS OF EDMUND

THREE SERIES of laws issued by Edmund are extant. Earlier editors, following MSS H and B, regarded I and II Edmund as parts of the same code (cf. II and III Edgar, I and II Canute), but Schmid pointed out that in MS D only I Edmund is given, and Liebermann, arguing from internal evidence (e.g. the existence of a special preamble for II Edmund where the king's name is repeated; see further *Gesetze*, III. p. 125), also supports the view that they are two separate codes.

I Edmund was promulgated at a Council which met at London at Easter. The year cannot be exactly determined, but the earliest possible date, as Liebermann points out, seems to be 942; for it was in that year that Oda became Archbishop of Canterbury (see Stubbs, *Registr. Sacr. Angl.* p. 25). In the year 943 Archbishop Wulfstan supported Anlaf (see *Sax. Chr.* D), but his signature is again affixed to royal documents in 944 (see Kemble, Nos. 399–402; Birch, Nos. 791 f., 794 f., 798 f.), 945 (Birch, 803, 807) and 946 (Kemble, 406, 409; Birch, 816). The code must be referred therefore to the years 942 or 944–6. It is distinctly ecclesiastical in tone and suggests comparison with the *Constitutiones Odonis* (Spelman, *Concilia* I. pp. 415 ff.).

II Edmund offers no evidence as to the time or place of its promulgation. It is notable for its regulations with regard to vendetta, and seems to be closely connected with the fragment entitled *Be Wergilde* (see Notes).

III Edmund likewise contains no indication as to its date, but it was promulgated at *Culinton*, i.e. probably Colyton in Devonshire (see Notes). An oath of allegiance to the king is demanded from all his subjects. It contains also various regulations with regard to theft, the tracking of unknown cattle etc., which are based upon earlier laws, especially II Edward and II–VI Æthelstan.

I Edmund is contained in MSS D (C.C.C. 201), H (Textus Roffensis) and B (C.C.C. 383) as well as in Lambarde's edition and in the Quadripartitus. Part of the preamble is also found in G (Brit. Mus. Cotton Nero A 1). II is found in H and B, in Lambarde's edition and in the Quadripartitus, while III has been preserved only in the Quadripartitus. For the relationship of the various MSS see Liebermann, III. pp. 124, 126, 128.

THE LAWS OF EDGAR

King Edgar is definitely named in the preambles to two series of laws, the first of which consists of two codes, an ecclesiastical and a secular. A fourth code dealing with the administration of the hundred is in general attributed to him also, and referred to as I Edgar. No king's name is mentioned in it, but it is obviously later than the time of Edmund (cf. cap. 2).

The only one of these codes which can be dated with any certainty is IV Edgar. The references which it contains to a severe plague and to Æthelwine and Oslac suggest that it belongs to the year 962 or 963 (see Notes and Liebermann, III. p. 138). Internal evidence (see Notes) shows that it was preceded in time by II and III Edgar, and also by the code to which the title I Edgar is given.

The evidence adduced for attributing this nameless code to Edgar is fully stated and discussed by Liebermann (see III. pp. 130–1). He draws attention to the injunction in III Edg. 5 that the hundred court shall be attended "as has been previously ordained," and notes the connection between III Edg. 7, 1 and cap. 2, 1 of the nameless code. He points out also the entire lack of evidence for the promulgation of any codes of law by either Edred or Edwig, but acknowledges the scantiness of the sources for such evidence. The fact that in IV cap. 2 a Edgar refers to the prerogatives of his father, and makes no mention of his immediate predecessors, is a further, though not very strong, argument in support of the view that neither of these two kings issued any laws. His conclusion, however, is that this nameless code can be dated for certain only between the years 946 and about 961. With the exception of the last two clauses (see Notes) the regulations bear upon the administration of the hundred.

The code divided by editors into II and III Edgar was apparently promulgated at Andover (cf. IV Edg. 1, 4). II deals exclusively with ecclesiastical affairs and particularly with the payment of church dues. It shows resemblances to passages in the so-called Canons enacted under King Edgar (see Thorpe, *Anc. Laws*, II. pp. 244–288). III draws a good deal upon earlier laws, especially I and II Edward and I and II Æthelstan. It contains definite and clearly stated regulations regarding the administration of justice, the meetings of the borough and county courts, the general employment of the surety system, and the establishment of uniform weights and measures.

IV is described not as a *gerædnis* but as a *gewrit* and was issued at a place called *Wihtbordesstan* which has not been satisfactorily identified (see Liebermann, III. p. 139). The style of the code is noteworthy, especially in the first part which deals with ecclesiastical affairs and reads like a homily. The secular half assures autonomy to the Danes, but at the same time enforces the observance of certain regulations in every part of the realm. The secular decrees of Edgar are as a whole notably progressive.

Three copies of I are extant, namely an A.S. text in MS B and two Latin translations in the Quadripartitus and the Consiliatio Cnuti respectively. II and III are preserved in MSS G, A (Brit. Mus. Harley 55), D, in Lambarde's edition and in Somner's transcript, while a Latin translation is found in the Quadripartitus, and a few clauses appear in the Instituta Cnuti. Two A.S. copies of IV are extant in MSS F (Brit. Mus. Cotton Nero E 1) and C (C.C.C. 265, p. 222), both dating from about 1030–60, while a Latin version which follows C is found also in C.C.C. 265, p. 217. For the relationship between the various texts see Liebermann, III. pp. 130, 133 f., 138.

The following text has been taken from MS D in the case of I Edm., II and III Edg.; from MS B in the case of II Edm. and I Edg.; and from MS C in the case of IV Edg.

I EDMUND

Her onginneð Eadmundes gerædnes[1].

Eadmund cyngc gesamnode micelne sinoð to Lundenbirig on
ða halgan easterlican tíd ægðer ge godcundra háda ge world-
cundra; ðar wæs Óda arcebiscop[2] 7 Wulfstan arcebiscop 7
manega oðre biscopas smeagende ymbon heora sawla ræd[3] 7 þara
þe him underþeodde wæron.

1. [Be gehadeda manna clænnisse.][4]

   Ðæt is æres[t][5] þæt hi budon[6], þæt þa halgan hadas þe Godes
   folc læron sculon lifes bisne, ðæt hi heora clænnesse healdan
   be heora hade, swa werhades swa wifhades, swa hwaðer swa
   hit sy. 7 gif hi swa ne don, þonne syn hi þæs wyrðe þe on
   ðam canone cweð, and þæt[7] hi þolian worldæhta 7 gehalgodre legerstowe, buton hi gebetan.

2. [Be teoþungum 7 cyricsceatum.]

   Teoðunge we bebeodað ælcum Cristene[8] men be his Cristen-
   dóme, and ciricsceat 7 Romfeoh 7 sulhælmessan[9]. And gif
   hit hwa don nelle, si he amansumod.

3. [Be monslihte.]

   Gif hwa Cristenes mannes blód ageote, ne cume he na on
   ðæs cyninges neawiste[10], ær he on dædbote ga, swa him biscop
   tæce 7 his scrift him wisige.

4. [Be nunna hæmede 7 forlygre.]

   Se þe wið nunnan hæme, gehalgodre legerstowe ne sy he
   wyrðe—buton he gebete—þe ma þe manslaga; þæt ilce we
   cwædon be æwbrice.

5. [Be cyricena gebetunge.]

   Eac we gecwædon, þæt ælc biscop béte Godes hus on his
   agenum, 7 eac þone cyningc minegige, þæt ealle Godes circan
   syn wel behworfene[11], swa us micel þearf is.

6. [Be mánsworum 7 liblacum.]

   Ða ðe mansweriað 7 liblac wyrcað beon[12] hi a fram ælcum
   Godes dæle aworpene, buton hi to rihtre dædbote gecirran
   þe geornor[13].

---

[1] *Eadmundes cyninges asetnysse* H; om. B.   [2] Om. H, B, Ld.
[3] *saul ared* B; *sawla ared* Ld.
[4] The Rubrics in this code are found in Ld. only.   [5] H, B; *æres* D.
[6] *þ. h. b.* om. H, B, Ld.   [7] *cwæð : ðæt is* H, B, Ld.   [8] *Cristenum* H, B, Ld.
[9] *c.* 7 *ælmesfeoh* H, B, Ld.   [10] *ánsyne* H; *neawæste, gyf he cyninges man sy* B, Ld.
[11] *behweorfene* H; *behwofene* B; *behofene* Ld.
[12] *syn* H, B, Ld.   [13] *þ. g.* om. H, B, Ld.

I EDMUND

Here begins Edmund's ordinance.

King Edmund has convened at London, during the holy season of Easter, a great assembly both of the ecclesiastical and secular estates. Archbishop Oda[1] and Archbishop Wulfstan[2] and many other bishops have there been taking counsel for the welfare of their [own] souls and [the souls] of those who have been placed under their charge.

1. This is their first injunction: that those in holy orders whose duty it is to teach God's people by the example of their life[1] should observe the celibacy befitting their estate, whether they be men or women. If they fail to do so, they shall incur that which is ordained in the canon, and[2] they shall forfeit their worldly possessions and burial in consecrated ground, unless they make amends.

2. We enjoin upon every Christian man, in accordance with his Christian profession, to pay tithes[1] and church-dues[2] and Peter's Pence and plough-alms[3]. And if anyone refuses to do so, he shall be excommunicated.

3. If anyone sheds the blood of a Christian man[1], he shall not come anywhere near[2] the king[3] until he proceeds to do penance, as the bishop appoints for him or[4] his confessor directs him.

4 He who has intercourse with a nun, unless he make amends, shall not be allowed burial in consecrated ground any more than a homicide. We have decreed the same with regard to adultery.

5. Likewise we have ordained that every bishop shall restore[1] the houses of God on his own property[2], and also exhort the king that all God's churches be well put in order, as we have much need [that they be].

6. Those who commit perjury[1] and practise sorcery[2] shall be cast out for ever from the fellowship of God[3], unless they proceed with special zeal to undertake the prescribed penance.

II EDMUND

Eadmund cyning cyð eallum folce, ge yldrum ge gingrum, ðe
on his anwealde syn¹, ðæt ic smeade mid minra witena geðeahte,
ge god[cund]ra hada² ge læwedra, ærest, hu ic mæhte Cristendomes mest aræran.

§ 1. Ðonne ðuhte us ærest mæst ðearf, þæt we ure gesib-
sumnesse 7 geþwærnesse fæstlicost us betweonan
heoldan gynd ealne minne anwald. Me egleð swyðe
7 us eallum ða unrihtlican 7 mænigfealdan gefeoht ðe
betwux us sylfum syndun; ðonne cwæde we:

1. [Be manslihte.]³
Gif hwa heonanforð ænigne man ofslea, þæt he wege sylf ða
fæhðe, butan he hy⁴ mid freonda fylste binnan twelf monðum
forgylde be fullan were, sy swa boren swa he sy.

§ 1. Gyf hine ðonne seo mægð forlæte 7 him foregyldan
nellen, ðonne wille ic þæt eal seo mægð sy unfah, butan
ðam hand[d]ædan⁵, gif⁶ hy him syððan ne doð mete ne
munde.

§ 2. Gif ðonne syððan hwilc his maga hine feormie, ðonne
beo he scyldig ealles ðæs þe he age wið ðone cyning,
7 wege ða fæhðe wið þa mægðe, forðam hi hine forsocan
ær.

§ 3. Gyf ðonne⁷ of ðære [oðre]⁸ mægðe hwa wrace do on
ænigum oðrum men butan on ðam rihthanddædan, sy
he gefah wið ðone cyning 7 wið ealle his frynd 7 ðolie
ealles ðæs he age.

2. [Be ðon ðe mon oþerne on cyricean gesece oþþe on cyninges
burh.]
Gif hwa cyrcan gesece oððe mine burh 7 hine man ðær sece
oððe yflige—ða ðe ðæt don⁹ syn ðæs ylcon scyldige ðe hit
her beforan cweð.

3. [Be fyhtwite 7 manbote.]
7 ic nelle þæt ænig fyhtewite oððe manbot¹⁰ forgifen sy.

---

¹ synd H. ² godra hada B, Ld; hadedra H.
³ The Rubrics in this code are found in Ld. only. ⁴ him Ld.
⁵ H; handædan B, Ld. ⁶ 7 hi Ld.
⁷ hwa ðonne on ðær mægþ wræce dô Ld.
⁸ H. ⁹ doð H. ¹⁰ H; manbote B, Ld.

II EDMUND

I, King Edmund[1], inform all people, both high and low[2], who are under my authority, that I have been considering, with the advice of my councillors both ecclesiastical and lay, first of all how I could best promote Christianity[3].

§ 1. Now, it has seemed to us first of all especially needful that we steadfastly maintain peace and concord among ourselves throughout all my dominion. I myself and all of us are greatly distressed by the manifold illegal deeds of violence which are in our midst[1]. We have therefore decreed:

1. Henceforth, if anyone slay a man, he shall himself [alone] bear the vendetta, unless with the help of his friends he pay composition for it, within twelve months[1], to the full amount of the slain man's wergeld, according to his inherited rank.

   § 1. If, however, his kindred abandon him and will not pay compensation on his behalf, it is my will that, if afterwards they give him neither food nor shelter[1], all the kindred, except the delinquent, shall be free from vendetta.

   § 2. If, however, any of his kinsmen harbour him thereafter, then, inasmuch as they had previously disclaimed him, that kinsman shall forfeit all his property to the king, and shall incur vendetta with the kin [of the slain man].

   § 3. If, however, anyone from the other kindred take vengeance on any man other than the actual delinquent, he shall incur the hostility of the king and of all his friends[1], and shall suffer the loss of all that he possesses.

2[1]. If anyone flees [for sanctuary] to a church or to my premises[2], and anyone attacks or injures him there, those who do so shall incur the penalty[3] which has already been stated.

3. My will is that no fine for fighting[1] or compensation for a slain dependent[2] be remitted.

4. [Be blodgeote.]

Eac ic cyðe, þæt ic nelle socne habban [þone ðe mannes blod geote]¹ to minum hirede, ær he hæbbe g[od]cunde² bote underfangen³ ⁊ wið ða mægðe gebet⁴—on bote befangen— ⁊ to ælcum rihte gebogen, swa biscop him tæce ðe hit on his scyre sy.

5. [Þæncunge ðæm ðe wið ðyfþe fylstaþ.]

Eac ic ðancie Gode ⁊ eow eallum, ðe me fylston⁵, ðæs friðes ðe we nu habbað æt ðam ðyfðam⁶; ðonne gelyfe ic to eow, þæt ge willan fylstan to ðyssum swa micle bet, swa us is eallum mare ðearf ðæt hit gehealden sy.

6. [Be mundbryce ⁊ hamsocne.]

Eac we cwædon be mundbryce ⁊ be hamsocnum: se ðe hit ofer ðis do, þæt he þolie ealles ðæs he age ⁊ sy on cyniges dome hwæðer he lif age.

7. [Be fæhþe.]

Witan scylon fæhðe sectan⁷: ærest æfter folcrihte slaga⁸ sceal his forspecan⁹ on hand syllan ⁊ se forspeca magum, þæt se slaga wille betan wið mægðe.

§ 1. Ðonne syððan gebyreð þæt man sylle ðæs slagan forspecan on hand, þæt se slaga mote mid griðe nyr ⁊ sylf wæres¹⁰ weddian.

§ 2. Ðonne he ðæs beweddad hæbbe, ðone finde he ðærto wæreborh.

§ 3. Ðonne þæt gedon sy, ðonne rære man cyninges munde; of ðam dæge on XXI nihton gylde man healsfang; ðæs on XXI nihton manbote; ðæs on XXI nihton¹¹ ðæs weres ðæt frumgyld.

---

¹ Om. B, H; *þon ðe m. b. geate* Ld.   ² H, Ld; *gec.* B.   ³ H, Ld; *-gan* B.
⁴ *ðam ægðe gebet* B; *þā ægðer gebet* H; *ðæm mægðe gebete* Ld.
⁵ *wel f.* H.   ⁶ *æt ð. ðyfþe gesette* Ld.   ⁷ *settan* Ld.
⁸ Ld; *-rihtes laga* B, H.   ⁹ *forspræcan* Ld.   ¹⁰ *weres* Ld.
¹¹ *nih'* B; *niht* H, Ld.

4[1]. Further, I declare that I forbid anyone [who commits homicide][2] to have right of access[3] to my household, until he has undertaken to make amends as the church requires, and has made—or set about making[4]—reparation to the kin, and has submitted to every legal penalty prescribed by the bishop in whose diocese it is.

5[1]. Further, I thank God and all of you, who have given me full support, for the immunity from thefts which we now enjoy. I therefore confidently expect of you, that you will be all the more willing to give your support towards this [maintenance of the public peace][2], in proportion as its observance is a more urgent matter for us all.

6. Further, with respect to violation of [the king's][1] 'mund' and attacks on a man's house[2], we have ordained that he who commits either of these after this shall forfeit all that he possesses, and it shall be for the king to decide whether his life shall be preserved.

7[1]. The authorities[2] must put a stop to[3] vendettas. First, according to public law, the slayer shall give security to[4] his advocate[5], and the advocate to the kinsmen [of the slain man], that he (the slayer) will make reparation to the kindred.

§ 1. After that it is incumbent upon the kin of the slain man to give security to the slayer's advocate, that he (the slayer) may approach[1] under safe-conduct[2] and pledge himself to pay the wergeld.

§ 2. When he has pledged himself to this, he shall find a surety for the payment of the wergeld.

§ 3. When that is done, the king's 'mund'[1] shall be established. In twenty-one days from that time *healsfang*[2] shall be paid; in twenty-one days after that 'manbot' (the compensation due to the slain man's lord), and twenty-one days after that the first instalment of the wergeld.

III EDMUND[1]

[2][I. De juratione[3] quae fiebat Eadmundo regi. II. De furę[4]. III. Qui[5] alterius hominem receperit vel ad dampnum aliquem manutenuerit. IIII. De servo fure. V. Ignotum[6] pecus non emendum sine testimonio. VI. De investigando pecore furato. VII. Ut quisque[7] suos faciat credibiles; et de infamatis; et de eis[8] qui haec praecepta negligunt.]

Haec est institutio quam Eadmundus rex et episcopi sui cum sapientibus suis instituerunt apud Culintonam de pace et juramento faciendo[9].

1. Imprimis, ut omnes jurent in nomine Domini, pro quo sanctum[9] illud sanctum est, fidelitatem Eadmundo regi, sicut homo debet esse fidelis domino suo, sine omni controversia et seductione[10], in manifesto, in occulto, et[11] in amando quod amabit, nolendo quod nolet; et[12] a die qua[13] juramentum hoc dabitur, ut nemo concelet hoc in fratre vel proximo suo plus quam in extraneo.

2. Vult etiam, ut ubi fur pro certo cognoscetur, twelfhindi et twihindi[14] consocientur et exuperent eum[15] vivum vel mortuum, alterutrum quod poterunt; et qui aliquem eorum infaidiabit qui in ea quaestione fuerint[16], sit inimicus regis et omnium amicorum eius[17]; et si quis adire negaverit et coadjuvare nolit, emendet regi CXX s.—vel secundum hoc perneget quod nescivit—et hundreto XXX s.

3. Et nolo ut aliquis recipiat alterius hominem, priusquam quietus sit erga omnem manum quae[18] rectum quaerat ab eo; et qui aliquem manutenebit et firmabit ad dampnum faciendum, custodiat, ut repraesentet eum ad emendandum, vel ipse componat quod alius componere debebat[19].

---

[1] *Instituta regis Ædmundi suorumque hic incipiunt* T.
[2] This table of contents is found in M, Hk, Br but not in T.
[3] *sacramento fidelitatis regi Edmundo faciendo* Br.
[4] *furibus capiendis* Br.   [5] *De illo qui* Br.
[6] *De illis qui emunt ignota pecora s. t.* Br.   [7] *Quisquis homines suos* Br.
[8] *haec p. negligentibus* Br.   [9] Om. T.   [10] *seditione* Br.   [11] Om. Br.
[12] Om. M, T.   [13] *ad te qua* M, *quam* Hk; *antequam* Br.
[14] *et twih.* om. Hk; *twifhindi* M, Br; *twifhyndi* T.   [15] *eum in* T.
[16] *fuerit* T.   [17] *eorum* M, Hk, Br.   [18] *qui* T.   [19] *debeat* Hk, *Br.*

III EDMUND

These are the provisions for the preservation of public peace[1] and the swearing of allegiance which have been instituted at Colyton[2] by King Edmund and his bishops, together with his councillors.

1. In the first place, all shall swear in the name of the Lord, before whom that holy thing is holy[1], that they will be faithful to King Edmund[2], even as it behoves a man to be faithful to his lord, without any dispute or dissension[3], openly or in secret[4], favouring what he favours and discountenancing what he discountenances[5]. And from the day on which[6] this oath shall be rendered, let no-one conceal the breach of it in a brother or a relation of his, any more than in a stranger.

2[1]. Further, it is his will, that where a man is proved to be a thief, nobles and commoners shall unite and seize him, alive or dead, whichever they can. And he who institutes a vendetta against any of those who have been concerned in that pursuit shall incur the hostility of the king and of all his friends[2], and if anyone shall refuse to come forward and lend his assistance, he shall pay 120 shillings to the king[3]— or deny knowledge of the affair by an oath of equivalent value—and 30 shillings to the hundred[4].

3[1]. And it is my will that no-one receive [into his service] one who has been in the service of another man, until he be quit [of all charges preferred against him] from any quarter where justice is sought from him; and he who shall support and harbour anyone who perpetrates crime[2] shall see to it that[3] he bring him to make compensation, or shall himself pay what is due from the other.

4. Et dictum est[1] de servis: si qui[2] furentur[3], senior ex eis capiatur et occidatur vel suspendatur, et aliorum singuli verberentur ter et extoppentur[4], et truncetur minimus digitus in signum.

5. Et nemo barganniet vel ignotum pecus recipiat qui non habeat testimonium summi praepositi vel sacerdotis vel hordarii[5] vel portirevae.

6. Et dictum est de investigatione[6] et quaesitione [pecoris furati][7], ut[8] ad villam pervestigetur, et non sit foristeallum aliquod[9] illi vel aliqua prohibitio itineris vel quaestionis.

§ 1. Et si vestigium illud de terra illa[10] non possit educi, quaeratur ubicunque suspectum fuerit ac dubium.

§ 2. Et si aliquis accusetur illic, adlegiet se sicut ad hoc pertinebit, et [stet ipsum pro superjuramento. Et qui quaesitionem huiusmodi prohibebit][11] reddat captale et regi cxx s. Et si quis refragaverit et[12] resistat et rectum facere nolit, emendet regi cxx s.

7. Et omnis homo credibiles faciat homines suos et omnes qui in pace et terra sua sunt.

§ 1. Et omnes infamati et accusationibus ingravati sub plegio redigantur.

§ 2. Et praepositus vel tainus, comes vel villanus, qui hoc facere nolet aut[13] disperdet, emendet cxx sol. et sit dignus eorum quae supra dicta[14] sunt.

---

[1] d. e. om. Br.   [2] qui si M, Hk; qui om. T.   [3] f. simul ut T.
[4] M, Hk; -torp- Br; -top- T.   [5] ordalii M, Hk, Br.
[6] vestigatione Hk, T.   [7] Om. M, Hk, T.   [8] Hk, Br, T; non M.
[9] Hk, Br, T; -quid M.   [10] ipsa T.   [11] Om. M, Hk, Br.
[12] vel T.   [13] ad M, Hk; ac T.   [14] qui s. dicti T.

4. And we have declared with regard to slaves that, if a number of them commit theft, their leader shall be captured and slain, or hanged, and each of the others shall be scourged three times and have his scalp removed[1] and his little finger mutilated as a token of his guilt.

5[1]. And no-one shall make a purchase or receive strange cattle unless he has as witness the high-reeve or the priest or the treasurer or the town-reeve[2].

6. And we have declared with regard to the tracking and pursuit of stolen cattle, that thorough investigation shall be made at the village[1], and that no obstacle shall be placed in the way thereof[2] or anything to prevent the pursuit and search[3].

§ 1[1]. And if the track cannot be followed beyond the bounds of that estate, search shall be made wherever suspicion or doubt attaches.

§ 2. And if anyone is accused there, he shall clear himself in the manner required by the case, and the track shall serve as an oath[1] on behalf [of the accuser]; and he who hinders a search of this kind shall pay the value of the stock and 120 shillings to the king[2]. And if anyone offers opposition and resistance and refuses to comply with the law, he shall pay a fine of 120 shillings to the king.

7[1]. And every man shall act as surety for his men and for all those who are under his protection and on his estate[2].

§ 1[1]. And all men of ill repute and those who have been frequently accused[2] shall be placed under surety.

§ 2[1]. And the reeve or the thegn, the noble or commoner[2] who refuses to do this, or disregards it, shall pay a fine of 120 shillings, and incur the penalties which have been stated above[3].

I EDGAR

Ðis is seo gerædnyss hu mon þæt[1] hundred haldan sceal.

1. Ærest, þæt hi heo gegaderian á ymb feower wucan, 7 wyrce
ælc man oðrum riht.

2. Þæt men[2] faran on cryd æfter ðeofan[3].
Gyf neod on handa stande, cyðe hit man ðam hundredesmen,
7 he syððan ðam teoðingmannum; 7 faran ealle forð, ðær
him God wisige, þæt hi tocuman moton; do ðam ðeofe his
riht, swa hit ær Eadmundes cwide wæs.

   § 1. 7 sylle mon þæt ceapgyld ðam ðe þæt yrfe age; 7 dǽle
   man þæt oðer on twa—healf ðam hundrede, healf ðam
   hlaforde—butan mannum; 7 fo se hlaford to ðam
   mannum.

3. And se man ðe ðis forsitte 7 ðæs hundredes dóm forsace,
7 him mon eft þæt illce gerecce, gesylle man ðam hundrede
xxx peninga 7 æt ðam æftran cyrre syxtig penega, half ðam
hundrede, half ðam hlaforde.

   § 1. Gyf hit ðriddan siðe dó, sylle healf pund; æt ðam
   feorðan cyrre ðolie ealles ðæs ðe he age 7 beo útlah[4],
   buton him se cyng eard alyfe.

4. And we cwǽdon be uncuðum yrfe, þæt nan man næfde,
buton hé hæbbe ðæs hundredesmanna gewitnyssa oððe ðæs
teoðingmannes, 7 se sy wel getrýwe.

   § 1. 7 buton þara oðer hæbbe, nele him mon nænne team
   geþafian.

---

[1] *þæt h. h. s. Ærest* has been omitted in the text and added in the margin in
the 12th cent.
[2] *m̃.*   [3] The rubric is in the margin, in red ink.
[4] *utlaht—t* struck out later.

I EDGAR[1]

This is the ordinance concerning the administration of the hundred[1].

1. In the first place, they[1] shall assemble without fail every four weeks[2], and every man shall do justice to his fellow.

2[1]. That men go without delay[2] in pursuit of thieves.

If the need is urgent, the chief official of the hundred[3] shall be informed, and shall forthwith inform the chief officials of the tithings[3], and all shall go forth, as God shall direct them, until they succeed in coming upon the thief[4]. He shall receive his deserts as has already been decreed by Edmund[5].

§ 1. And the value of the livestock[1] shall be paid to its owner, and the remainder [of the thief's property]— all except his men—shall be divided in two, half [being given] to the hundred, and half to his lord who shall also take over his men.

3. And whosoever neglects this[1], and ignores the authority[2] of the hundred—and the charge is established against him subsequently[3]—shall pay 30 pence[4] to the hundred, and on the second occasion 60 pence, half to the hundred and half to his lord.

§ 1. If he does it a third time, he shall pay half a pound[1]. On the fourth occasion he shall suffer the loss of all that he possesses and be outlawed, unless the king allow him to remain in the country.

4[1]. And with regard to strange cattle, we have declared that no-one shall keep any such, except with the cognisance of the men of the hundred[2] or with that of the chief official of the tithing; and he must be a thoroughly trustworthy man.

§ 1. And unless he has the cognisance of one or other of these, he shall not be permitted to vouch to warranty.

5. Eac we cwædon, gyf him hundred bedrife tród on oðer
   hundred, þæt mon cyðe ðam hundredesmen[1], 7 he ðonne
   ðær midfare.

   § 1. Gyf he hit forsitte, gesylle ðam cynge ðrittig scill'.

6. Gyf hwá riht forbuge 7 uthleape, forgylde þæt angylde se
   ðe hine to ðam hearme geheold.

   § 1. And gyf hine man teó, þæt he hine utsceóte, geladige
        hine swa hit on lande stande.

7. On hundrede swa on oðer gemote we wyllað þæt mon
   folcriht getæce æt ælcere spæce, 7 andagie hwænne man
   þæt gelæste.

   § 1. 7 se ðe ðone andagan brece—buton hit sy ðurh hla-
        fordes geban—gebete mid xxx scill', 7 to gesetton
        dæge gelæste þæt he ær sceolde.

8. Hryðeres belle[2], hundes hoppe[2], blæshorn—ðissa ðreora ælc
   bið anes scill' weorð; 7 ælc is melda geteald.

9. Ðæt isen ðe bið to ðrimfealdum ordale, þæt wege III pund[3].

---

[1] m̃ with *anna* added above in later handwriting; *men* Lieb.
[2] 7 added in later handwriting.
[3] 7 *to anfaldum an pund,* added in the margin in later handwriting.

5. We have further declared, that if one hundred follow up a track into another hundred, notice shall be given to the chief official of the latter[1], and he shall then take part in the search.

   § 1. If he neglects to do so, he shall pay 30 shillings[1] to the king.

6[1]. If anyone evades the law and escapes, he who has supported him in wrongdoing shall pay the damage[2].

   § 1. And if he is accused of abetting him in his escape, he shall clear himself according to the established custom of the district[1].

7. In the hundred, as in other courts[1], it is our will that every case be treated in accordance with the public law and have a date fixed for its decision.

   § 1. And he who fails to appear at the appointed time— unless prevented by a summons[1] from his lord—shall pay 30 shillings[2] as compensation and perform on a fixed date what he should have done before.

8[1]. A cow's bell, a dog's collar[2] and a horn for blowing[3]—each of these three shall be worth a shilling, and each is reckoned as an informer[4].

9[1]. The iron for the triple ordeal shall weigh three pounds.

II EDGAR

Her is Eadgares cynincges gerædnes[1].

Ðis is seo gerædnes þe Eadgar cyngc mid his witena geþeahte gerædde, Gode to lofe 7 him silfum to cynescype 7 [eallum his leodscype][2] to þearfe.

1. Ðæt synd þonne ærest, þæt Godes cirican syn ælces[3] rihtes wyrðe.

§ 1. 7 man agife ælce teoðunga to ðam ealdum mynstrum[4] þe seo hyrnes tohyrð; 7 þæt sy þonne swa gelæst, ægðer ge of ðegnes inlande ge of neatlande[5], swa hit seo sulh gegange[6].

2. [Be cyricsceat.][7]

Gif hwa þonne þegna sy þe on his boclande circan hæbbe þe legerstow on sy, gesylle þone[8] þriddan dæl his agenra teoðunga into his circan.

§ 1. Gif hwa circan hæbbe þe legerstow on [ne][2] sy, do[9] he of þam nigoðan dæle[10] his preoste þæt þæt he wille.

§ 2. 7 ga ælc ciricsceat into ðam ealdan mynstre be ælcum frigan heorðe[11].

§ 3[12]. Gelæste man sulhælmessan þonne xv niht beon onufan eastran.

3. [Be teoþungum.]

7 sy ælcere geoguðe teoðinge gelæst be pentecosten 7 ðara eorðwæstma be emnihte 7 ælc ciricsceat to Martinus[13] mæssan, be þam fullan wite þe seo domboc tæcð.

§ 1. Gif[14] hwa þonne ða teoðunge gelæstan nelle, swa we gecweden habbað, þonne[1] fare þæs cyninges gerefa to 7 þæs biscopes 7 þæs mynstres mæssepreost 7 niman unðances þone teoðan dæl to þam mynstre ðe hit toge-

---

[1] Om. G, A. Ld.   [2] G, A, Ld; om. D.
[3] Added in late handwriting in G; om. Ld.
[4] þ. ealdan mynstre G, Ld; þ. ealdan mynstrum A.
[5] geneatlande G, A; neatland Ld.   [6] swa swa his sulh gega G, Ld.
[7] The rubrics are found in Ld. only.   [8] g. he þane (ðonne) G, Ld.
[9] ðonne do G, Ld.   [10] þ. nigan (nigon, nygan) dælum G, A, Ld.
[11] eorðe G (h added later above the line), Ld.   [12] Om. G, Ld, Q.
[13] c. sy gelæst be M. G, Ld.   [14] 7 gyf (gif) G, A, Ld.

II EDGAR

Here is King Edgar's ordinance.

This is the ordinance which King Eadgar has enacted, with the advice of his councillors, for the glory of God, and his own royal dignity[1], and the good of all his people[2].

1. This is the first provision, that God's churches shall be entitled to all their prerogatives[1].

    § 1[1]. And all tithes shall be paid to the old churches[2] to which obedience is due; and payment shall be made both from the thegn's demesne land and the land held by his tenants[3]—all that is under the plough[4].

2[1]. If, however, there is a thegn who, on the land which he holds by title-deed, has a church to which is attached a graveyard, he shall pay the third part of his own tithes to his church.

    § 1. If anyone has a church to which there is no graveyard attached, he shall pay what he will to his priest out of the next tenth part[1].

    § 2. And every church-due for every free household[1] shall go to the old church.

    § 3[1]. Plough-alms shall be rendered 15 days[2] after Easter.

3[1]. And the tithe of all young animals shall be rendered by Pentecost, and that of the fruits of the earth by the Equinox, and every church due shall be rendered by Martinmas, under pain of the full penalty[2] which the written law[3] prescribes.

    § 1[1]. If, however, anyone refuses to render tithes in accordance with what we have decreed, the king's reeve, and the bishop's reeve, and the priest of the church shall go to him, and, without his consent, shall take the tenth part for the church to which it is due, and the next

birige, 7 tæcan¹ him to ðam nigoðan dæle, 7 todæle man
ða eahta dælas on twa, 7 fo se landhlaford² to healfum,
to healfum se biscop, si hit cyninges man si hit þegnes.

4. [Be þon heorþpeninge.]
    7 sy ælc heorðpænig agifen be Petres mæssedæg.

§ 1. 7 se ðe hine³ to ðam andagan gelæst næbbe, læde hine
to Rome 7 ðarto eacan þrittig p', 7 bringe þonne⁴
switelunge þæt he þar swa micel betæht hæbbe; 7 þonne
he ham cume, gilde þam cyninge hundtwelftig scill'.

§ 2. 7 gif he hine eft sillan nelle, læde hine eft to Rome 7
oðre swilce bote; 7 þonne he ham cume, gilde þam
cynge twahund scill'.

§ 3. Æt þam þriddan siðe⁵, gif he þonne git nelle, þolige
ealles ðæs þe he age.

5. [Be freolsdægum 7 fæstenum.]
    7 healde man ælces Sunnandæges freolsunga⁶ fram Sæternes-
dæges nontide⁷ oð Monandæges⁸ lihtinge, be þam wite ðe seo⁹
domboc tæce¹⁰, 7 ælcne oðerne mæssedæg swa he beboden sy¹¹.

§ 1. 7 man ælc⁹ bebodon fæsten healde mid ælcere georn-
fulnesse [7 ælces Frigedæges fæsten, buton hit freols sy]¹².

§ 2¹³. 7 gelæste man sawlsceat æt ælcan Cristenan men to
ðam mynstre þe hit togebirige.

§ 3¹³. 7 stande ælc ciricgrið swa swa hit betst stod.

---

¹ G, A, Ld.   Cf. VIII Atr. 8; I Cn. 8, 2; *tæce* D.   ² *hlaford* Ld.   ³ *ðonne* G, Ld.
⁴ *þonne þanon* s. G; *þænne þonon* s. A; *ðone ðonon* Ld.
⁵ *cyrre* G, Ld.   ⁶ *freols* G, Ld.   ⁷ *f. nontide þæs* s. G, Ld.
⁸ *ðæs* M. G, Ld.   ⁹ Om. G, Ld.   ¹⁰ *tæcð* G, A, Ld.
¹¹ *beo* G, A Ld.   ¹² A; om. G, D Ld.   ¹³ Om. G, Ld, Q.

tenth shall be allotted to him[2], and the eight [remaining] parts shall be divided in two, and the lord of the manor[3] shall take half and the bishop half, whether the man be under the lordship of the king or of a thegn.

4. And every hearth-penny[1] shall be paid by St Peter's Day.

§ 1[1]. And he who has failed to make payment by the appointed time shall take it to Rome, and 30 pence in addition thereto, and shall bring thence evidence that he has there handed over that amount; and when he comes home, he shall pay 120 shillings to the king.

§ 2. And if he again refuses to give it, he shall take it again to Rome, and hand over the same sum as compensation, and when he comes home, he shall pay 200 shillings to the king.

§ 3. And on the third occasion, if he still refuses, he shall suffer the loss of all that he possesses.

5[1]. And every Sunday shall be observed as a festival from noonday on Saturday till dawn on Monday, under pain of the penalty which the written law prescribes; and every other feast-day according to the regulations appointed for it.

§ 1. And every fast which has been appointed shall be rigorously observed, [and the fast every Friday, unless it be a festival].

§ 2[1]. And payment for the souls of the dead shall be rendered to the church to which it is due on behalf of every Christian man.

§ 3. And every right of sanctuary possessed by the church[1] shall be maintained according to the highest standards of the past[2].

III EDGAR

Eadgares cynincges gerædnes[1].

1. [Weoruldcund gerædnysse.][2]

Þis is ðonne seo worldcunde gerædnes þe ic wille þæt man healde.

§ 1. Þæt is þonne ærest[3] þæt ic wille, þæt ælc man sy folcrihtes wurðe, ge earm ge éadig, 7 heom man rihte domas deme.

§ 2. 7 sy on ðare bote swilc forgifnes, swilce[4] hit for Gode gebeorhlic sy 7 for worlde aberendlic.

2. [Be ðone ðe mon cyng gesece 7 be ðæm were.]

7 ne gesece nan man þone cyngc for nanre spræce, buton he æt ham rihtes [wyrðe][5] beon ne mote, oððe riht abiddan ne mæg[6].

§ 1. Gif þæt riht to hefig sy, secan[7] siððan þa lihtinge to ðam cynge.

§ 2. 7 æt nanum botwyrðum gilte ne forwyrce man mare þonne his wer.

3. [Be unrihtum dome.]

7 se dema, þe oðrum woh deme[8], gesille þam cynge hund-twelftig[9] scill' to bote—buton he[10] mid aðe gecyðan durre, þæt he hit na rihtor ne cuðe—7 þolige áá his þegenscipes, buton he hine[11] æt ðam cynge gebicge, swa[12] he him geþafian wille; 7 ofmanige[13] scirebiscop[14] þa bote to ðæs cynges handa.

4. [Be ðon ðe mon oþerne forsecgaþ.]

And se þe oðerne mid woge forseccan wille, þæt he aðor oððe feo oððe freme[15] þe wyrsa sy, gif þonne se oðer þæt[3] geunsoðian mæge þæt him man onsecgan wolde, sy he his tungan scildig, buton he hine mid his were forgilde.

---

[1] Om. G, A, Ld.   [2] The rubrics are found in Ld only.
[3] Om. G, Ld.   [4] swilce swilce A.   [5] G, A; wyrþ Ld; om. D.
[6] mæge G, A, Ld.   [7] sece G, A, Ld.   [8] onwoh gedeme G, Ld.
[9] ...twelftig. G₂ begins here after torn out pages.   [10] buton h. hit G₂.
[11] h. eft G; eft Ld.   [12] swa swa A.
[13] D, G₂; amanige G, A, Ld.   [14] þære scyre b. G, A, G₂, Ld.
[15] D, G₂; feo oððe feore G, A (vel freme written above feore in A), Ld.

III EDGAR

King Edgar's ordinance.

1. My will is further[1] that the following be observed as a secular ordinance.

§ 1[1]. In the first place, my will is that every man[2], rich or poor[3], obtain the benefit of the public law and be awarded just decisions.

§ 2. And that there be such remission in the case of compensations as shall be justifiable in the sight of God and acceptable in the eyes of men[1].

2[1]. And no-one shall apply to the king about any case, unless he cannot obtain the benefit of the law or fails to command justice at home[2].

§ 1. If the law is too oppressive, he shall apply to the king for mitigation[1].

§ 2. And no man shall forfeit more than his wergeld for any offence for which compensation may be paid[1].

3[1]. And a judge[2] who gives a false judgment against another man shall pay 120 shillings as compensation to the king, unless he is prepared to declare on oath that he did not know how to give a more just decision; and he shall forfeit for ever his rank as a thegn, unless he redeem it from the king on such terms as the king will allow him. And the bishop of the diocese shall exact the compensation on the king's behalf.

4. And if anyone seeks to accuse another man falsely, so that he is injured either in property or in reputation[1], and if the second man can refute the charge which the first has sought to bring against him, the first shall forfeit his tongue, unless he redeem himself with his wergeld.

5. [Be gemotum.]

7 sece man hundredes gemot[1] swa hit ǽr geset wæs.

§ 1. 7 hæbbæ man þriwa on geare buruhgemot 7 tuwa scirgemot.

§ 2. 7 ðar beo on þare scire biscop[2] 7 se ealdorman, 7 ðar ægðer tæcan Godes[3] riht ge worldriht.

6. [Be borgum.]

7 finde him ælc man þæt he borh habbe; 7 se borh hine[4] to ælcon rihte gelǽde 7 gehealde.

§ 1. 7 gif hwa ðonne woh wirce 7 utaberste[5], abere se borh þæt he beran[6] scolde.

§ 2. Gif hit þonne[7] þeof[8] beo, 7 gif he hine þonne[7] binnan XII monðum gelangian mæge, agife hine to rihte, 7 him man agife þæt he ær geald[9].

7. [Be tyhtbysigum.]

7 se þe tihtbisig sy 7 folce ungetrywe 7 þas gemot forbuge þrywa[10], þonne scifte[11] man of þam gemote ða ðe him toridan, 7 finde þonne[12] git borh, gif he mæge.

§ 1. Gif he þonne ne mæge, gewilde man hine swa hwaðer swa[13] man mæge, swa cucune swa deadne, 7 niman[14] eal þæt he age, 7 gilde man ðam teondan[15] his ceapgild angildes, 7 fo se hlaford[16] elles[17] to healfum, to healfum þæt hundred.

§ 2. 7 gif aðer oððe mæg oððe fremde ða rade forsace, gilde þam cyninge hundtwelftig scill'.

§ 3. 7 gesece se æbæra þeof þæt þæt he gesece, oððe se þe on hlafordsearwe gemet sy, þæt hi næfre feorh ne gesecan, buton se cyningc him feorhgeneres unne[18].

---

[1] *hundredgemót* G, A; *hundrede gemote* Ld.
[2] *ðær sciregemote bisceop* Ld.   [3] *ge G.* G, A, G₂, Ld.
[4] *h. þonne* G, A, G₂, Ld.   [5] *utoðberste* G, Ld; *utætberste* A, G₂.
[6] *aberan* G, A, Ld.   [7] Om. G, A, G₂, Ld.   [8] *þyfð* G; *ðyfþe* Ld.
[9] *sealde* G, Ld.   [10] Om. G, Ld.
[11] *sceawie (-ige)* G, Ld; *sceapige* A; *scawie* G₂.   [12] *f. him þ.* G, A, Ld.
[13] *hine swaðor (-er) m. m.* G, A, Ld; *hine mon swæðer m. m.* G₂.
[14] *nime man* G, G₂, Ld.   [15] *teonde* G, A, G₂; *ða teonde* Ld.
[16] *landhlaford* G, Ld.   [17] Om. G, Ld.
[18] *buton...unne* om. G, A, G₂, Ld.

5. And the hundred court shall be attended as has been previously ordained[1].

> § 1[1]. And the borough court shall be held three times in the year and the county court twice[2].

> § 2[1]. And the bishop of the diocese and the ealdorman[2] shall be present, and shall direct the observance of[3] both ecclesiastical and secular law.

6. And every man shall see that he has a surety[1], and this surety shall bring and keep him to [the performance of] every lawful duty.
> § 1. And if anyone does wrong and escapes[1], his surety shall incur what the other should have incurred[2].

> § 2. If the case be that of a thief[1] and his surety can lay hold of him within twelve months, he shall deliver him up to justice, and what he has paid shall be returned to him.

7[1]. And if anyone who has a bad reputation and is unworthy of public confidence[2] fails to attend the court-meetings three times, men shall be chosen[3] from the meeting who shall ride to him[4], and he may then still find a surety, if he can.

> § 1[1]. And if he cannot do so, they shall seize him as they can, either alive or dead, and they shall take all that he has, and shall pay to the accuser the unaugmented value of his goods[2]; and the lord of the manor shall take half [of what remains], and the hundred half.

> § 2. And if anyone, either kinsman or stranger[1], refuses to ride [against him], he shall pay the king 120 shillings.

> § 3[1]. And the proved thief[2], or he who has been discovered in treason against his lord[3], whatever refuge he seeks, shall never be able to save his life, unless the king grant that it be spared[4].

8. [Be mynetum 7 gemettum.]
7 gange[1] án mynet ofer ealne þæs cyninges anweald, 7 þone
nan man ne forsace.

§ 1. 7 gange án[2] gemet 7 an gewihte[3], swilce man on
Lundenbirig 7[4] on Wintaceastre healde.

§ 2. 7 ga seo wæge wulle to cxx p'[5], 7 nan man hig undeoror[6] ne sille.

§ 3[7]. 7 gif hwa hi þonne undeoror sille, oððe eawunga oððe
dearnunga, gilde ægðer þam cynge lx[8] scill' ge se þe
hi sille ge se þe hi bicge.

IV EDGAR

Her is geswutelod on þisum gewrite, hu Eadgar cyncg wæs
smeagende, hwæt to bote mihte æt þam færcwealme þe his
leodscype swyðe drehte 7 wanode, wide gynd his anweald.

1. Ðæt is þonne ærest þæt him þuhte 7 his witum, þæt ðus
gerad ungelimp mid synnum 7 mid oferhyrnysse Godes
beboda geearnod wære, 7 swyðost mid þam oftige þæs
neadgafoles þe Cristene men Gode gelæstan scoldon on heora
teoðingsceattum. He beþohte 7 asmeade þæt godcunde be
woruldgewunan:

§ 1. Gif geneatmanna hwylc forgymeleasað his hlafordes
gafol 7 hit him to ðæm rihtandagan ne gelæst, wen is,
gyf se hlaford mildheort bið, þæt he ða gymeleaste to
forgyfenesse læte 7 to his gafole buton witnunge fó.

§ 2. Gyf he ðonne gelomlice þurh his bydelas his gafoles
myngað 7 he ðonne aheardað 7 hit þencð to ætstren-
genne, wen is, þæt ðæs hlafordes grama to ðam swyðe
weaxe, þæt he him ne unne naðer ne æhta ne lifes:

---

[1] ga G, Ld.   [2] g. a. om. G, Ld.   [3] 7 a. g. om. G, Ld.
[4] on L. 7 om. G, Ld.   [5] ealfan (healf.) punde G, G₂.
[6] hie n. m. ná deoror G, Ld; n. m. hy na undeoror A, G₂.
[7] Om. G, Ld.   [8] A, G₂; xl D.

8¹. And one coinage² shall be current throughout all the king's realm, and no-one shall refuse it.

§ 1. And there shall be one system of measurement¹, and one standard of weights², such as is in use in London and in Winchester³.

§ 2. And a wey¹ of wool shall be sold for 120 pence, and no-one shall sell it at a cheaper² rate.

§ 3¹. And if anyone sells it at a cheaper rate, either openly or secretly, both he who sells it and he who buys it shall pay 60 shillings² to the king.

IV EDGAR

¹Notification is hereby given in this order², that King Eadgar has been considering what remedy could be found for the plague³ which has greatly afflicted and reduced his people throughout the length and breadth of his dominion.

1. In the first place, he and his councillors are of opinion that misfortune such as this has been merited because of sin and disregard of God's commands¹, and especially through the withholding of the tribute which Christian people should render to God by their tithes. He has been thinking over and considering the ways of God² by an analogy with human actions:

§ 1. If any tenant¹ neglects the payment due to his lord and does not render it to him on the appointed day, it is to be expected that, if the lord is merciful, he will grant forgiveness for the neglect and take his payment without exacting a penalty.

§ 2. If, however, through his bailiffs¹ he repeatedly claims his rent, and the tenant proves obstinate, and thinks to stand out against it², it is to be expected that the lord's anger will grow so great that he will grant him neither property nor life³.

§ 3. Swa is wén þæt ure Drihten dó þurh ða gedyrstignysse þe folces men wiðhæfton þære gelomlican myngunge þe ure lareowas dydon ymbe þæt neadgafol ures Drihtnes —þæt syn ure teoðunga 7 cyricsceattas.

§ 4. Ðonne beode ic 7 se arcebisceop, þæt ge God ne gremian, ne naðer ne geearnian ne þone færlican deað þises andweardan lifes, ne huru þone toweardan écere helle, mid ænigum oftige Godes gerihta; ac ægðer ge earm ge eadig þe ænige teolunga hæbbe, gelæste Gode his teoðunga mid ealre blisse 7 mid eallum unnan, swa seo gerædnys tæce þe mine witan æt Andeferan geræddon 7 nu eft æt Wihtbordesstane mid wedde gefæstnodon.

§ 5. Ðonne beode ic minum gerefan, be minum freondscype 7 be eallum þam ðe hi ágon, þæt hi styran ælcum þara ðe þis ne gelæste 7 minra witena wed abrecan mid ænegum wacscype wille, swa swa him seo foresæde geradnes tæce; 7 on ðære steore ne sy nan forgyfnes.

§ 5a. Gyf he swa earm bið þæt he aþer deð oððe þa Godes wanað, his sawla to forwyrde, oððe waccor mid modes graman hy behwyrfð þonne þæt he him to agenum teleð, þonne him micele agenre is þæt him æfre on écnysse gelæst, gyf he hit mid unnan 7 mid fulre blisse dón wolde.

§ 6. Ðonne wille ic, þæt ðas Godes gerihta standan æghwær[1] gelice on minum anwealde;

§ 7. 7 ða Godes þeowas þe ða sceattas underfoð, þe we Gode syllað, libban clænan life, þæt hy ðurh ða clænnysse ús to Gode þingian mægen;

---

[1] F; *ægðer* C.

§ 3. It is to be expected that our Lord will act in like manner, because of the audacity with which laymen have withstood the repeated admonitions given [us] by our teachers with regard to the payments which we are in duty bound to render to our Lord, namely, our tithes and church-dues.

§ 4. I and the archbishop[1] enjoin, therefore, that you do not, by withholding any of God's dues, provoke Him to wrath, and incur either the sudden death[2] [which is befalling you] in this present life or, still worse, the death to come in everlasting hell[3]; but everyone, both rich and poor, whose property has yielded him any-thing[4], shall, with all gladness and with all willingness, render his tithes to God, as is prescribed by the ordinance which my councillors enacted at Andover[5], and have now confirmed by solemn declaration[6] at Wiht-bordestan.

§ 5. Further, I enjoin upon my reeves, on pain of forfeiting my friendship and all they possess, to deal in the manner prescribed by the aforesaid ordinance with everyone who fails to perform this and, by any re-missness on his part, consents to violate the solemn declaration of my councillors. And there shall be no remission of the [prescribed] punishment.

§ 5a. If he is so debased[1] as either to curtail what is due to God[2], to the ruin of his soul, or, with angry heart, to attend to it less diligently than to what he accounts his own, [he ought to realise that][3] what endures for him to all eternity will be much more his own, if he has been willing to give his tribute with gladness and with all willingness.

§ 6. Further, it is my will that these ecclesiastical dues be everywhere[1] alike throughout my dominion.

§ 7[1]. And that the servants of God who receive the dues which we render to Him shall live a pure life, so that, by virtue of their purity, they may intercede for us with God.

§ 8. 7 ic 7 mine þegnas wyldan ure preostas to ðan þe ure saula hyrdas us tæcað, þæt syndon ure bisceopas, þe we næfre mishyran ne sceolon on nan þara ðinga þe hi us for Gode tæcað, þæt we ðurh þa hyrsumnysse, þe we heom for Gode hyrsumiað, þæt ece líf geearnian, þe hy us towemað mid lare 7 mid bysene godra weorca.

2. Woruldgerihta ic wille þæt standen on ælcum leodscype swa gode swa hi mon betste aredian mæge, Gode to gecwemnysse 7 me to fullum cynescype 7 earmum 7 eadegum to ðearfe 7 to friðe.

2a. 7 to ælcere byrig 7 on ælcere scyre hæbbe ic mines cyne- scypes gerihta swa min fæder hæfde, 7 mine þegnas hæbben heora scipe on minum timan swa hi hæfdon on mines fæder.

§ 1. 7 ic wille þæt woruldgerihta mid Denum standan be swa godum lagum, swa hy betste geceosan mægen.

§ 1a. Stande þonne mid Englum þæt ic 7 mine witan to minra yldrena domum geyhton, eallum leodscype to ðearfe.

§ 2. Sy þeahhwæðere þes ræd gemæne eallum leodscype, ægðer ge Englum ge Denum ge Bryttum, on ælcum ende mines anwealdes, to ðy þæt earm 7 eadig mote agan þæt hi mid rihte gestrynað, 7 þeof nyte hwær he þeofte[1] befæste ðeah he hwæt stele, 7 him swa geborgen sy, heora unwilles, þæt heora to feola ne losien.

3. Ðæt þonne his[2] þæt ic wille, þæt ælc mann sy under borge ge binnan burgum ge buton burgum.

§ 1. 7 gewitnes[3] sý geset to ælcere byrig 7 to ælcum hun- drode:

---

[1] þyfþe F.   [2] D. is þ. F.   [3] F; gehitnæs C.

§ 8. And that I and my thegns shall enforce upon our priests[1] the duties prescribed for us by the guardians of our souls, namely our bishops, whom we ought never to disobey in any of those matters which they, as representatives of God, prescribe for us, so that we, through the obedience which we show them as representatives of God, may inherit the eternal life to which they draw us by their teaching and by the example of good works.

2[1]. My will is that the rights of the laity[2] be maintained in every province[3] at the best standard which can be devised, in accordance with what will be acceptable to God[4], and will preserve my royal dignity unimpaired, and tend to the advantage and security of rich and poor.

2a. And that in every borough and in every county I possess my royal prerogatives as my father[1] did, and that my thegns keep their rank[2] in my lifetime[3] as they did in my father's.

§ 1. And it is my will that the rights of the laity be maintained among the Danes in accordance with the best constitution[1] which they can determine upon.

§ 1a. Among the English, however, the additions which I and my councillors have made to the laws of my ancestors[1] shall be observed, for the benefit of the whole nation[2].

§ 2. The following measure, however, shall apply generally to the whole nation—to the English, Danes[1] and Britons[2] in every part of my dominion—to the end that rich and poor may possess what they have lawfully acquired; and that thieves, even if they steal anything, may not know where to deposit their stolen goods; and that, little as they may like it, such precautions be taken against them that very few of them may escape.

3. My will is, further, that every man be under surety[1], whether he live within a borough or in the country[2].

§ 1. And a body of standing witnesses shall be appointed for every borough and for every hundred.

4. To ælcere byrig xxxvi¹ syn gecorene to gewytnesse.

5. To smalum burgum 7 to ælcum hundrode xii, buton ge má wyllan.

6. 7 ælc mon mid heora gewytnysse bicge 7 sylle ælc þeora ceapa þe he bicgcge oððe sylle aþer oððe burge oððe wæpengetace².

§ 1. 7 heora ælc, þonne hine man ærest to wytnesse³ gecysð, sylle þone að, þæt he næfre, ne for feo ne for lufe ne for ege, ne ætsace nanes þara þinga þe he to gewytnesse wæs, 7 nan oðer þingc on gewytnesse ne cyðe butan þæt án þæt he geseah oððe gehyrde.

§ 2. 7 swa geæðedra⁴ manna syn on ælcum ceape twegen oððe þry to gewitnysse.

7. 7 se ðe æfter ænegum⁵ ceape ride, cyðe his neahgeburum ymbe hwæt he ride; 7 ðonne he ham cume, cyðe eác on hwæs⁶ gewitnysse he ðone ceap gebohte.

8. Gif he þonne unmyndlunge ceap áredige ut on hwylcere fare, buton he hit ær cydde þa he útrád, cyðe hit þonne he ham cyme; 7 gyf hit cuce orf bið, mid his tunscipes gewitnysse on gemænre læse gebringe.

§ 1. Gif he swa ne deð ær fif nihtum, cyðan hit þæs tunes men þam hundrodes ealdre, 7 beon buton wite ægðer ge hy sylfe ge heora hyrdas; 7 ðolige þæs orfes ðe hit þider brohte, for ði þe he hit his neahgeburum cyðan nolde, 7 fó se landrica to healfon 7 to healfan þæt hundred.

9. Gif hit þonne ofer v niht ungecyd on gemænre læse wunað, þolige þæs orfes swa we ær cwædon, 7 ðara hyrda ælc ðolige ðære hyde, 7 ðæs ne sy nan forgyfnes, gesecan⁷ þæt hi gesecan⁷; 7 he ðeahhwæðere cyðe on hwæs gewitnysse he þæt orf bohte.

---

¹ F; xxxiii. C.   ² on w. F.   ³ gewitnysse F.
⁴ geæþdera F.   ⁵ F; agenum C.   ⁶ F; ðæs C.   ⁷ -en F.

4. 36[1] persons shall be chosen as witnesses for every borough.

5. 12 [shall be chosen] for small boroughs and for every hundred, unless you desire more.

6. And every man shall buy or sell in the presence of these witnesses all the goods which he buys or sells either in a borough or in a wapentake[1].

   § 1. And each of them, when he is first chosen as a witness, shall swear an oath that he will never, for money[1] or favour or fear[2], deny any of the things of which he has been witness, or declare in his testimony anything except only what he has seen or heard.

   § 2. And two or three men who have taken the oath in this manner shall be present as witnesses at every transaction.

7. And he who sets out[1] to make any purchase shall inform his neighbours of the object of his journey; and when he comes home, he shall also declare who was present as witness when he bought the goods.

8. If, however, he makes a purchase unexpectedly, when he is away on some journey or other, and he had not given notice of it when he set out, he shall do so when he comes home; and, if it is livestock, he shall bring it to the common pasture with the cognisance of the village to which he belongs.

   § 1. If he does not do so within 5 days, the villagers shall inform the head of the hundred[1], and neither they nor their herdsmen shall be fined; and he who brought the livestock there shall forfeit it, because he has failed to give notice of it to his neighbours, and the lord of the manor shall take half and the hundred half.

9. If, however, it remains unnotified on the common pasture for more than 5 days, he shall forfeit the livestock as we have stated, and each of the herdsmen shall undergo the lash[1], and there shall be no remission of that punishment, whatever refuge they seek; and the man himself shall declare none the less who was present as witness when he bought the livestock.

10. Gif he ðonne cenð þæt he hit mid gewitnysse bohte þara
    manna þe to gewitnysse genamode synt, aðer oððe on byrig
    oððe on hundrode, 7 se hundrodes[1] ealdor þæt geacsoð þæt
    hit soð is, þolige þeah þæs orfes, for ði þe he hit his neah-
    geburum cyðan nolde ne his hundrodes ealdre, 7 næbbe his
    na maran hearm.

11. Gyf he þonne cænne þæt he hit mid gewitnysse bohte, 7 þæt
    leas bið, sy he þeof 7 ðolige heafdes 7 ealles ðæs þe he age;
    7 healde se landhlaford þæt forstolene orf 7 ðæs orfes ceap-
    gyld, oð þæt se agenfrigea þæt[2] geacsige 7 mid gewitnesse
    him þæt orf geahnige.

12. Þonne wille ic þæt stande mid Denum swa gode laga swa
    hy betste geceosen; 7 ic heom á geþafode 7 geðafian wille,
    swa lange swa me lif gelæst, for eowrum hyldum þe ge me
    symble cyddon.

    § 1. 7 ðæs wilnige þæt ðes án dom on swylcere smeagunge
    sy ús eallon gemæne, to gebeorge 7 to friðe eallum
    leodscype.

13. 7 ic wille þæt tunesmen 7 heora hyrdas habban þas ylcan
    smeagunge on minum cucum orfe 7 on minra þegena, ealswa
    hy habbað on heora agenum.

    § 1. Gif hit þonne min gerefa oððe ænig oðer man, riccre
    oððe unriccre, onscunað 7 ungerysena gebyt aðer oððe
    tunesmannum oððe heora hyrdon, ceose Dene be lagum
    hwylce steore hy be ðan healdan willað.

14. Mid Anglum ic hæbbe gecoren 7 mine witan, hwæt seo steor
    beon mæge, gif ænig man mid ánbyrdnysse beginð oððe mid
    ealle ofslyhð ænigne þara þe ymbe þas smeagunge bið 7 þæt
    dyrne orf ameldað, oððe þara ænigne þe on soðre gewitnesse
    bið [7][3] mid his soðe þæne unscyldigan ahret 7 ðæne scyldigan
    rihtlice fordeð.

---

[1] *hundrodest* C; *hundredes* F.   [2] F; *agenfrige að* C.
                            [3] F; om. C.

10. If, however, he makes it known that he has bought it with the cognisance of the men who have been nominated as witnesses, either in a borough or in a hundred[1], and the head of the hundred learns that his statement is true, he shall none the less forfeit the livestock, because he has failed to give notice of it to his neighbours or to the head of his hundred, but he shall suffer no greater loss[2].

11. If, however, he makes it known that he has bought it in the presence of witnesses, and that statement proves false, he shall be regarded as a thief, and shall forfeit his head and all that he possesses; and the lord of the manor shall keep the stolen livestock, or[1] its equivalent value, till the owner hears of it, and proves his claim to the livestock with the help of witnesses.

12. Further, it is my will that the Danes continue to observe the best constitution which they can determine upon[1]. I[2] have always granted you such a concession and will continue to do so, as long as my life lasts, because of the loyalty[3] which you have constantly professed to me.

   § 1. But I desire that this one decree relating to investigations such as these[1] shall apply equally to us all[2], for the protection and security of the whole population.

13. And it is my will that villagers and their herdsmen shall have the same right of investigation with regard to my livestock and that of my thegns as they have with regard to their own.

   § 1. If, however, any reeve of mine or any other man[1], whether of high or low position, refuses this, and offers any indignity to either the villagers or their herdsmen, the Danes shall determine, according to their constitution, what penalty they will fix for this offence.

14. I and my councillors have determined what the penalty[1] shall be among the English, if any man ventures[2] to offer resistance or slays outright anyone who is engaged in this investigation and who gives notice of the concealed cattle, or anyone who is giving true witness and, by his veracity, saves the innocent and brings just doom upon the guilty.

§ 1. Þonne wille ic þæt symble mid eow gehealden sý þæt ge to friðes bote gecoren hæfdon mid micclum wisdome 7 me swyðe gecwemlice.

§ 2. 7 ðas eaca sy ús eallum gemæne þe on ðissum iglandum wuniað.

15. Þonne fyrðrige Oslác eorl 7 eall here þe on his[1] ealdordome wunað, þæt ðis stande, Gode to lofe 7 ure ealra saula to ðearfe 7 eallum folce to friðe.

§ 1. 7 write man manega gewrita be ðisum 7 sende ægðer ge to Ælfere ealdormen ge to Æþelwine[2] ealdormen, 7 hi gehwyder, þæt ðes ræd cuð sy ægðer ge earmum ge eadigum.

16. Ic beo eow swyðe hold hlaford þa hwyle þe me lif gelæst, 7 eow eallum swyðe bliðe eom, for ði þe ge swa georne ymbe frið syndon.

---

[1] F; ðis C.   [2] F; Ægelwine C.

§ 1. Further, it is my will that the provisions which you have made, with great wisdom and very acceptably to me, for the improvement of public security, be continually observed among you.

§ 2. But this addition shall apply generally to all of us[1] who dwell in these islands.

15. Further, Earl Oslac[1] and all the population[2] dwelling in his earldom shall promote the observance of this, to the praise of God, and for the good of the souls of all of us, and the security of the whole nation.

§ 1. And many copies of this order shall be made and sent to both the ealdormen, Aelfhere[1] and Aethelwine[2], and they shall distribute them in all directions, so that this measure shall be known both to rich and poor.

16. I will be a very gracious lord to you as long as my life lasts. I am very well pleased with you all[1], because you are so zealous for the preservation of the public peace.

PROMISSIO REGIS

The Anglo-Saxon version of the Coronation oath given here is taken from the eleventh century MS Cotton Cleopatra B XIII (Cp). It is contained also in the sixteenth century MS Oxford Bodley Junius 60 into which it was copied from the eleventh century MS Cotton Vitellius A VII (Cv) now destroyed (see Liebermann, I. p. 214).

It is evidently a translation of the oath included in the Latin coronation ritual of which four recensions, dating from the tenth to the fourteenth centuries, are extant (see Legg, *English Coronation Records*). The consecration of English kings is recorded as early as the eighth century (see *Sax. Chr.* ann. 785), and Liebermann suggests that the liturgy and oath may date from the ninth century at least. None of the three MSS representing the earliest recension, however, is earlier than the tenth century (see Liebermann, III. p. 144). One of them is traditionally connected with Egbert, Archbishop of York (d. 766, see Stubbs, *Registr. Sacr. Anglic.* p. 10), and may be a copy of a Pontifical of his, though there is no real evidence in favour of this ascription. The second recension falls before 973 and may have been employed at the coronation of Edgar (see Ramsay, *Athenæum*, 29 March 1902, p. 401). It spread to the Continent where it was used at coronations both in France and Italy (see Legg, *op. cit.* p. 14). The A.S. version has points in common with both these forms. The third recension is found in MSS of the twelfth century, while the fourth, which dates from the fourteenth century, is contained in the *Liber regalis* (see Legg, *op. cit.* p. 81).

The preamble of the Anglo-Saxon version names Dunstan as the archbishop officiating at the ceremony, and gives the place as Kingston. Dunstan consecrated Edgar (973), Edward (975) and Æthelred (978 or 979), but the coronation of Edgar took place at Bath (see *Sax. Chr.* A) and it is not certain where Edward was crowned. Æthelred, however, was crowned at Kingston (see *Sax. Chr.*; Florence of Worc., ed. Thorpe, I.

p. 146; Henry of Hunt., Rolls Series, p. 167), so that this document is generally taken to refer to him. Liebermann, however, does not preclude the possibility of its referring to Edward, and consequently leaves it in doubt as to whether the event mentioned belongs to 975 or 978.

The coronation oath is followed both in Cp and Ju by a commentary detailing the duties of a Christian king (see Wright and Halliwell, *Reliquiae Antiquae* II. p. 194; Stubbs, *Mem. of St Dunstan*, p. 356). Liebermann directs attention to the general resemblance between this passage and the section entitled *Be eorðlicum cyninge* in the Institutes of Polity (ed. Thorpe, *Anc. Laws*, II. p. 304) as well as Wulfstan's Homilies (ed. Napier, p. 266 f.). In tone and phraseology also it suggests comparison with V and VI Æthelred. He is of opinion that this addition may have been due to the Anglo-Saxon translator.

PROMISSIO REGIS[1]

Ðis gewrit is gewriten stæf be stæfe be þam gewrite þe Dunstan arcebisceop sealde urum hlaforde æt Cingestune, þa on dæg þa hine man halgode to cinge, 7 forbead him ælc wedd to syllanne butan þysan wedde þe he up on Cristes weofod léde, swa se bisceop him dihte:

1. On þære halgan þrinnesse naman! Ic þreo þing beháte Cristenum folce 7 me underðeoddum:

   § 1. án ærest, þæt Godes cyrice 7 eall Cristen folc minra gewealda soðe sibbe healde;

   § 2. oðer is, þæt ic reaflac 7 ealle unrihte þing eallum hádum forbeode;

   § 3. þridde, þæt ic beháte 7 bebeode on eallum dómum riht 7 mildheortnisse, þæt us eallum arfæst 7 mildheort God þurh þæt his ecean miltse forgife, se lifað 7 rixað.

Finit.

[1] *Sacramentum vel Pr. r. in consecratione* Ju.

PROMISSIO REGIS

This document has been copied, letter by letter, from that which Archbishop Dunstan[1] gave to our lord at Kingston[2], on the day when he was consecrated as king, forbidding him to give any pledge[3] except this one which he laid upon Christ's altar, as the bishop directed him:

1. In the name of the Holy Trinity![1] I promise three things to the Christian people who are under my authority[2]:

   § 1[1]. Firstly, that true peace shall be assured to[2] the church of God and to all Christian people in my dominions.

   § 2[1]. Secondly, I forbid robbery and all unrighteous deeds by all classes of society.

   § 3[1]. Thirdly, I promise and enjoin justice and mercy in the decision of all cases, in order that God, who liveth and reigneth, may in his grace and mercy be brought thereby to grant us all his eternal compassion.

THE LAWS OF ÆTHELRED

THE LAWS OF ÆTHELRED

Eight series of laws issued by Æthelred are extant, together with short fragments of two other series. They fall naturally into two groups, I–IV being concerned with secular affairs while V–X are almost entirely ecclesiastical in content.

Of the first four codes the only one which can be dated with any certainty is II. It contains the terms of peace made between Æthelred and his councillors and a force of so-called 'Danes,' of which one of the leaders was Olaf Tryggvason (see Notes). It would seem that money was paid to invading forces both in 991 and 994—on the first occasion after the battle of Maldon in which Byrhtnoth, Ealdorman of Essex, was defeated and killed (see *Sax. Chr.* ann. 991 E, F, where, however, none of the Danish leaders is mentioned by name); on the second occasion after a considerable part of the country had been ravaged by Olaf (*ib.* ann. 994 E, F). Archbishop Sigeric is mentioned in the Chronicle only in connection with the former transaction and he died in the autumn of 994 before terms could have been arranged with the invaders. Liebermann therefore, for this and other reasons (see III. p. 149 f.), concludes that the treaty given here accompanied the former transaction[1]. On the latter occasion Olaf was baptised—and we know that after his return to Norway he was a most zealous Christian—but there is no reference to this here.

The treaty, as distinguished from that between Alfred and Guthrum, is entirely concerned with the personal relations between the two parties. The invading army obviously had no intention of permanently settling in the country. Clauses 8 and 9 have no intrinsic connection with what precedes, and are regarded by Liebermann as an independent piece, of legislation. He attributes them to a date about 1000 in view both of their style and of their contents (cf. III Atr. 6, 1 and II Cn. 24, 2, which apparently mark later developments in the system of vouching to warranty).

---

[1] See also Schmid, p. li; Freeman, *Norman Conq.* I. p. 278; Steenstrup, *Normannerne*, III. p. 238, IV. p. 56 f.; Stevenson, *Crawford Ch.* p. 120; Plummer, *Sax. Chr.* II. p. 173; Hodgkin, *Hist. of Engl.* p. 381; Oman. *Engl. bef. Conq.* p. 558.

I and III have points in common and may have been issued about the same time. Both refer to an earlier assembly at Bromdun, and clauses found in I are repeated in III (see Notes). I is particularly concerned with the districts under English Law (see Preamble), whereas III, with its regulations for the Five Boroughs, its Scandinavian money-system and its Northern terms, seems specially intended for the Danelaw. I was enacted at Woodstock in Mercia (cf. IX), III at Wantage in Wessex. At the latter place a notable assembly met in 997 (cf. Kemble, No. 698), and hence III is attributed to that year by Kemble (*Saxons in England*, II. p. 257), Schmid (p. li) and Freeman (*Norman Conquest*, I. p. 295). Liebermann, however, does not consider this conclusion justified, although he attributes both codes to the period preceding Æthelred's exile in 1013. He notes that the laws issued after his return lay particular stress on the necessity for loyalty to one royal lord—an injunction which does not appear in either of these. Both codes contain definite regulations with regard to legal procedure and stand in line with the laws of Æthelstan and Edgar.

In IV no king's name is mentioned but it almost certainly belongs to the reign of Æthelred. The order observed in referring to both sections of the people (i.e. *Dani et Angli*, cap. 8), and the insistence upon the fixed relationship of 15 ores to a pound (cap. 9, 2), point to a period when Danish influence was particularly strong. That it was not issued during the reign of Canute, however, seems evident from the fact that the Danes are not mentioned among those enjoying special trade privileges. Liebermann points out, in addition to these considerations, that Normandy appears in peaceful intercourse with England (cap. 2, 5 f.), and that relations between the Danes and English inhabitants of the country are apparently amicable. He consequently attributes the code to a date between 991—the year of the treaty between Æthelred and Richard, Duke of Normandy (see Notes)—and 1002, when the violent outbreak of hatred against the Danes was followed by the ravages and final conquest of Sweyn, 1003–1014. The code combines an account of the special regulations in force at London (chiefly with regard to the payment of toll and the trading rights of foreigners) with general decrees (mainly with regard to the coinage), applicable apparently to the whole country. The first part is particularly interesting for the light it sheds not only on the topography of London about the year 1000, but also on the trade of N.W. Europe at the time. As a document relating particularly to London it stands beside VI Æthelstan, the Charter of Henry I (Hn Lond) and the *Libertas Londoniensis* (see Liebermann, I. p. 673).

The last codes of Æthelred's reign are thoroughly ecclesiastical in tone and homiletic in style, full of tiresome repetitions and injunctions, but giving small sign of any practical policy with regard to the difficulties of the time. They bear witness to the strong influence exercised by Archbishop Wulfstan of York, to whose sermons whole passages afford close parallels (see Notes).

Codes V and VI are alike in substance, though individual differences justify their being regarded as independent. Certain clauses in VI (e.g. caps. 5, 2; 12 ff.; 32 ff.; 34) are not found in V, while additional passages, probably due to scribes, are peculiar to certain MSS (e.g. V D, caps. 32, 1-5; VI D and K, caps. 41-49; VI K, caps. 50-53). Liebermann supports Schmid's suggestion that both codes are descended from the same ordinance issued at King's Enham in 1008 (cf. X Preamble, cap. 3 ff.; VI Preamble and Note; V Heading G). The arrangement of both is practically the same, and both deal with the duties of Christian men in general, also the duties of clerics and the rights and revenues of the Church. The promotion of public security is enjoined, also attention to the repair of bridges and fortifications, to military service and to the fitting out of ships. A Latin paraphrase of VI, written in a very inflated style, is valuable for the additional information which it supplies in the preamble and in the concluding paragraph (see Notes).

Code VII is preserved in the Quadripartitus and in an Anglo-Saxon copy. In spite of differences in arrangement these point back to a common ancestor—an edict issued at Bath in a year of invasion when Michaelmas fell sometime between Thursday and Sunday (cf. VII, cap. 2, 3*a*; VII (A.S.), cap. 1). The years possible, as Liebermann points out, are 992-5, 998-1000, 1004-6, 1009-11 and 1015. The absence of reference to the approaching end of the world dreaded in the year 1000 (cf. Ælfric, *Homilies*,

R.

4

ı. pp. 578, 608; ıı. p. 370) suggests that the edict belongs to a later date, while the heading of the Anglo-Saxon version recalls *se ungemetlica unfriðhere* which began its ravages on the south and east of England in August 1009 (see *Sax. Chr.*). There is no clue however to the exact date. The occasion obviously was one of great national stress owing to the attacks of the Danes, and the purpose of the edict was to enforce the observance of Christian duties and to appoint certain special days in that year for fasting and prayer. It is particularly interesting for the light it sheds on the terror inspired by the invaders, and also notable for its entire lack of reference to practical measures of defence. Other traces of this edict of penitence are to be found in Wulfstan's Homilies (ed. Napier, pp. 169–175).

The heading of VIII in MS D ascribes it to the year 1014. No king's name is mentioned in the preamble, but resemblances both in content and phraseology to V and VI, and more particularly to Wulfstan's sermon of 1014, are in favour of accepting that date as correct. The arrangement in this code is more logical than in those preceding, and several new and important regulations appear with regard to the grading of churches, the division of tithes and the trial of members of the clergy. The expression of a desire to revive the better conditions of former days, as established by Æthelstan, Edmund and Edgar (cap. 43), is noteworthy, even though the point of view is purely ecclesiastical.

The fragments IX and X were first included by Liebermann in his edition of the Laws. The preamble and two clauses of IX are preserved in Hickes' *Thesaurus Linguarum Septentrionalium* ıı. p. 232, the MS having been burnt. In the preamble the place of assembly is named as Woodstock (cf. I), while the two extant clauses are repetitions from V and VI. For the text of X (preserved in MS Christina 946 in the Vatican at Rome) I am indebted to Liebermann's edition. The preamble, which has echoes of Edmund and Edgar, explains the aim of law-giving, while the only two extant clauses are quotations from V.

As regards the MSS of the other codes—I and II are preserved in B (from which the present text is taken), in Lambarde's edition (drawn from B and a lost MS) and in Q, while I is also found in H; III is found in H and Q; IV only in Q; V is preserved in D (from which the present text is taken), G and G$_2$ (the two latter in the same codex but in different handwriting); VI is found in K (from which the present text is taken) and partly in D; VII in Q and D; VIII in D, while the first section entitled *Be Cyricgriðe* is also found in G among a series of pieces of the same type. A few clauses appear likewise in the *Consiliatio Cnuti*. For the relationship of the various MSS see Liebermann, III. pp. 146, 149, 156, 169, 178, 182.

I ÆTHELRED

Æðelredes lage[1].

Ðis is seo gerædnys[2] þe Æþelred cining 7 his witan geræddon, eallon folce to friðes bote, æt Wudestoce on Myrcena lande, æfter Engla lage.

1. [Be borgum.][3]
Þæt is, ðǽt ælc freoman getreowne borh hæbbe, þæt se borh hine to ælcon rihte gehealde, gyf he betyhtlad wurðe.

§ 1. Gyf he ðonne tyhtbysig sy, gange to ðam ðreofealdan ordale.

§ 2. Gyf se hlaford sæcge þæt him naðor ne burste ne að ne ordal syððan þæt gemot wæs æt Bromdune, nime se hlaford him twegen getreowa ðegenas innan ðam hundrede 7 swerian þæt him næfre að ne burste ne he[4] ðeofgyld ne gulde—buton he ðone gerefan hæbbe ðe ðæs wyrðe sy þe þæt don mæge.

§ 3. Gyf se að ðonne forðcume, ceose se man ðonne, ðe ðær betyhtlad sy, swa hweðer swa he wylle, swa anfeald ordal swa pundes wurðne að, innan ðam ðrim[5] hundredan, ofer ðrittig penega.

§ 4. Gyf hi ðonne að syllan ne durron, gange to ðam ðrifealdan ordale.

§ 5. Gyf he ðonne ful wurðe, æt ðam forman cyrre bete ðam teonde twygylde 7 ðam hlaforde his were 7 sette getreowe borgas þæt he ælces yfel[es][6] eft geswice.

§ 6. And æt ðam oðran cyrre ne sy ðær nan oðer bot buton þæt heafod.

§ 7. Gyf he ðonne uthleape 7 þæt ordal forbuge, gylde se borh ðam teonde his ceapgyld 7 ðam hlaforde his were ðe his wites wyrðe sy.

§ 8. And gyf mon ðone hlaford teo, þæt he be his ræde[7] uthleope 7 ær unriht worhte, nime him fif ðegnas to 7 beo him sylf syxta 7 ladie hine ðæs.

---

[1] Om. Ld; *Æþelredes cyninges gerædnisse* H. [2] H; *þa gerædnysse* B.
[3] The rubrics are found only in Ld. [4] Om. Ld. [5] H, Ld; *drim* B.
[6] *yfeles* H; *yfel* B; *yfle* Ld. [7] H, Ld; *hræde* B.

I ÆTHELRED

Æthelred's laws[1].

This is the ordinance[1] which King Æthelred and his councillors have enacted, at Woodstock in Mercia[2], for the promotion of public security[3], wherever English law prevails[4].

1. Namely, that every freeman shall have a trustworthy surety[1] who shall hold him to the performance of every legal duty, if he has been accused.

§ 1[1]. If, however, he is of bad reputation, he shall go to the triple ordeal.

§ 2. If his lord asserts that he (the accused) has failed neither in oath nor in ordeal since the assembly was held at Bromdun[1], he (the lord) shall choose two trustworthy thegns within the hundred, and they shall swear that neither has his oath ever failed nor has he been convicted of stealing—unless the lord have a reeve[2] who is qualified to discharge this duty.

§ 3. If the oath is forthcoming, the man who is accused there shall choose whichever he will, either the simple ordeal or an oath equivalent to a pound in value, [supported by compurgators found] within the three hundreds[1], [in the case of any object] over 30 pence [in value][2].

§ 4. If they dare not give the oath, he (the accused) shall go to the triple ordeal[1].

§ 5. If he is found guilty, on the first occasion he shall pay the accuser double value and his wergeld[1] to his lord[2], and shall appoint trustworthy sureties[3] that henceforth he will desist from every kind of misdeed.

§ 6. And on the second occasion he shall not be able to make any amends except by his head[1].

§ 7[1]. If he escapes and avoids the ordeal, his surety shall pay the value of his goods to the accuser and the wergeld of the accused to the lord who is entitled to the fines incurred by him.

§ 8[1]. And if the lord is accused of advising the man who had done wrong to escape, he shall choose five thegns, and shall himself make a sixth, and shall clear himself of the accusation.

§ 9. ⁊ gyf seo lad forðcume, beo he ðes weres wyrðe.

§ 9a. ⁊ gyf héo forð ne cume, fo se cyng to ðam were ⁊ beo se ðeof utlah wið eal folc.

§ 10. ⁊ hæbbe ælc hlaford his[1] hiredmen on his agenon borge.

§ 11. Gyf he ðonne betyhtlad wurðe ⁊ he ut oðhleape[2], gylde se hlaford ðæs mannes were ðam cynge.

§ 12. ⁊ gyf mon ðone hlaford téo, þæt he be[1] his ræde utleope, ladie hine mid fif ðegnum ⁊ beo him sylf sixta.

§ 13. Gyf him seo lad byrste, gylde ðam cynge his were ⁊ si se man utlah.

§ 14. ⁊ beo se cyng ælces ðara wita wyrðe ðe ða men gewyrcean þe boclond hæbben, ⁊ ne bete nan man for nanre tihtlan, buton hit sy ðæs cynges gerefan gewitnysse.

2. [Be ðeowmen ðe ful wyrþe.]
And gyf ðeowman ful wurðe æt þam ordale, mearcie man hine æt[3] ðam forman cyrran.

§ 1. ⁊ æt ðam oðran cyrre ne sy ðær nan bót buton þæt heafod.

3. [Be ðon ðe mon ne ceapige buton gewitnysse.]
⁊ þæt[4] nan man ne dó naðor: ne ne bycgge ne ne hwyrfe, buton he borh hæbbe ⁊ gewitnysse.

§ 1. And gyf hit hwa do, fo se landhlaford to ⁊ healde þæt órf, oð þæt mon wite hwa hit mid rihte áge.

4. [Be ðæm men ðe eallum folc ungetrywe sy.]
⁊ gyf hwylc man sy ðe eallon folce ungetrywe sy, fare ðæs cynges gerefa to ⁊ gebringe hine under borge þæt hine man to rihte gelǽde ðam ðe him onspæcon.

§ 1. Gyf he ðonne borh næbbe, slea man hine ⁊ hine[5] on ful lecge.

§ 2. ⁊ gyf hwá hine forne forstande, beon hi begen anes rihtes wyrðe.

§ 3. ⁊ se ðe þis forsitte ⁊ hit geforðian nylle, swa ure ealra cwide is, sylle ðam cynge hundtwelftig scill'.

---

[1] Added above in later handwriting in B.
[2] *uthleape* Ld.
[3] *þam ordale...æt.* Added in margin in later handwriting in B.
[4] Om. Ld.　　　　　[5] Om. H.

§ 9[1]. And if he succeeds in clearing himself, he shall be entitled to the wergeld.

§ 9a. And if he fails, the king shall take the wergeld, and the thief shall be treated as an outlaw[1] by all the nation.

§ 10[1]. And every lord shall be personally [responsible as] surety for the men of his own household.

§ 11. And if a man is accused and escapes, the lord shall pay his wergeld to the king.

§ 12[1]. And if the lord is accused of advising him to escape, he shall clear himself with [the help of] five thegns, himself making a sixth.

§ 13. If he fail to clear himself, he shall pay his (own)[1] wergeld to the king, and the man shall be an outlaw.

§ 14. And the king shall be entitled to all the fines which are incurred by men who hold land by title deed, and no-one [of these] shall pay the compensation following upon any charge, unless in the presence of the king's reeve.

2. And if a slave is found guilty at the ordeal, he shall be branded[1] on the first occasion[2].

§ 1[1]. And on the second occasion he shall not be able to make any amends except by his head.

3[1]. And no-one shall either buy or exchange anything, unless he have a surety and witnesses.

§ 1. And if anyone do so, the lord of the manor[1] shall seize and keep the stock, until it is known who is the rightful owner.

4[1]. And if there is anyone who is regarded with suspicion by the general public, the king's reeve shall go and place him under surety so that he may be brought to do justice to those who have made charges against him.

§ 1. If he has no surety, he shall be slain and buried in unconsecrated ground[1].

§ 2[1]. And if anyone interposes in his defence[2], they shall both incur the same punishment.

§ 3[1]. And he who ignores this, and will not further what we have all decreed, shall pay 120 shillings to the king.

II ÆTHELRED

Ðis synd ða friðmal 7 ða forword ðe Æthelred cyng 7 ealle his witan wið ðone here gedon habbað, ðe Anlaf 7 Iustin 7 Guðmund Stegitan sunu mid wæron.

1. Ðæt ærost, þæt woroldfrið stande betweox Æthelrede cynge 7 eallum his leodscipe 7 eallum ðam here ðe se cyng þæt feoh sealde æfter ðam formalan ðe Sigeric arcebiscop 7 Æðelwerd ealdormann 7 Ælfric ealdorman worhton, ða h[i][1] abædon æt ðam cynge, þæt hy mostan ðam læppan frið gebicgean, ðe hy under cynge[2] hand ofer hæfdon.

   § 1. 7 gif ænig sciphere on Englaland hergie, þæt we habban heora ealra fultum; 7 we him sculon mete findon, ða hwile ðe hy mid us beoð.

   § 2. 7 ælc ðæra landa ðe ænigne friðige ðæra ðe Ænglaland hergie, beo hit utlah wið us 7 wið ealne here.

2. [Be ceapscypum.][3]
   7 ælc ceapscip frið hæbbe ðe binnan muðan cuman, ðeh hit unfriðscyp sy, gyf hit undrifen bið.

   § 1. 7 ðeh hit gedriuen beo 7 hit ætfleo to hwilcre friðbyrig, 7 ða menn up ætberstan into ðære byrig, ðonne habban ða men frið 7 þæt hy him mid bringað.

3. [Be ðæs cyninges fryþmannum.]
   7 ælc agenra friðmanna frið hæbbe, ge on lande ge on wætere, ge binnan muðan ge butan.

   § 1. Gyf Æðelredes cynges friðman cume on unfriðland 7 se here ðærto cume, hæbbe frið his scip 7 ealle his æhta.

   § 2. Gyf he his scip upp getogen hæbbe oððon hulc geworhtne oððon[4] geteld geslagen—þæt he ðær frið hæbbe 7 ealle his æhta.

---

[1] Ld: *hu* B.   [2] *cynges* Ld.   [3] The rubrics are found only in Ld.
[4] *oððe on* Ld.

II ÆTHELRED

These are the terms of the truce and the agreement which King Æthelred and all his councillors have made with the (Viking) fleet led by Olaf[1] and Justin[2] and Guðmund[3], the son of Stegita.

1. In the first place, a general truce[1] shall be established between King Æthelred and all his subjects and the whole (Viking) fleet to which the king has paid tribute, in accordance with[2] the terms which Archbishop Sigeric[3] and Ealdorman Æthelweard and Ealdorman Ælfric[4] made, when they obtained the king's permission to purchase peace for the districts[5] which, subject to him, they ruled over[6].

    § 1. And if any hostile fleet harry in England[1], we shall have the help of all of them; and we shall be under the obligation of finding provisions[2] for them, as long as they remain with us[3].

    § 2. And every region[1] which affords protection to any of those who harry England shall be treated as an enemy [country] by us and all the aforesaid fleet[2].

2. And every merchant ship which enters an estuary, even if it belong to a region not included in the truce[1], shall be afforded protection, provided it is not pursued[2].

    § 1. And even if it is pursued and reach any town included in the truce[1] and the men escape into the town, protection is to be afforded to them and to what they bring with them.

3. But all of those who are specially included in the truce[1] are to enjoy the protection of the truce, whether on land or on water, whether within an estuary or not.

    § 1. If a subject of King Æthelred's who is included in the truce comes to a region to which it does not apply[1], and the aforesaid fleet arrives there, protection shall be afforded to his ship and all his goods.

    § 2. If he has drawn his ship ashore or built a hut or pitched a tent, protection shall be afforded to himself and to all his goods.

§ 3. Gyf he his æhta bere geman ðara unfriðmanna æhta into huse, ðolie his æhta, 7 æbbe sylf frið 7 feorh, gif he hine cyðe.

§ 4. Gyf se friðman fleo oððon feohte 7 nelle hine cyðan, gif hine man ofslea, licge ungylde[1].

4. [Be ðon ðe mon on scipe bereafod sy.]
Gyf man beo æt his æhtan bereafod, 7 he wite of hwilcum scipe, agyfe steoresman ða æhta oððon gange feowra sum tó 7 oðsace—7 beo him sylf fifta—þæt he hit ariht name, swa hit ær geforword wæs.

5. [Be monslege.]
Gyf Ænglisc man Deniscne ofsleo, frigman frigne, gylde hine mid xxv pundum, oððon man ðone handdædan agyfe; 7 do se Denisca ðone Engliscan ealswa, gif hine[2] ofslea.

§ 1. Gyf Englisc man Deniscne ðræl ofslea, gylde hine mid punde, 7 se Denisca Engliscne ealswa, gif he hine ofslea.

§ 2. Gyf eahta men beon ofslagene, ðonne is þæt friðbrec, binnan byrig oððon buto[n][3]. Binnan eahta mannum bete man þæt fullum were.

6. [Be friþbrec binnan byrig.]
Gyf hit binnan byrig gedon bið, seo friðbræc, fare seo buruhwaru sylf to 7 begyte ða[4] banan, cuce[5] oððe deade, heora nyh[s]tan[6] magas heafod wið heafde. Gyf hy nellan, fare se ealdorman to; gif he nelle, fare se cyning to; gif he nelle, licge se ealdordóm on unfriðe.

§ 1. Æt eallum slyht 7 æt ealre ðære hergunge 7 æt eallum ðam hearmum ðe ær ðam gedon wære, ær ðæt frið geset wære, man eall onweig[7] læte, 7 nan man þæt ne rece[8] ne bote ne bidde.

§ 2. 7 þæt naðor ne hy[9] ne we ne underfon oðres wealh ne oðres ðeof ne oðres gefan.

---

[1] orgylde Ld.   [2] g. he h. Ld.   [3] Ld; buto B.   [4] ðe Ld.
[5] cute B; cucne o. deadne Ld.   [6] nyhtan B, Ld.   [7] on wege Ld.
[8] wræce Ld.   [9] hine Ld.

§ 3. If he bears his goods into a house in common with those of the men not included in the truce[1], he shall forfeit his goods, but he himself shall have protection and his life [shall be spared], if he makes himself known.

§ 4. If a man included in the truce flees or fights and fails to make himself known, no compensation shall be paid for him[1], if he is slain.

4. If anyone has been robbed of his goods and he knows the ship by[1] which it has been done, the captain[2] shall restore the goods or shall go with four compurgators[3]—himself making a fifth—and deny [the charge, proving] that he was justified in taking them, according to the terms laid down above[4].

5. If an Englishman slays a Dane, both being free men, he shall pay 25 pounds[1] for him, or the actual delinquent shall be delivered up. And likewise in the case of a Dane who slays an Englishman.

§ 1. If an Englishman slays a Danish slave[1], he shall pay one pound[2] for him, and the Dane likewise for the English slave whom he slays.

§ 2. If eight men are slain, that constitutes a breach of the truce[1], whether in a town or in the open country. For less than eight men the full wergeld shall be paid as compensation.

6. If the breach of the truce takes place inside a town, the burghers themselves shall go and take the slayers alive or dead[1]—the nearest relatives[2] [of the slain men] shall take head for head[3]. If they fail to do so[4], the ealdorman[5] shall act; if he fails to do so, the king[5] shall act; if he fails, that earldom shall be excluded from the provisions of this truce[6].

§ 1. As regards all the slaughter and all the harrying and all the injuries[1] which were done[2] before the truce was made—all of them shall be forgotten, and no-one shall avenge them or demand compensation for them.

§ 2[1]. And neither of the two parties to the truce—neither they nor we—shall harbour a slave[2] belonging to the other party, or a thief pursued by them, or anyone who is involved in vendetta with them.

7. [Be landesmannes tyhte.]

7 gif man secge on landesmann þæt he orf stæle[1] oððon man
sloge, 7 hit secge an sceiðman 7 an landesman, ðonne ne
beo he nane[s][2] andsæces wyrðe.

§ 1. 7 gif heora menn slean ure eahta, ðonne beoð hy utlage
ge wið hy ge wið us, 7 ne beo nanre bote weorðe.

§ 2. Twa and twentig ðusend[3] punda goldes 7 seolfres man
gesealde ðam here of Ænglalande wið friðe.

8. [Be ðon ðe mon gefô ðe him losod wæs.]

Gyf hwa befo þæt him losod wæs, cenne se ðe he hit æt
befo, hwanon hit him come; sylle[4] on hand 7 sette borh,
þæt he bringe his geteaman in ðær hit besprecen bið.

§ 1. Gif he liuiendre handa team gecenne 7 sy on oðere
scire se ðe he to tymð, hæbbe swa la[n]gne[5] fyrst swa
ðærto gebyrige. Sette on ða hand ðe hit him sealde
7 bidde þæt he clænsie, gif he mæge.

§ 2. Gif he tofeóht, ðonne clænsnoð he ðene ðe hit ær æt
befangen wæs. Cenne he syððan hwanan hit him[4] come.

§ 3. Gif he cenne ofer I scira, hæbbe I wucena fyrst; gif he
cenne ofer II scira, hæbbe II wucena fyrst; gyf he cenna[6]
ofer III scira, hæbbe III wucena fyrst; ofor eallswa fela
scira swa he cenne, hæbbe swa fela wycena fyrst.

§ 4. 7 tyme[7] hit mon æure ðær hit ærost befangen beo[8].

9. [Be teamum.]

Hwilon stod þæt man sceolde ðrywa tyman ðær hit ærest
befangen wære, 7 syððan fylgean teame, swa hwær swa man

---

[1] Ld; *scæle* B.   [2] Ld; *nan ei* B.
[3] *n* added in later handwriting, B.   [4] Om. Ld.   [5] Ld; *lagne* B.
[6] *cenne* Ld.   [7] *cume* B, Ld; *tyme* Lieb.   [8] *wære* Ld.

7. And if a man of our country[1] is charged with having stolen cattle or with having slain anyone, and the charge is brought by one Viking[2] and one man belonging to this country, he shall not be entitled to make any denial.

§ 1[1]. And if their men slay eight of us, they shall be treated as outlaws both by them and by us, and shall not be allowed to settle the matter by any payment of compensation.

§ 2[1]. 22,000 pounds in gold and silver[2] have been paid out of England to the (Viking) fleet as the price of the truce.

[II Æthelred, Appendix.]

8. If anyone attaches what he has lost, the man in whose possession it is attached shall declare how it came to him. He shall give pledges and furnish surety that he will produce his warrantor, when the case shall be brought into court.

§ 1. If he vouches a living person to warranty and the man whom he vouches is in another county, he shall be granted as long adjournment as is necessary for the purpose[1]. He shall lay it to the charge of the man who sold it to him, and request him to justify the transaction, if he can.

§ 2. If the latter accepts the charge, he [thereby] clears the man in whose possession it has been attached. He himself shall afterwards declare how it came to him.

§ 3[1]. If he can specify the county in which the man whom he vouches to warranty lives, he shall have a week's adjournment; if he can locate him within two counties, he shall have two weeks; if within three, he shall have three weeks—the number of weeks' adjournment granted him shall correspond to the number of counties which he names.

§ 4. And vouching to warranty shall always[1] take place where the property has first been attached.

9. Formerly it was the rule that vouching to warranty for the first three times should take place where the goods were first attached, and afterwards[1] the process should be trans-

to cende. Ða geræddan[1] witan, þæt hit betere wære, þæt
man æure tymde ðær hit ærest befangen wære, swa longe
þæt man wiste hwær hit ætstandan wolde, ðy læs ðe mon
unmihtigne man to feor 7 to lange for his agenan swencte.
Swunce mare se ðe þæt unriht gestreon on his handa stode
7 læsse se ðe ðær ariht onspræce.

§ 1. Warige eac hine se ðe his agen[2] befoð: he to ælcan
teame hæbbe getrywne borh 7 beorge þæt he awoh ne
befo, ðy les ðe hine mon swence, swa he oðerne man
ðohte.

§ 2. Gyf hwa to deadan tyme—buton he yruenoman hæbbe
ðe hit clænsie—geswutelie mid gewitnysse, gif he mæge,
þæt he riht cenne se ðe hit tyme 7 clænsnige hine sylfne
mid ðam. Ðonne bið se deada besmiten, buton he frind
hæbbe ðe hine mid rihte clænsnian, swa he sylf scolde,
gif he mehte oðð liues wære.

§ 3. Gif he ðonne ðære freonda hæfð ðe þæt don durron,
ðonne berst se team, swa wel swa he liues wære 7 sylf
andsæc[3] worhte; stent ðonne ðeofscyldig se ðe hit on
handa hæfð, forðam a bið andsæc swiðere ðonne
onsagu.

§ 4. Eac betweox teame, gif hwa tofehð 7 na furðor team
ne cenð ac agnian wille, ne mæg mon ðæs wyrnan, gif
getrywe gewitnes him to agenunge rymð, forðam
agnung bið ner ðam ðe hæfð ðonne ðam ðe æftersprecð.

---

[1] -don Ld.   [2] Ld; hagen B.   [3] Ld; and sæt B.

ferred to the locality indicated (by the evidence of the
third person). Then the authorities decided that it would
be better for the vouching to warranty always to take place
where the property was first attached, until it should appear
where the process would end, lest a man of small means
should be burdened by long and distant journeys in order
to recover his property. The burden should rather be borne
by him who has in his possession property to which he is
not entitled, than by him who is putting forward a just
claim to it.

§ 1. Likewise, he who attaches his goods shall see to it that
he has trustworthy security[1] in every case of vouching
to warranty, and shall beware of attaching wrongly,
lest the burden which he had thought should be borne
by the other man should be laid upon him.

§ 2. If anyone vouches a dead person[1] to warranty—unless
he have an heir who can answer the charge—he who
vouches him to warranty shall show by means of witnesses, if he can, that he is acting justly, and by means
of them shall clear himself. Then the dead man will
be held guilty, unless he have friends who will clear
him according to the law, as he himself would have
been obliged to do, had he been able or had he been
alive.

§ 3. If, however, he has friends[1] who are prepared to do so,
the vouching to warranty shall fail as completely as if
he had himself been alive and had proved his denial.
Then he, in whose possession the goods are, will be held
guilty of theft[2], because denial is always stronger than
accusation.

§ 4. Further, in the course of vouching to warranty, if
anyone accepts and does not carry the process any
farther but desires to declare himself the owner [of the
goods][1], no-one can deny his claim, if trustworthy witnesses establish his ownership of the goods, for a priori
the actual possessor must be regarded as having more
right than the claimant[2].

III ÆTHELRED

Ðis syndon þa lága þe Æðelred cyng 7 his witan gerædd habbað æt Wánetingc to friðes bóte.

1. Ðæt is: þæt his grið stande swa forð swa hit fyrmest stód on his yldrena dagum, þæt þæt sy bótléas þæt he mid his agenre hánd sylð.

   § 1. 7 þæt grið, þæt se ealdormann 7 kinges geréfa on Fif burga geþincða sylle, bete man þæt mid xii hund'.

   § 2. And þæt grið þæt man sylleð on i burhgaþinðe[1], bete man þæt mid vi hundr̄; and þæ[t][2] man sylle on wǽpentáke, bete man þæt mid hundr̄, gif hit man brecð; and þæt man sylle on éalahuse, bete man þæt æt deadum menn mid vi healfmarce 7 æt cwicon mid xii óran.

2. And þæt þæt man cyðe mid gewitnesse, þæt nan man þæt ne awende æt cwícon þe ma þe æt déadon.

   § 1. 7 gange ælc man þæs to gewitnesse þe he durre on þam haligdóme swerian þe him man on hand sylð.

3. And lándcóp 7 hlafordes gifu þe he on riht age to gifanne 7 lahcóp 7 witword 7 gewítnes, þæt þæt stande þæt hit nan man ne awénde.

   § 1. 7 þæt man habbe gemót on ælcum wæpen[t]ace[3]; 7 gán út þa yldestan xii þegnas 7 se gerefa mid 7 swerian on þam haligdome þe heom man on hand sylle, þæt hig nellan nǽnne sacleasan man forsecgean ne nænne sacne forhélan.

---

[1] *burhga* (1) *þinðe* (1 written above the line) H; *unius burgi þincþa* Q.
[2] *þær* H.   [3] *-kace* H.

III ÆTHELRED

These are the constitutions[1] which King Æthelred and his councillors have enacted at Wantage[2] for the promotion of public security[3].

1. Namely, that the king's peace[1] shall continue to be maintained in accordance with the highest standards[2] observed in the days of his ancestors, so that breach of the peace which he establishes in person shall not be atoned for by any payment of compensation[3].

   § 1. But for breach of the peace which the ealdorman or[1] the king's reeve establishes in the Court of the Five Boroughs[2], 1200 of silver shall be paid as compensation.

   § 2. And for breach of the peace established in the court of one borough[1] 600 [of silver] shall be paid as compensation, and 100 for that established in a wapentake. In the case of breach of the peace in an ale-house, 6 half marks[2] shall be paid as compensation if a man is slain, and 12 ores if no-one is slain[3].

2. Secondly, declarations made with the support of witnesses shall be incontrovertible, whether the persons concerned be alive or dead[1].

   § 1. And a man shall appear as witness to such things[1] [only] as he is prepared to swear to on the relics[2] which are given into his hand.

3. And there shall be no interference with purchases of land[1], or gifts by a lord of what he has a legal right to bestow, or purchases of legal rights[2], or asseverations (which have been duly made) or testimonies[3] (which have been duly given).

   § 1. And a court shall be held in every wapentake, and the twelve leading thegns[1] along with the reeve shall go out and swear on the relics[2] which are given into their hands, that they will not accuse any innocent[3] man or shield any guilty[4] one.

§ 2. 7 niman þonne þa tihtbysian men þe mid þam gerefan [sace]¹ habbað, 7 heora ælc sylle vi healfmarc wedd, healf landrícan 7 healf wǽpentake.

§ 3. 7 ælc bicge him lage mid xii óran, healf landrican, healf wæpentake.

§ 4. 7 ælc tihtbysig man gange to þryfeldan órdale oððe gilde feowergilde.

4. Gif se hlaford þonne hine ladian wylle mid twam godum þegenum, þæt he næfre þeofgild né gúlde, siððan þæt gemót wæs on Brómdune, ne he betihlod nære, gange tó anfealdum órdale oððe gilde iiigilde.

§ 1. Gif he þonne ful beo, slea man hine, þæt him forberste se swéora; 7 gif he þæt ordal forbuge, gilde angylde þam agenan frian 7 landrícan xx óran 7 gá eft to þam órdale.

§ 2. And gif se ágena frígia nelle þæt ordal gesecean, gilde xx óran 7 sy his spæce forlóren; 7 he þeah gange þam landrícan to ordale oððe agife twygilde.

5. And gif hwa borhleas órf habbe 7 landrícan hit befón, agife þæt órf 7 gilde xx oran.

6. 7 ælc tíond áge geweald, swa hwæðer he wille, swa wæter swa ísen.

§ 1. 7 ælc téam 7 ælc ordal beo on þæs kyninges byrig.

§ 2. 7 gif he þæt ordal forfleo, gilde se borh hine be his were.

¹ Not in MS.; cf. causam Q.

§ 2. And then they shall arrest those men of bad repute against whom the reeve is taking proceedings[1], and each of them shall pay six half marks[2] as security, half to the lord of the manor and half to the wapentake[3].

§ 3. And each of them shall pay 12 ores[1], half to the lord of the manor and half to the wapentake. in order to obtain the benefit of the law.

§ 4[1]. And every man of bad repute shall go to the triple ordeal or pay fourfold [the value of the goods involved].

4[1]. If, however, his lord is willing to clear him, [swearing], along with two good thegns, that he has neither been convicted of theft nor been accused since the assembly was held at Bromdun, he shall go to the simple ordeal[2] or pay threefold [the value of the goods involved].

§ 1[1]. If then he is proved guilty, he shall be struck such a blow as shall break his neck. But if he evades the ordeal, he shall pay the value [of the goods] to their owner, and 20 ores[2] to the lord of the manor, and shall thereafter go to the ordeal.

§ 2. But if the owner [of the goods] shall fail to appear at the ordeal, he shall pay 20 ores and shall lose his case. But nevertheless the lord of the manor shall cause him (the thief) to go to the ordeal[1] or to pay double the value of the goods[2].

5. And if anyone has livestock acquired without surety[1], and manorial lords attach it[2], he shall give up the livestock[3] and pay 20 ores.

6[1]. And every accuser shall have the choice of whichever ordeal he desires [for the accused]—either ordeal by water or by iron.

§ 1. And every vouching to warranty[1] and every ordeal shall take place in a royal manor[2].

§ 2[1]. And if he (the accused) flees from the ordeal, his surety shall pay for him to the amount of his (the fugitive's) wergeld.

7. And gif hwa þeof clænsian wylle, lecge an c to wedde, healf
   landrican 7 healf cinges gerefan binnan port, 7 gange to
   þrimfealdan ordale.

   § 1. Gif he clæne beo æt þam ordale, nime úpp his mǽg; gif
   he þonne ful beo, licge þar he lǽg, 7 gilde an c.

8. And ælc mynetére þe man tihð þæt fals feoh sloge, syðð an
   hit forboden wæs, gange to þrimfealdan ordale; gif he ful
   beo, slea hine man.

   § 1. And nan mann ne áge nænne mynetere buton cyng.

   § 2. 7 ælc mynetere þe betihtlad sí, bicge him láh mid xii
   oran.

9. 7 nan mann hryðer ne sléa, buton he habbe twégra trywra
   manna gewitnesse, 7 he healde iii niht hyde 7 heafod;
   7 sceapes eallswa.

   § 1. 7 gif he þa hyde ǽr þam awég sylle, gilde xx oran.

10. 7 ælc flyma beo flyma on ælcum lande þe on ánum sy.

11. 7 nan man náge náne socne ofer cynges þegen buton cyng
    sylf.

12. And æt cynges spǽce lecge man vi healfmarc wedd 7 æt
    eorles 7 biscopes xii óran wedd 7 æt ælcum þegene vi óran
    wedd.

13. 7 gif man hwilcne man téo, þæt he þone man féde þe ures
    hlafordes grið tóbrocen habbe, ladige hine mid þrinna xii,
    7 se geréfa namige þa lade.

    § 1. And gif hine man mid him befare, béon hig begen ánes
    rihtes weorðe.

    § 2. 7 þæt dóm stande þar þegenas sámmǽle beon; gif hig
    sacan, stande þæt hig viii secgað; 7 þa þe ðær ofer-
    drífene beoð, gilde heora ælc vi healfmarc.

7[1]. And if anyone seeks to clear a thief, he shall deposit 100 [of silver] as security[2], half with the lord of the manor[3] and half with the king's town-reeve[4] and he shall go to the triple ordeal.

§ 1. And if he prove innocent at the ordeal, he shall remove his kinsman [from his grave in unconsecrated ground][1]. If, however, he be guilty, the thief shall lie where he is, and he himself shall pay 100 [of silver][2].

8. And every moneyer who is accused of striking false coins, after it was forbidden[1], shall go to the triple ordeal; if he is guilty, he shall be slain.

§ 1. And no-one except the king[1] shall have a moneyer.

§ 2[1]. And every moneyer who is accused shall pay 12 ores in order to obtain the benefit of the law.

9. And no-one shall kill a cow unless he has two trustworthy men as witnesses, and he shall keep the hide and the head[1] for three days; and those of a sheep likewise.

§ 1. And if he disposes of the hide before that, he shall pay 20 ores[1].

10. And everyone who is an outlaw in one district shall be an outlaw everywhere.

11[1]. And no-one shall have jurisdiction over a thegn of the king except the king himself.

12. And in the case of an action brought by[1] the king, 6 half-marks shall be deposited as security, and in the case of one brought by an earl or a bishop, 12 ores, and of one brought by a thegn, 6 ores as security.

13. And if anyone is accused of furnishing with food a man who has broken our lord's peace, he shall clear himself with three times twelve[1] compurgators who shall be nominated by the reeve.

§ 1. And if he (the accused) is found in his company, they shall both incur the same penalty[1].

§ 2. And a verdict in which the thegns are unanimous[1] shall be held valid; if they disagree, the verdict of eight[2] of them shall be valid, and those who are outvoted[3] in such a case shall each pay 6 half-marks[4].

§ 3. 7 þar þegen áge twegen costas, lufe oððe lage, 7 he
þonne lufe geceose, stande þæt swa fæst swa sé dom.

§ 4. 7 se ðe ofer ðæt láde geþafie oððe se þe hy sylle, gilde
VI healfmarc.

14. And se þe sitte úncwydd 7 uncrafod on his áre on life, þæt
nan mann on his yrfenuman ne spéce æfter his dæge.

15. And se þe reafað man leohtan dæge 7 he hit kyþe to þrim
túnan, þæt he ne beo nanes fryðes weorðe.

16. 7 þa myneteras þe inne wuda wyrceð oððe elles hwær, þæt
þa bion heora feores scyldig, buton se cyning heom arian
wille.

IV ÆTHELRED

[Item rex Lundoniae.][1]

[2][De institutis Lundoniae; et primum: quae[3] portae observa-
bantur[4]. [2.] De teloneo dando ad Bilingesgate. [3.] De teloneo
retento. [4.] De hamsocna vel in porto[5] vel in via regia[6].
[5.] De falsariis et eis consentientibus. Et de cum falsa moneta
deprensis[7]. [6.] Et de monetariis[8].]

1. Ealdredesgate[9] et Cripelesgate[10] (id est portas illas) ob-
servabant[11] custodes.

2. Ad Billingesgate si advenisset una navicula—I obolus
tolonei[12] dabatur; si maior et haberet[13] siglas[14]—unum den.

§ 1. Si adveniat ceol vel hulcus, et ibi iaceat—quatuor d.
ad teloneum[15].

§ 2. De navi plena lignorum—unum lignum ad tol'[16].

§ 3. In ebdomada pañ'[17] teloñ[18] III diebus: die Dominica et[19]
die Martis et[19] die Iovis.

---

[1] R.   [2] This table of contents is found in M, Hk, Br.   [3] *quod* Br.
[4] *-buntur* Br.   [5] *-tu* Br.   [6] *-gis* Br.
[7] Instead of *Et...depr.* Br has: [6.] *De sonantibus pecuniam puram.* [7.] *De
mercatoribus qui falsum et lactum afferunt ad portum.* [8.] *De suasione regis contra
falsum operantes.*
[8] [9]...*m. et ubi erunt* Br.   [9] T; *Aaldretes* R; *Aldretes* M, Hk; *Aldredes* Br.
[10] *Crypeleg.* T; *Cyrpuleg.* M, Hk; *Ciryclegate* Br.   [11] *-bunt* Br.
[12] *thel.* T, Br.   [13] *habet* T, M, Hk, Br.   [14] *gulas* R, T.
[15] *a. t. dentur* Br.   [16] *a. t. detur* Br.   [17] R, T; *panū* M; *panum* Br.
[18] *thelonium detur* Br.   [19] Om. M, Hk, Br.

§ 3. And where a thegn has two alternatives[1] before him—
amicable agreement or legal proceedings—and he de-
cides upon the former, it shall be as binding as a legal
decision.

§ 4. And he who subsequently[1] permits a man to clear
himself [of a transaction], and [likewise] he who offers
to clear himself shall pay 6 half-marks.

14. And if a man dwells on his property free from claims and
charges[1] during his lifetime, no-one shall bring an action
against his heirs[2] after his death.

15. And if a man robs another in daylight[1], and the latter makes
the deed known in three villages[2], he shall not be entitled
to protection[3] of any kind.

16[1]. And moneyers who work in a wood[2] or elsewhere[3] shall
forfeit their lives, unless the king is willing to pardon them.

IV ÆTHELRED

1. The gates called Aldersgate[1] and Cripplegate[1] (i.e. the actual
gates) were in the charge of guards.

2. If a small ship came to Billingsgate[1], 1 half-penny was paid
as toll; if a larger ship with sails, 1 penny was paid.

§ 1. If a barque or a merchantman[1] arrives and lies there,
4 pence is paid as toll.

§ 2. From a ship with a cargo of planks, one plank is given
as toll.

§ 3. On three days of the week toll for cloth[1] [is paid]—
on Sunday and Tuesday and Thursday[2].

§ 4. Qui ad pontem venisset[1] cum uno[2] bato ubi piscis inesset[3], ipse mango[4] unum obolum dabat[5] in telon., et de una[2] maiori nave unum d.

§ 5. Homines de Rotomago qui veniebant cum vino vel craspisce[6] dabant[7] rectitudinem sex sol. de magna navi et viginti frustum de ipso craspisce[6].

§ 6. Flandrenses et Ponteienses et Normannia et Francia monstrabant res suas et extolneabant.

§ 7. Hogge et Leodium et Nivella qui pertransibant[8] ostensionem dabant et telon.

§ 8. Et homines imperatoris qui veniebant in[9] navibus suis bonarum legum digni tenebantur sicut et nos.

§ 9. Praeter[10] discarcatam[11] lanam et dissutum unctum, et tres porcos vivos licebat eis emere in naves suas.

§ 10. Et non licebat eis aliquod forceapum facere burhmannis, et dare toll' suum et in sancto natali Domini duos grisengos pannos et unum brunum et decem libras piperis et cirotecas quinque hominum et duos caballinos tonellos[12] aceto plenos; et totidem in pascha.

§ 11. De dosseris cum gallinis i gallina telonei, et de[13] uno dossero cum ovis v ova telonei, si veniant ad mercatum.

§ 12. Smeremangestrae (quae mangonant in caseo et butiro) xiiii diebus ante natale Domini unum den., et septem diebus ante[14] natale Domini[15] unum alium[16].

3. Si portireva vel tungravio compellet[17] aliquem vel alius praepositus quod teloneum supertenuerit, et homo respondeat quod nullum tolneum[18] concelaverit quod iuste dare[2] debuisset[19], iuret hoc se vii°[20] et sit quietus.

§ 1. Si appellet quod tolneum[21] dedit[22], inveniat cui dedit et sit quietus.

---

[1] *veniat* Br.   [2] Om. M, Hk, Br.   [3] *inest, unus ob. dabatur* Br.
[4] *magno* M, Hk.   [5] *dabit* R.   [6] *craspice* R.
[7] *dabant...craspisce* om. M, Hk, Br.   [8] *per terras ibant* T, M, Hk, Br.
[9] *cum* M, Hk, Br.   [10] *Praeter...v. l. eis* om. M, Hk, Br.   [11] *discartatam* T.
[12] *tolennos* M; *collennos* Hk; *colennos* Br.   [13] Om. M, Hk.   [14] *post* Br.
[15] M, Hk, Br.   [16] *u. a. denarium ad theloneum* Br.
[17] *v. alius p. compellat aliquem* Br.   [18] R; *teloneum* T, M, Hk, Br.
[19] *debuit* Br.   [20] vi° M, Hk, Br.   [21] R, T; *telon.* M, Hk; *thel.* Br.
[22] *dederit* Br.

§ 4. A merchant who came to the bridge[1] with a boat containing fish paid 1 half-penny as toll, and for a larger ship 1 penny.

§ 5. Men of Rouen[1], who came with wine or blubber-fish[2], paid a duty[3] of 6 shillings for a large ship and 5 %[4] of the fish.

§ 6. Men from Flanders[1] and Ponthieu and Normandy and the Isle of France exhibited their goods and paid toll[2].

§ 7. Men from Huy[1] and Liège and Nivelles who were passing through (London)[2] paid a sum for exhibition[3] and toll.

§ 8. And subjects of the Emperor[1] who came in their ships[2] were entitled to the same privileges[3] as ourselves.

§ 9. Besides wool, which had been unloaded[1], and melted fat[2], they were also permitted to buy three live pigs[3] for their ships.

§ 10. But they were not allowed any right of pre-emption[1] over the burgesses, and [they had] to pay their toll[2], and at Christmas[3] two lengths of grey cloth[4] and one length of brown and 10 pounds of pepper[5] and five pairs of gloves and two saddle-kegs[6] of vinegar, and the same at Easter.

§ 11. From hampers[1] with hens, one hen [is given] as toll, and from one hamper of eggs, five eggs as toll, if they come to the market.

§ 12. Women who deal in dairy produce[1] (i.e. cheese and butter) pay 1 penny a fortnight before Christmas, and another penny a week before Christmas.

3. If the town-reeve or the village reeve[1] or any other official[2] accuses[3] anyone of having withheld[4] toll, and the man replies that he has kept back no toll which it was his legal duty to pay, he shall swear to this with 6 others and shall be quit of the charge.

§ 1. If he declares[1] that he has paid toll, he shall produce the man to whom he paid it, and shall be quit of the charge.

§ 2. Si tunc hominem invenire non possit cui dederit[1], reddat ipsum tolneum et persolvat et[2] quinque libras regi.

§ 3. Si cacepollum advocet quod ei teloneum dedit, et ille neget, perneget ad Dei iudicium et in nulla alia lada[3].

4. Et diximus: homo qui hamsocnam faciet intra[4] portum sine licentia et summam infracturam aget[5] de placito unge-bendeo[6], vel qui aliquem innocentem affliget[7] in via regia, si iaceat[8], iaceat in ungildan ækere.

§ 1. Si pugnet antequam sibi[9] rectum postulet ac vivat, emendet regis[10] burhbrece quinque libris.

§ 2. Si curet[11] amicitiam ipsius porti, reddat nobis triginta sol. emendationis, si rex hoc concedat nobis.

5. Etiam dixerunt quod nichil eis interesse videbatur inter falsarios et mercatores qui bonam pecuniam portant ad falsarios et ab ipsis emunt ut inpurum et minus appendens operentur, et inde mangonant[12] et barganiant, et eos etiam qui conos faciunt in occultis et vendunt falsariis pro pecunia et incidunt alterius monetarii nomen[13] in eo et non ipsius immundi.

§ 1. Unde visum est sapientibus omnibus, quod isti tres homines unius rectitudinis essent digni.

§ 2. Et si aliquis eorum accusetur, sit[14] Anglicus sit trans-marinus, ladiet se pleno ordalio.

§ 3. Et constituerunt, monetarii cur[15] manum perdant et ponatur super ipsius monetae fabricam.

§ 4. Et monetarii[16], qui in nemoribus operantur[16] vel alicubi[17] similibus fabricant, vitae suae culpabiles sint, nisi rex velit eorum misereri.

---

[1] *dedit* Br.　　[2] R; om. T, M, Hk, Br.　　[3] *laga* T.　　[4] *faciat inter* R.
[5] *age* Hk; *agat* Br.　　[6] R; *-dro* T, M, Hk, Br.　　[7] *-gat* Br.
[8] *s. i.* om. Br.　　[9] Om. M, Hk, Br.　　[10] Om. T.　　[11] *-at* M, Hk.
[12] *mag.* M, Hk.　　[13] *monetam mundam et n. ipsam immundam* Br.
[14] *si* R.　　[15] *cur mon.* M, Hk; *quod mon.* Br.　　[16] Om. Br.
[17] *alibi* T, M, Hk, Br.

§ 2. If, however, he cannot produce the man to whom he paid it, he shall pay the actual toll and as much again[1] and 5 pounds to the king[2].

§ 3. If he vouches the tax-gatherer[1] to warranty[2] [asserting] that he paid toll to him, and the latter denies it, he shall clear himself by the ordeal and by no other means of proof.

4. And we[1] have decreed that a man who, within the town, makes forcible entry into another man's house without permission and commits a breach of the peace[2] of the worst kind...[3] and he who assaults an innocent person on the king's highway[4], if he is slain, shall lie in an unhonoured grave[5].

§ 1[1]. If, before demanding justice, he has recourse to violence, but does not lose his life thereby[2], he shall pay 5 pounds for breach of the king's peace[3].

§ 2. If he values the good-will[1] of the town itself, he shall pay us[2] 30 shillings[3] as compensation, if the king will grant us this concession.

5. Further, they[1] have decided that no distinction is to be drawn between those who issue base coin, and traders who take good money to such men and bribe[2] them to produce [from it] coin which is defective in quality and weight[3] with which they trade and buy, and, thirdly, those who make dies in secret and sell them to coiners for money, engraving upon them a name which is that of another moneyer and not that of the guilty one.

§ 1. It has therefore been determined by the whole council that these three [classes of] men shall incur the same punishment[1].

§ 2. And if one of them is accused, whether he be an Englishman or a foreigner, he shall clear himself by the full ordeal[1].

§ 3[1]. And they have decreed that[2] coiners shall lose a hand, and that it shall be fastened up over the mint.

§ 4[1]. And moneyers who carry on their business in woods or work in other such places shall forfeit their lives, unless the king is willing to pardon them.

6. Et praecipimus ne quis pecuniam puram et recte appendentem sonet, monetetur in quocumque portu monetetur[1] in regno meo, super overhirnessam meam.

7. Et diximus de mercatoribus qui falsum et lacum[2] afferunt ad portum, ut advocent si possint.

§ 1. Si non possint[3], werae suae culpa sit[4] vel vitae suae, sicut rex volet[5], vel eadem lada se innoxient quam praediximus, quod in ipsa pecunia nil immundum sciebant unde suam negotiationem exercuerunt.

§ 2. Et habeat postea dampnum illud ex incuria sua, ut cambiat[6] ab institutis monetariis purum et recte[7] appendens.

§ 3. Et portirevae qui falsi huius consentanei[8] fuerint, eiusdem censurae digni sint[9] cum falsis monetariis, nisi rex indulgeat eis vel se possint[10] adlegiare eodem cyrað[11] vel ordalio praedicto.

8. Et rex suadet et mandat episcopis suis et comitibus et aldremannis et praepositis omnibus, ut curam adhibeant[12] de illis qui tale falsum operantur et portant per patriam, sicut praemissum[13] est, utrobique cum Danis et Anglis.

9. Et ut monetarii pauciores sint quam antea fuerint[14]: in omni summo portu III[15], et in omni alio portu sit unus monetarius.

§ 1. Et illi habeant suboperarios suos in suo crimine, quod purum faciant et recti ponderis, per eandem witam quam praediximus.

---

[1] *monetur* M, Hk, Br; *in q. p. m.* om. R.   [2] *laccum* M, Hk; *lactum* Br.
[3] *s. n. p.* om. R.   [4] *culpabiles sint* Br.   [5] *velit* Br.   [6] Om. M, Hk, Br.
[7] *rectum* Br.   [8] *falso cons.* Br.   [9] *sunt* R, T.   [10] *possit* R, T.
[11] *cir.* R; *syrað* M, Hk; *sirath* Br.   [12] *-eat* R.   [13] *prom.* R, T.
[14] *-runt* Br.   [15] *sint tres monctarii* Br.

6. And we enjoin that no-one shall refuse pure money of the proper weight, in whatever town[1] in my kingdom it be coined, under pain of incurring the fine for insubordination to me.

7. And we have decreed with regard to traders who bring money which is defective in quality and weight to the town, that they shall name a warrantor if they can.

   § 1. If they cannot do so, they shall forfeit their wergeld or their life, as the king shall decide[1], or they shall clear themselves by the same method[2] as we have specified above, [asserting] that they were unaware that there was anything counterfeit about the money with which they were carrying on their business.

   § 2. And afterwards such a trader shall pay the penalty of his carelessness by having to change [his base money] for pure money of the proper weight obtained from the authorised moneyers[1].

   § 3[1]. And town-reeves who have been accessories to such a fraud shall be liable to the same punishment as coiners, unless the king pardon them, or they can clear themselves by a similar oath of nominated jurors[2], or by the ordeal specified above[3].

8. And the king advises and commands his bishops and earls and ealdormen[1] and all his reeves that, both[2] among the Danes and the English[3], they be on the watch for those who coin such base money and spread it abroad through the country, as has been stated above.

9. And moneyers shall be fewer in number than they have been in the past. In every principal town[1] [there shall be] three, and in every other town [there shall be] one.

   § 1. And they shall be responsible for the production by their employees of pure money of the proper weight, under pain of incurring the same fine[1] as we have fixed above.

§ 2. Et ipsi qui portos[1] custodiunt, efficiant per overhernes-
sam meam, ut omne pondus sit marcatum ad pondus
quo pecunia mea recipitur; et eorum singulum signetur
ita, cur[2] xv[3] orae libram[4] faciant.

§ 3. Et custodiant omnes monetam, sicut vos docere praecipio et omnes elegimus.

V ÆTHELRED

In nomine Domini[5].

Ðis is seo gerædnes, þe Engla cyninge [7][6] ægðer [ge][6] gehadode
ge læwede witan gecuron 7 geræddon.

1. Þis[7] þonne ærest, þæt we ealle[8] ænne God lufian 7 wurðian
7 ænne Cristendom georne healdan 7 ælcne hæðendom mid
ealle awurpan[9]; 7 þæt we habbað ealle ægðer ge mid worde
ge mid wedde gefæstnod, þæt we under anum cynedome
ænne Cristendom healdan willað.

§ 1. 7 ure[s][10] hlafordes gerædnes 7 his witena is[11], þæt man
rihte lage[12] up arære 7 ælce unlage georne afille, 7 þæt
man læte æghwilcne man beon rihtes wurðe, 7 [þæt][6]
man frið 7 freondscipe rihtlice healde [innan þysan earde
for Gode 7 for worolde][6].

2. 7 ures hlafordes gerædnes 7 his witena is, þæt man Cristene
men 7 unforworhte of earde ne sylle, ne huru on hæðene
þeode[13], ac beorge[14] georne þæt man þa sawla ne forfare þe
Crist mid his agenum life gebohte.

---

[1] porcos R, T.   [2] quod Hk.
[3] Om. Br.   [4] bilibram inst. of o. l. T.
[5] I. n. D., anno dominicae incarnationis MVIII G; Be Angolwitena gerednesse G₂.
[6] G, G₂; om. D.   [7] Ðæt is G; Ðæt G₂.
[8] w. e. fram synnan georne gecyrran 7 ure misdæda geornlice betan 7 æ. G. G₂.
[9] The rest of the sent. is omitted in G₂.   [10] ures G; ure D.
[11] 7 witena gerædnes is G₂ (throughout).   [12] laga G, G₂.
[13] leode G, G₂.   [14] b. man G, G₂.

§ 2. And those who have the charge of towns shall see to it, under pain of incurring the fine for insubordination to me, that every weight is stamped according to the standard employed in my mint[1]; and the stamp used for each of them shall show that the pound contains 15 ores[2].

§ 3. And the coinage is to be maintained by all at the standard which I lay down in your instructions, in accordance with the decision at which we have all arrived.

V ÆTHELRED

In the name of the Lord[1].

This is the ordinance which has been determined upon and enacted by the king of England[1] and his councillors, both ecclesiastic and lay[2].

1. The first provision is: that we all[1] love and honour one God[2], and zealously observe one Christian faith[3], and wholly renounce all heathen practices[4]. We have confirmed, both by word and by pledge, our firm intention of observing one Christian faith under the authority of one king[5].

   § 1[1]. And the decree of our lord and of his councillors is, that justice shall be promoted and all injustice zealously suppressed, and that every man shall be allowed the benefit of the law[2], and that peace and good-will[3] shall be duly maintained [within this land in matters both religious and secular[4]].

2[1]. And it is the decree of our lord and his councillors, that Christian men who are innocent of crime shall not be sold out of the land[2], least of all to the heathen[3], but care shall diligently be taken that the souls which Christ bought with his own life[4] be not destroyed.

3. 7 ures hlafordes gerædnes 7 his witena is, þæt man Cristene men for ealles to litlum to deaðe ne fordeme[1]; ac elles geræde man friðlice steora folce to þearfe, 7 ne forspille for litlum Godes handgeweorc 7 his agenne ceap þe he deore gebohte.

4. 7 ures hlafordes gerædnes 7 his witena is, þæt ælces hades men georne gebugan, for Gode 7 for worlde, ælc to ðam rihte þe him to gebirige. And huruþinga Godes þeowas— biscopas 7 abbodas, munecas 7 minicena, preostas 7 nunnan —to rihte gebugan 7 regollice libban 7 for eal Cristen folc geornlice þingian.

5. And ures hlafordes gerædnes 7 his witena is, þæt muneca gehwilc þe ute sy of mynstre 7 regoles ne gime, do swa him þearf is: gebuge georne into mynstre mid eallum ead-mettum, 7 misdæda geswice 7 bete swiðe georne þæt he abrocen hæbbe; geþence word 7 wed þe[2] he Gode betæhte.

6. And se munuc, þe mynster næbbe, cume [him][3] to[4] scire-biscope 7 trywsige hine sylfne wið God 7 wið men, þæt he huru þreo þingc þananforð behealdan[5] wille, þæt is his clænnesse 7 munuclice scrudware 7 þeowian his Drihtene swa wel swa he betst mæge; 7 gif he þæt gelæste, þonne bið he wyrðe þæt hine man þe bet healde, wunige þar he wunige.

7. And canonicas þar seo ár sý þæt hi beoddern 7 slæpern habban magan, healdan heora mynster mid rihte 7 mid clænnisse, swa heora regol tæce; oððe riht is þæt he[6] þolige þare are se ðe þæt nelle.

8. And ealle mæssepreostas we biddað 7 lærað þæt hi beorgan heom silfum wið Godes irre.

---

[1] G, G₂; -demde D. [2] þæt G₂.
[3] Written in the margin in a handwriting of the same period.
[4] Om. G. [5] healdan G, G₂. [6] Om. G, G₂.

3[1]. And it is the decree of our lord and his councillors, that Christian men shall not be condemned to death for too trivial offences, but, on the contrary, merciful punishments[2] shall be determined upon for the public good, that the handiwork of God, and what he purchased for himself at a great price, be not destroyed for trivial offences.

4[1]. And it is the decree of our lord and his councillors, that men of every estate shall readily submit, in matters both religious and secular, to the duty which befits them; and most of all the servants of God, bishops and abbots, monks and nuns[2], priests and women under religious vows[2], shall submit to their duty, and live according to their rule, and zealously intercede[3] for all Christian people.

5[1]. And it is the decree of our lord and his councillors, that every monk, who is out of a monastery[2] and who is not observing a rule, shall do what is his duty, namely, he shall readily return into the monastery with all humility, and desist from his misdeeds, and zealously make amends for the transgressions he has committed. Let him remember the vows[3] which he rendered to God.

6. And the monk who has no monastery[1] shall come to the bishop of the diocese, and shall vow to God and to men henceforth to observe three things at least, namely, celibacy, and the wearing of the monastic habit, and the service of his Lord to the best of his ability. And if he carries out this vow, he shall be entitled to be treated with greater consideration[2], wherever he may dwell.

7[1]. And canons[2], wherever their property admits of their having a refectory and a dormitory, shall maintain regularity and celibacy in their foundation, as their rule prescribes; otherwise it is right that he who refuses to do so should forfeit his endowment[3].

8[1]. And we pray and admonish all priests to guard against incurring the wrath of God.

9. Fulgeorne hi wi[t]an[1] þæt hi nagan mid rihte þurh hæmed-
þinge wifes gemanan.

§ 1. 7 se þe þæs geswican wille 7 clænnesse healdan, habbe
he Godes mildse, 7 þar to eacan to worldwurðscipe þæt
he sy þegenweres 7 þegenrihtes wurðe, ge on life ge
on legere.

§ 2. 7 se þe þæt nelle, [þæt his hade gebyrige][2], wanige his
wurðscipe ge for Gode ge for worlde.

10. And æghwilc Cristen man[3] unriht hæmed georne forbuge
7 godcunde laga rihtlice healde.

§ 1. 7 sy ælc cirice on Godes griðe 7 on ðæs cynges 7 on
ealles Cristenes folces.

§ 2. And æni man heonan forð cirican ne ðeowige, ne ciric-
mangunge mid unrihte ne macyge, ne ciricðen ne utige
buton biscopes geþeahte.

11. 7 gelæste man Godes gerihta georne[4] æghwilce geare.

§ 1. Þæt is sulhælmessan[5] xv niht onufan eastron 7 geoguðe
teoðunge be pentecosten 7 eorðwæstma be ealra halgena mæssan [7 Romfeoh be Petres mæssan][2] 7
leohtgescot þriwa on geare.

12. 7 sawlsceat is rihtast þæt man symle gelæste æt openum
græfe.

§ 1. 7 gif man ænig lic of rihtscriftscire elles hwar lecge,
gelæste man sawlsceat swa ðeah into ðam mynstre þe
hit to hirde.

§ 2. 7 ealle Godes rihta friðige[6] man georne, ealswa hit
þearf is.

§ 3. 7 freolsa 7 fæstena rihtlice healde[7].

13. Sunnandæges freols healde man georne swa ðarto gebirige.

§ 1. 7 cipinga 7 folcgemota on ðam halgan dæge geswice
man georne.

---

[1] G, G₂; *wican* D.   [2] G, G₂; om. D.   [3] *m. eac* G, G₂.
[4] Om. G₂.   [5] *s. huru* G₂.   [6] *gerihta fyrðrige* G, G₂.
[7] *h. man r.* G, G₂.

9[1]. They know full well[2] that they have no right to marry.

§ 1[1]. But he who will turn from marriage and observe celibacy shall obtain the favour of God, and in addition, as worldly honour, he shall enjoy the wergeld and the privileges of a thegn, both during his life and after his death[2].

§ 2[1]. And he who will not do [what befits his order] shall impair both his ecclesiastical and his civil status.

10[1]. And all Christian men shall carefully avoid illicit unions, and duly observe the laws of the church.

§ 1[1]. And all churches shall be under the special protection of God and of the king and of all Christian people.

§ 2[1]. And no-one henceforth shall oppress[2] the church, or make it an object of improper traffic[3], or turn out a minister of the church without the bishop's consent.

11[1]. And ecclesiastical dues shall be promptly rendered every year.

§ 1. Namely, plough-alms fifteen days[1] after Easter, and the tithe of young livestock at Pentecost, and [the tithe] of the fruits of the earth at the feast of All Saints[2], [and Peter's Pence by St Peter's Day], and light dues three times in the year[3].

12[1]. And it is best that payment for the souls of the dead should always be rendered before the grave is closed.

§ 1[1]. And if any body is buried elsewhere than in the parish to which it properly belongs, the payment shall nevertheless be made to the church to which the deceased belonged.

§ 2[1]. And all God's dues shall be promptly rendered[2], as the occasion requires.

§ 3[1]. And festivals and fasts shall be duly observed.

13[1]. The festival of Sunday shall be diligently observed in a fitting manner.

§ 1. And marketings[1] and meetings shall be strictly abstained from on the holy day.

14. And sancta Marian freolstide ealle wurðian[1] man georne, ærest mid fæstene 7 siððan mid freolse.

    § 1. 7 to æghwilces apostoles heahtida[2] fæste man[3] 7 freol-sige; butan to Philippus 7 Iacobus freolse ne beode we nan fæsten [for þam eastorlican freolse][4].

15. Elles oðre freolsa 7 fæstena healde man georne, swa swa þe heoldon þa ðe betst heoldon.

16. 7 sancte Eadwardes mæssedæg witan habbað gecoran[5] þæt man freolsian sceal ofer eal Englaland on xv kl. Apr'.

17. 7 fæstan ælce Frigedæg, buton hit freols sy.

18. 7 ordol 7 aðas sindon tocweðen[6] freolsdagum 7 ymbren-dagum[7] 7 ab[8] Adventum Domini oð xiiii niht ofer midde-wintres tid[9] 7 fram Septuagesima oð xiiii[10] niht ofer eastron.

19. 7 beo ðam halgum tidan, ealswa hit riht is, eallum Cristenum mannum sóm 7 sib gemæne, 7 ælc sacu getwæmed.

20. 7 gif hwa oðrum scule borh oððe bote æt worldlican þingan, gelæste hit georne ær oððe æfter.

21. 7 si ælc wuduwe þe hi silfe mid rihte healde[11] on Godes griðe 7 on ðæs cynges.

    § 1. 7 sitte ælc xii monað werleas; ceose siððan þæt heo sylf wille.

22. 7 æghwilc Cristen man do swa him ðearf is—gime his Cristendomes georne 7 gewunige gelomlice to scrifte[12] 7 un-forwandodlice his synna gecyðe 7 geornlice bete swa swa him man tæce.

    § 1. 7 gearwige eac to huselgange oft 7 gelome gehwa hine silfne.

    § 2. 7 word 7 weorc fadige mid rihte 7 að 7 wed wærlice healde.

---

[1] weorðie G; weorðige G₂. [2] -tide G, G₂. [3] f. m. georne G₂.
[4] G, G₂; om. D. [5] -en G, G₂. [6] D, G; tocwedene G₂.
[7] rihtymb. G, G₂. [8] fram G, G₂.
[9] oð octabas Epiphanię (-ige) G, G₂. [10] xv G, G₂.
[11] gehealde G, G₂. [12] G, G₂; Criste D.

14[1]. And all St Mary's festivals[2] shall be zealously honoured, first with fasting and afterwards with festivity.

§ 1[1]. And at the festival of every apostle there shall be fasting and festivity, except that at the festival of Philip and James[2] we enjoin no fast [because of the Easter festival][3].

15[1]. Otherwise, festivals and fasts shall be strictly observed in accordance with the highest standards of the past[2].

16[1]. And the authorities have decided that St Edward's[2] festival shall be celebrated throughout England on the 18th of March.

17[1]. And a fast [shall be observed] every Friday, unless it be a festival.

18[1]. And trial by ordeal and [the rendering of] oaths are forbidden during festivals and on Ember days, and from the Advent[2] till a fortnight after Christmas[3], and from the Septuagesima[4] till a fortnight after Easter.

19[1]. And at the holy festivals, as is fitting, there shall be peace and concord among all Christian men, and every dispute shall be laid aside.

20[1]. And if anyone owes another a debt or compensation in connection with secular matters, he shall render it readily either before or after [the festival].

21[1]. And all widows who lead a respectable life shall enjoy the special protection of God and of the king.

§ 1[1]. And each of them shall remain without a husband for a year, after which she may decide as she herself desires.

22[1]. And every Christian man shall do what is his duty: he shall pay zealous regard to his Christian profession, and shall frequently go to confession, and freely confess his sins, and readily make amends as is prescribed for him.

§ 1[1]. And everyone shall also prepare himself frequently and often for receiving the sacrament.

§ 2[1]. And he shall order his words and deeds aright and carefully abide by his oath and his pledge.

23. 7 æghwilc unriht awurpe man georne of þisum earde þæs[1] man don[2] mæge.

24. 7 swicollice dæda 7 laðlice unlaga ascunige man swiðe, þæt is: falsa gewihta 7 woge gemeta 7 lease gewitnessa [7 fracodlice ficunga][3];

25. 7 egeslice manswara 7 deofollice dæda on morðweorcan 7 on manslihtan, on stalan 7 on strudungan[4], on gitsungan 7 on gifernessan, on ofermettan 7 on oferfillan, on swiccræftan 7 on mistlican lagbrycan, on hadbrican 7 on æwbrican [7 on freolsbrycan, on fæstenbrycan][5] 7 on mæniges cynnes misdædan.

26. Ac lufige man Godes riht heonan forð georne wordes 7 dæda; þonne wurð þisse þeode sona God milde.

　　§ 1. 7 beo man georne ymban friðes bote 7 ymbe feos bote æghwar on earde, 7 ymbe burhbote 7 ymbe bricbote[6] æghwar on earde[7] on æghwilcum ende, 7 ymbe firdunga[8], áá þonne neod sy, be þam þe man geræde.

27. 7 ymbe scipfirðrunga, swa man geornost mæge[9], þæt æghwilc geset sy sona ofer eastron æghwilce geare.

28. And gif hwa buton leafe of firde gewænde þe se cyninge silf on sy, plihte him silfum oððe wergilde[10].

　　[§ 1[11]. 7 se þe elles (ham)[12] of fyrde gewende, beo se cxx scill' scyldig.]

29. 7 gif ænig amánsumad man, buton hit friðbena sy, on ðæs cynincges neawiste ahwar gewunige, ær ðam þe he hæbbe godcunde bote georne gebogene, þonne plihte he to[13] him silfum oððe to[14] his æhtan.

30. 7 gif hwa ymbe cyninc[15] sirewe, beo[16] his feores scildig, buton[17] he hine ladige be þam deopestan þe witan gerædan.

---

[1] þæsþe G, G₂.　　[2] gedon G, G₂.　　[3] G, G₂.
[4] G, G₂; scrutungan D.　　[5] G₂.　　[6] 7 y. bricb. om. G.
[7] æ. on e. om. G, G₂.　　[8] f. eac G, G₂.
[9] gif man þæt geræde, added above in the twelfth cent. in G₂.
[10] h. s. 7 ealre his are G.　　[11] G, G₂; om. D.　　[12] G₂.
[13] Om. G; added above later in G₂.　　[14] h. s. 7 eallan G, G₂.
[15] y. cyninges feorh G, G₂.　　[16] sy he G, G₂.
[17] 7 gif he ladian wille do þæt be ðæs cynges wergylde oððe mid þryfealdan ordale on Engla lage inst. of buton...gerædan G, G₂.

23[1]. And every injustice shall be zealously cast out from this land as far as is possible.

24[1]. And deceitful deeds and hateful injustices shall be strictly avoided, namely, untrue weights[2] and false measures[2] and lying testimonies[3] [and shameful frauds[4]];

25[1]. and horrible perjuries and devilish deeds, such as murders and homicides, thefts and robberies[2], covetousness and greed, gluttony and intemperance[3], frauds and various breaches of the law, violations of holy orders[4] and of marriage, [breaches of festivals and of fasts], and misdeeds of many kinds.

26[1]. But the law of God shall henceforth be zealously cherished both in word and in deed; then forthwith God will have mercy upon this nation.

§ 1[1]. And the promotion of public security and the improvement of the coinage[2] in every part of the country, and the repairing of fortresses[3] and of bridges[3] throughout the country on every side, and also the duties of military service[3] shall always be diligently attended to, whenever the need arises, in accordance with the orders given.

27[1]. And the fitting out of ships[2] as diligently as possible, so that in every year they may all be equipped soon[3] after Easter.

28[1]. And if anyone deserts an army which is under the personal command of the king[2], it shall be at the risk of [losing] his life or his wergeld[3].

[§ 1. And he who deserts any other army shall forfeit 120 shillings[1].]

29[1]. And if any excommunicated man, unless it ·be one who is a suppliant for protection, remains anywhere near the king, before he has readily submitted to the amends required by the church, it shall be at the risk of [losing] his life or[2] his possessions.

30[1]. And if anyone plots against the king, he shall forfeit his life, unless he clears himself by the most solemn oath[2] determined upon by the authorities[3].

31. 7 gif hwa forsteal oððe openne wiðercwide ongean lahriht
     Cristes oððe cyninges ahwar gewyrce, gilde swa wer swa
     wite swa lahslite, a be þam þe seo dæd sy.

> § 1. 7 gif he ongean riht geonbyrde oððe æhlip gewirce,
> 7[1] hine man þonne þurh þæt[2] afille, licge ægilde eallum
> his freondum.

32. 7 æfre alecgan[3] heonan forð þa unlaga þe ure[4] hlaford oft
     7 gelome silf het alecgan.

> § 1[5]. Ðæt is þonne án ærest æt ðam ætfengan þe swicigende
> manswican lufedan be westan, þe mænigne man ge-
> swænctan 7 on unriht gedrehtan.

> § 2. 7 oðer is, þæt gewitnessa ne moston standan, þeah hi
> fulgetreowe wæron 7 hi swa sædan swa hi to woldon
> swerian.

> § 3. Ðridde is æt swigean, þæt man wolde sweogian 7 on
> æftergængan eft siððan sprecan þæt man on forgængan
> næfre becliopode.

> § 4. 7 be norðan stod seo unlagu, þæt man moste banweorc
> on unsacne secgan, 7 þæt scolde standan, gif hit wurde
> swa gecyðed ydæges sona.

> § 5. Ac þæt unriht alegde ure hlaford; þæt he ma mote.

[33[6]. 7 æghwylce unlaga alecge man georne.]

> § 1. Forðam þurh þæt hit sceal on earde godian to ahte,
> þæt[7] man unriht alecge 7 rihtwisnesse lufige for Gode
> 7 for worlde[8].

34. Ealle we sculon ænne God lufian 7 wurðian 7 ænne Cristen-
     dom georne healdan[9] 7 ælcne hæðendom mid ealle awurpan.

---

[1] o. r. þurh æhlyp geonbyrde 7 swa gewyrce þæt G, G$_2$.
[2] þ. þ. þ. om. G, G$_2$.   [3] alicgan G, G$_2$.
[4] þe ær þysan wæran to gewunelice wide G, G$_2$.
[5] §§ 1–5 are found only in D.   [6] G, G$_2$.   [7] þe G, G$_2$.
[8] f. w. Amen G$_2$.   [9] 7 æ. C. g. h. om. G.

31[1]. And if anyone is guilty of offering obstruction or open
opposition anywhere to the law of Christ or of the king, he
shall pay either wergeld[2] or fine[3] or *lahslit* according to the
nature of the offence.

§ 1. And if he offers resistance to the course of justice or
commits a breach of the law[1], and through that brings
about his own death, no compensation shall be paid for
him to any of his friends.

32. And there shall henceforth be an end to the unjust practices
which our lord himself has frequently and often com-
manded us to stop[1].

§ 1[1]. Firstly, with regard to the process of attaching property,
to which crafty rogues in the west[2] have been much
addicted and by which many people have been harassed
and unjustly oppressed.

§ 2. Secondly, that the testimony of witnesses was not
allowed to be valid, although they were thoroughly
trustworthy and were willing to swear to [the truth of]
their statements.

§ 3[1]. Thirdly, with regard to the practice of bringing forward, after long silence, claims against an heir which
had never been made against his predecessor.

§ 4. And in the north there has prevailed the unjust practice
of bringing accusations of homicide against a guiltless[1]
man, and such an accusation was held to be valid, if it
was made at once on the very day [of the homicide].

§ 5. But this practice has been stopped by our lord. May
he succeed in stopping more!

[33[1]. And injustice of every kind shall be zealously suppressed.]

§ 1[1]. For it is only by the suppression of injustice and the
love of righteousness, in matters both religious and
secular, that any improvement shall be obtained in the
condition of our country.

34. It is the duty of us all to love and honour one God, and
zealously uphold one Christian faith, and wholly renounce
all heathen practices.

35.   7 uton ænne cynehlaford holdlice healdan 7 lif 7 land samod ealle werian, swa wel swa we betst magon, 7 God ælmihtigne inweardre heortan fultumes biddan.

    § 1[1]. Sit nomen Domini benedictum.

VI ÆTHELRED

Be witena gerædnessan.

Þis syndan þa gerædnessa þe Engla rædgifan gecuran 7 gecwædan 7 geornlice lærdan þæt man scolde healdan.

1.   7 þæt is þonne ærest þæra biscpa frumræd, þæt we ealle fram synnum georne gecyrran, þæs þe we don magan, 7 ure misdæda andettan georne 7 geornlice betan 7 ænne God rihtlice lufian 7 weorðian 7 ænne Christendom anrædlice healdan 7 ælcne hæþendom georne forbugan 7 gebedrædene aræran georne us betweonan 7 sibbe 7 some lufian georne 7 anum cynehlaforde holdlice hyran 7 georne hine healdan mid rihtan getrywðan.

2.   7 witena gerædnes is, þæt abbodas 7 abbodissan heora agen lif rihtlice fadian 7 eac heora heorda wislice healdan 7 þæt ælces hades men georne gebugan for Gode 7 for worolde, ælc to þam rihte þe him to gebyrige, 7 huruþinga Godes þeowas—biscpas 7 abbodas, munecas 7 mynecena, canonicas 7 nunnan—to rihte gecyrran 7 regollice libban 7 for eall Cristen folc þingian georne.

3.   7 witena gerædnes is, þæt muneca gehwilc þe ute of mynstre sy 7 regoles ne gyme, do swa him þearf is: gebuge georne into mynstre mid eallum eaðmettum 7 misdæda geswice 7 bete swyþe georne þæt he abrocen hæbbe; geþence word 7 wedd þe he Gode betæhte.

<hr>

[1] Om. G; s. n. D. b. et rel. G₂.

35¹. And let us loyally support one royal lord, and all of us together defend our lives and our country, to the best of our ability, and from our inmost heart pray to God Almighty for help.

§ 1¹. Blessed be the name of the Lord.

VI ÆTHELRED

Concerning the ordinances of the councillors.

These are the ordinances¹ which the councillors² of England have decided and agreed upon, earnestly enjoining that they should be observed³.

1¹. And first of all, the primary ordinance² of the bishops is, that we all zealously turn from sins, as far as we can, and readily confess our misdeeds, and zealously make amends, and duly love and honour one God, and unanimously uphold one Christian faith, and zealously renounce all heathen practices, and earnestly promote among us the habit of prayer, and zealously cherish peace and concord³, and loyally obey one royal lord, and readily support him with due fidelity⁴.

2¹. And the decree of the councillors is², that abbots and abbesses shall order their own lives aright, and also keep their flocks with wisdom, and that men of every estate shall readily submit in matters both religious and secular to the duty which befits them, and most of all the servants of God—bishops and abbots, monks and nuns, canons and women under religious vows—shall revert to a proper discharge of their duties and live according to their rule³, and earnestly intercede for all Christian people. ′

3¹. And the decree of the councillors is, that every monk who is out of a monastery² and who is not observing a rule, shall do what is his duty, namely, he shall readily return into the monastery with all humility, and desist from his evil ways, and zealously make amends for the transgressions he has committed. Let him remember the vows which he rendered to God.

§ 1. ⁊ se munuc, þe mynster næbbe, cume to scirebiscop ⁊
trywsige hine sylfne wið God ⁊ wið men, þæt he huru
þreo þing þanon forð healdan wille, þæt is his clænnesse
⁊ munuclice scrudware ⁊ þeowian his Drihtne swa wel
swa he betst mæge; ⁊ gif he þæt gelæste, þonne bið he
weorðe þæt hine man þe bet healde, wunige þær he
wunige.

4. ⁊ canonicas þær seo ar sy þæt he beodern ⁊ slæpern habban
magan, healdan heora mynster mid clænnesse, swa heora
regol tæce, oððon riht is þæt þolige þære are se þe þæt nelle.

5. ⁊ ealle Godes þeowas, ⁊ huruþinga sacerdas, we biddað ⁊
lærað, þæt hy Gode hyran ⁊ clænnesse lufian ⁊ beorhgan
him sylfum wið Godes yrre.

§ 1. Fulgeorne hi witan þæt hy nagon mid rihte þurh ænig
hæmedþing wifes gemanan.

§ 2. Ac hit is þe wyrse þe sume habbað twa oððe ma, ⁊ sum,
þeh he forlæte þa he ær hæfde, he be lifiendre þære eft
oþere nimð, swa ænigan Cristenan man ne gedafenað
to donne.

§ 3. ⁊ se ðe þæs geswican wille ⁊ clænnesse healdan, hæbbe
he Godes miltse ⁊ þær to eacan, to woroldweorðscipe,
þæt he sy þegenweres ⁊ þegenrihtes wyrþe, ge on life
ge on legere.

§ 4. ⁊ se þe þæt nelle, þæt his hade gebyrige, wanige his
weorðscipe ægðer ge for Gode ge for worolde.

6. ⁊ la gyt we willað biddan freonda gehwylcne ⁊ eal folc eac
læran georne, þæt hy inwerdre heortan ænne God lufian ⁊
ælcne hæþendom georne ascunian.

7. ⁊ gif wiccan oððe wigeleras, scincræftcan oððe horcwenan,
morðwyrhtan oððe mánsworan ahwar on earde wurðan
agytene, fyse hy man georne ut of þysan earde ⁊ clæ[n]sige[1]
þas þeode, oþþe on earde forfare hy mid ealle, butan hy
geswican ⁊ þe deoppor gebetan.

---

[1] clæs. K.

§ 1[1]. And the monk who has no monastery[2] shall come to the bishop of the diocese, and shall vow to God and to men henceforth to observe three things at least, namely, celibacy, and the wearing of the monastic habit, and the service of his Lord to the best of his ability. And if he carries out this vow, he shall be entitled to be treated with greater consideration, wherever he may dwell.

4[1]. And canons, wherever their property admits of their having a refectory and a dormitory, shall maintain celibacy in their foundation, as their rule prescribes; otherwise it is right that he who refuses to do so should forfeit his endowment[2].

5[1]. And we pray and enjoin all the servants of God, and priests above all, to obey God and practise celibacy and guard against incurring the wrath of God.

§ 1[1]. They know full well that they have no right to marry.

§ 2[1]. But some are guilty of a worse practice in having two or more [wives], and others, although they forsake their former wives, afterwards take others while these are still alive—a thing which is unfitting for any Christian man to do.

§ 3[1]. But he who will turn from marriage and observe celibacy shall obtain the favour of God, and in addition, as worldly honour, he shall enjoy the wergeld and the privileges of a thegn, both during his life and after his death.

§ 4. And he who will not do what befits his order shall impair both his ecclesiastical and his civil status.

6[1]. And now behold, we will beseech all our friends[2] and likewise earnestly enjoin upon the whole nation, to love one God from their inmost heart, and zealously shun all heathen practices.

7[1]. And if wizards or sorcerers, magicians[2] or prostitutes, those who secretly compass death or perjurers be met with anywhere in the land, they shall be zealously driven from this land and the nation shall be purified; otherwise they shall be utterly destroyed in the land, unless they cease from their wickedness and make amends to the utmost of their ability.

8. ⁊ witena gerædnes is, þæt man rihte laga up arære for Gode ⁊ for worolde ⁊ æghwilce unlaga georne afylle;

§ 1. ⁊ þæt man heonan forð læte manna gehwylcne, ge earmne ge eadigne, folcrihtes wyrðe;

§ 2. ⁊ þæt man frið ⁊ freondscipe rihtlice healde innan þysan earde for Gode ⁊ for worolde.

9. ⁊ witena gerædnes is, þæt man Christene men ⁊ unforworhte of earde ne sylle, ne huru on hæþene þeode; ac beorge man georne þæt man þa sawla ne forfare þe Crist mid his agenum life gebohte.

10. ⁊ witena gerædnes is, þæt man Christene men for ealles to lytlan to deaðe ne forræde. Ac elles geræde man friðlice steora, folce to þearfe, ⁊ ne forspille for lytlum Godes agen handgeweorc ⁊ his agenne ceap þe he deore gebohte.

§ 1. Ac æghwilce dæde toscade man wærlice ⁊ dom æfter dæde medemige be mæþe, swa for Gode sy gebeorhlic ⁊ for worolde aberendlic.

§ 2. ⁊ geþence swyþe georne se þe oþrum deme, hwæs he sylf gyrne, þonne he þus cweðe: "Et dimitte nobis debita nostra" et reliqua.

11. ⁊ we læ欟ð swyþe geornlice þæt æghwilc Christen man unriht hæmed georne forbuge ⁊ Christene lage rihtlice healde.

12. ⁊ æfre ne geweorðe þæt Christen man gewifige in VI manna sibfæce on his agenum cynne, þæt is binnan þam feorþan cneowe, ne on þæs lafe þe swa neah wære on woroldcundre sibbe, ne on þæs wifes nydmagan þe he ær hæfde.

§ 1. Ne on gehalgodre ænigre nunnan, ne on his gefæderan, ne on ælætan ænig Cristen man ne gewifige æfre; ne na ma wifa þonne an hæbbe, ac beo be þære anre, þa hwile þe heo libbe, se þe wille Godes lage gyman mid rihte ⁊ wiþ hellebryne beorgan his sawle.

8[1]. And the decree of the councillors is, that justice shall be promoted in matters both religious and secular, and all injustice zealously suppressed;

§ 1[1]. and that henceforth all men, both rich and poor, shall be allowed the benefit of the law;

§ 2[1]. and that peace and goodwill shall be duly maintained within this land in matters both religious and secular.

9[1]. And it is the decree of the councillors that Christian men who are innocent of crime shall not be sold out of the land, least of all to the heathen, but care shall diligently be taken that the souls which Christ bought with his own life be not destroyed[2].

10[1]. And the decree of the councillors is, that Christian men shall not be condemned to death for too trivial offences, but, on the contrary, merciful punishments shall be determined upon, for the public good, that the handiwork of God and what he purchased for himself at a great price be not destroyed for trivial offences.

§ 1[1]. But every deed shall be carefully distinguished and judgment meted out in proportion to the offence, as shall be justifiable in the sight of God and acceptable in the eyes of men[2].

§ 2[1]. And he who judges another shall earnestly consider what he himself desires when he says: "Forgive us our trespasses" etc.

11[1]. And we very earnestly enjoin upon every Christian man carefully to avoid illicit unions and duly to observe the laws of the church.

12[1]. And it must never happen that a Christian man marries among his own kin within six degrees of relationship[2], that is, within the fourth generation[3], or with the widow of a man as nearly related to him[4] as this, or with a near relative of his first wife's.

§ 1. And a Christian man must never marry a professed nun or his godmother[1] or a divorced woman, and he shall never have more wives than one, but he who seeks to observe God's law aright and to save his soul from hell-fire[2] shall remain with the one as long as she lives.

13. 7 sy ælc cyrice on Godes griþe 7 on þæs cynges 7 on ealles Cristenes folces.

14. 7 sy ælc cyricgrið binnan wagum 7 cyninges handgrið efen unwemme.

15. 7 ænig man heonan forð cyrican ne þ[e]owige¹ ne cyricmangunge mid unrihte ne macige, ne cyricþén ne utige butan biscopes geþehte.

16². 7 gelæste man Godes gerihta æghwilce geare rihtlice georne, þæt is sulhælmessan huru xv niht ofer eastron.

17. 7 geogoðe teoþunge be pentecosten 7 eorðwæstma be ealra halgena mæssan.

18. 7 Romfeoh be Petres mæssan.
    § 1³. 7 cyricsceat to Martinus mæssan.

19. 7 leohtgescot þriwa on geare.

20. 7 saulsceat is rihtast þæt man symble³ gelæste aa³ æt openum⁴ græfe.

21. 7 gif man ænig lic of riht[scrift]scire⁵ elles hwar lecge, gelæste man þone saulsceat swa þeh into þam mynstre þe hit to hyrde.
    § 1. 7 ealle Godes gerihta fyrþrige⁶ man georne, ealswa hit þearf is.

22. 7 freolsa 7 fæstena healde man rihtlice.
    § 1. Sunnandæges freols healde man georne swa þærto gebyrige; 7 cypinga 7 folcgemota 7 huntaðfara 7 worldlicra weorca on þam halgan dæge geswice man georne.
    § 2. 7 sancta Marian heahfreolstida⁷ ealle³ weorðige man georne, ærest mid fæstene 7 syþþan mid freolse.
    § 3. 7 to æghwilces apostoles heahtide fæste man georne, butan to³ Philippus 7 Iacobus freolse ne beode we nan fæsten for þam easterlican⁸ freolse, butan hwa wille⁹.
    § 4. Elles oðre freolsa 7 fæstena healde man georne, swa swa þa heoldan þa þe betst heoldan.

---

¹ þow. K.   ² At this point MS D begins.   ³ Om. D.
⁴ ðam op. D.   ⁵ rihtscire K; rihtre scriftscire D.   ⁶ friðige D.
⁷ freolst. D.   ⁸ eastran dæges fr. D.   ⁹ b. hw. w. om. D.

13¹. And every church shall be under the special protection of God and of the king and of all Christian people.

14¹. And every right of sanctuary within the walls of a church, and the protection granted by the king in person shall remain equally inviolate.

15¹. And no-one henceforth shall oppress the church, or make it an object of improper traffic, or turn out a minister of the church without the bishop's consent.

16¹. And ecclesiastical dues shall be promptly and duly rendered every year, namely, plough-alms at the latest fifteen days after Easter.

17. And the tithe of young livestock at Pentecost, and that of the fruits of the earth at All Hallows.

18. And Peter's Pence by St Peter's Day.
§ 1¹. And church dues at Martinmas.

19¹. And light dues three times in the year.

20¹. And it is best that payment for the souls of the dead should always be rendered before the grave is closed.

21¹. And if any body is buried elsewhere than in the parish to which it properly belongs, the payment shall nevertheless be made to the church to which the deceased belonged.
§ 1¹. And all God's dues shall be promptly rendered, as the occasion requires.

22¹. And festivals and fasts shall be duly observed.
§ 1¹. And the festival of Sunday shall be diligently observed in a fitting manner; and marketings and meetings and hunting expeditions² and secular employments shall be strictly abstained from on the holy day.
§ 2¹. And all St Mary's high-festivals shall be zealously honoured, first with fasting and afterwards with festivity.
§ 3. And at the festival of every apostle fasting shall be strictly observed, except that at the festival of Philip and James we enjoin no fast, because of the Easter festival, unless anyone desires to fast.
§ 4. Festivals and fasts otherwise shall be strictly observed in accordance with the highest standards of the past.

23. ⁊ ymbren fæstena¹ swa swa sanctus Gregorius Angelcynne
sylf hit² gedihte.

[§ 1³. And sancte Eadwardes mæssedæg witan habbað gecoran þæt man freolsian sceal ofer eall Englaland on
xv kl. Aprilis.]

24. ⁊ fæste man ælce Frigedæg, butan hit freols sy.

25. ⁊ ordal ⁊ aþas ⁊ wifunga æfre⁴ syndan tocwedene heah-
freolsdagum⁵ ⁊ rihtymbrenum⁶ ⁊ fram Adventum Domini
oð octabas Epiphanige ⁊ fram Septuagessima oð xv niht
ofer eastran.

§ 1. And beo þam halgan tidan, ealswa hit riht is, eallum
Cristenum mannum sibb ⁊ som gemæne ⁊ ælc sacu
totwæmed.

§ 2. ⁊ gif hwa oðrum scyle borh oððe bote æt woroldlican
þingan, gelæste hit him georne ær oððon æfter.

26. ⁊ sy ælc wydewe, þe hy sylfe mid rihte gehealde, on Godes
griðe ⁊ on þæs cynges.

§ 1. ⁊ sitte ælc xii monað werleas; ceose syþþan þæt heo
sylf wille.

27. ⁊ æghwilc Christen man do swa him þearf is: gyme his
Christendomes georne ⁊ gewunige gelomlice to scrifte⁷ ⁊
unforwandodlice his synna gecyðe ⁊ geornlice bete, swa swa
him man tæce.

§ 1. ⁊ gearwige eac to huslgange huru þriwa on geare gehwa
hine sylfne þe his agene þearfe wille understandan⁸, swa
swa him þearf is.

28. ⁊ word ⁊ weorc freonda gehwilc fadige mid rihte ⁊ að ⁊ wedd
wærlice healde.

§ 1. ⁊ æghwilc unriht aweorpe man georne of þysan earde
þæs þe man don mæge.

---

¹ D; *ymbren ⁊ fæstena* K.   ² Om. D.   ³ D; om. K.   ⁴ *⁊ w. æ.* om. D.
⁵ *heah* superscribed in later hand.   ⁶ *rihtymbrendagum* D.
⁷ *to his scr.* D.   ⁸ *und. cunne* D.

23[1]. And the fasts of the Ember Days [shall be observed] as St Gregory himself prescribed for the English nation.

   [§ 1[1]. And the authorities have decided that St Edward's festival shall be celebrated throughout England on the 18th of March.]

24[1]. And a fast [shall be observed] every Friday, unless it be a festival.

25[1]. And trial by ordeal, and [the rendering of] oaths, and marriages[2] are always forbidden during festivals, and on legally appointed Ember days, and from the Advent till the Octave of Epiphany, and from the Septuagesima till fifteen days after Easter.

   § 1[1]. And at the holy festivals, as is fitting, there shall be peace and concord among all Christian men, and every dispute shall be laid aside.

   § 2. And if anyone owes another a debt or compensation in connection with secular matters, he shall render it to him readily either before or after [the festival].

26[1]. And all widows who lead a respectable life shall enjoy the special protection of God and of the king.

   § 1. And each of them shall remain without a husband for a year, after which she may decide as she herself desires.

27[1]. And every Christian man shall do what is his duty: he shall pay zealous regard to his Christian profession, and shall frequently go to confession, and freely confess his sins, and readily make amends, as is prescribed for him.

   § 1. And everyone who seeks to understand what is for his own good shall also prepare himself for sacrament at least three times in the year, as is his duty.

28[1]. And everyone of our friends[2] shall order his words and deeds aright, and strictly abide by his oath and pledge.

   § 1[1]. And every injustice shall be zealously cast out from this land, as far as it is possible to do so.

§ 2[1]. 7 swicollice dæda 7 laðlice unlaga ascunige man swyðe,
þæt is false gewihta 7 woge gemeta 7 lease gewitnessa
7 fracodlice ficunga 7 fule forligra 7 egeslice mánswara
7 deoflice dæda on morðweorcum 7 on manslihtan, on
stalan 7 on strudungan, on gitsungan 7 on gifernessan,
on ofermettan 7 on oferfyllan, on swiccræftan 7 on
mistlican lahbrican, on æwbrican 7 on hadbrican, on
freolsbricon 7 on fæstenbricon, on cyricrénan 7 on
mæniges cynnes misdædan.

29. 7 la understande man georne þæt eal swylc is to leanne 7
næfre to lufianne.

30. Ac[2] lufige man Godes riht heonan forþ georne wordes 7
weorces[3]; þonne[4] wyrð þysse þeode sona God milde.

31. Wutan eac ealle ymbe friþes bote 7 ymbe feos bote smeagean
swyðe georne.

32. Swa ymbe friþes bote swa þam bondan sy selost 7 þam
þeofan sy laþost;

§ 1. 7 swa ymbe feos bote þæt an mynet gange ofer ealle
þas þeode butan ælcon false.

§ 2. 7 gemeta 7 gewihta rihte man georne, 7 ælces unrihtes
heonan forð geswice.

§ 3. 7 burhbota 7 bricbota aginne man georne on æghwilcon
ende[5] 7 fyrdunga eac 7 scipfyrdunga ealswa, a þonne
neod[6] sy, swa swa man geræde[7] for gemænelicre neode.

33[8]. 7 wærlic bið þæt man æghwilce geare sona æfter eastron
fyrdscipa gearwige.

34. 7 gyf hwa folces fyrdscip awyrde, gebete þæt georne 7
cyninge þa munde; 7 gif hit man amyrre þæt hit ænote
weorðe, forgylde hit fullice 7 cyninge þone mundbrice.

---

[1] Caps. 28 § 2–29 (end) om. D.   [2] 7 D.   [3] dæda D.
[4] þ. wurð us Godes miltse þe gearuwre D.   [5] on æg. e. om. D.
[6] fyrd. eac swa, á þ. þearf D.   [7] s. s. m. ger. om. D.
[8] Caps. 33–39 (end) om. D.

§ 2[1]. And deceitful deeds and hateful injustices shall be strictly avoided, namely, untrue weights, and false measures, and lying testimonies, and shameful frauds, and foul adulteries, and horrible perjuries, and devilish deeds such as murders and homicides, thefts and robberies, covetousness and greed, gluttony and intemperance, frauds and various breaches of the law, violations of marriage and of holy orders, breaches of festivals and of fasts[2], sacrilege[3], and misdeeds of many kinds[4].

29[1]. And now behold it must be clearly understood[2] that all such are to be censured and not to be indulged in.

30[1]. But God's law shall henceforth be zealously cherished in word and in deed; then God will forthwith be gracious towards this people.

31[1]. Further, let us all earnestly take thought for the promotion of public security and the improvement of the coinage.

32[1]. Public security shall be promoted in such a way as shall be best for the householder[2] and worst for the thief.

§ 1[1]. And the coinage shall be improved by having one currency, free from all adulteration, throughout all the country.

§ 2[1]. And weights and measures shall be corrected with all diligence, and an end put to all unjust practices.

§ 3[1]. And the repairing of fortifications and of bridges shall be diligently undertaken on every side, and also the provision of military and naval forces, whenever the occasion demands, as may be ordered for our common need.

33[1]. And it is a wise precaution to have warships made ready every year soon after Easter.

34[1]. And if anyone damages a national warship, he shall with all diligence make compensation for it, and shall pay to the king the fine due for breach of his "mund"[2]; and if it be destroyed[3] so as to be useless, he shall pay for it in full, and shall give the king the fine due for breach of his "mund."

35. 7 gif hwa of fyrde butan leafe gewende þe cyning sylf on
sy, plihte his are.

36. 7 gif morðwyrhtan oððe mansworan oððe æbære manslagan
to þam geþristian þæt hy on þæs cyninges neaweste gewunian, ær þam þe hy habban bote agunnen for Gode 7 for
worolde, þonne plihton hy heora are 7 eallon heora æhten,
butan hit friðbenan syndan.

37. 7 gyf hwa ymbe cyninges feorh syrwe, sy he his feores
scyldig 7 ealles þæs þe he age, gif hit him ongesoþod weorðe;
7 gif he hine ladian wille 7 mage, do þæt be þam deopestan
aðe oþþe mid þryfealdan ordale on Ængla lage, 7 on Dena
lage be þam þe heora lagu sy.

38. 7 gif hwa forsteal ongean lahriht Cristes oþþe cyninges
ahwar gewyrce, gylde wer oþþe wite be þam þe seo dæd sy;
7 gif he geonbyrde 7 sylf gewyrce þæt hine man afylle,
licge ægylde.

39. 7 gif hwa nunnan gewemme oþþe wydewan nydnæme,
gebete þæt deope for Gode 7 for worolde.

40. 7 smeage man symle on æghwilce[1] wisan hu man fyrmest
mæge ræd aredian, þeode to þearfe and rihtne Christendom
swyþost aræran 7 æghwilce unlaga geornost afyllan.

§ 1. Forþam þurh þæt hit sceal on earde godian to ahte, þe
man unriht alecge 7 rihtwisnesse lufige for Gode 7 for
worlde.

41[2]. Nu wille we eac læran Godes þeowas georne, þæt hy huru
hy sylfe wærlice beþencan 7 þurh Godes fultum clænnesse
lufian 7 georne heora bocum 7 gebedum fylgean 7 dæges 7
nihtes oft 7 gelome clypian to Christe 7 for eal Christen folc
þingian georne.

---

[1] *ælce* D.   [2] Om. D.

35[1]. And if anyone deserts an army which is under the personal command of the king, it shall be at the risk of losing his property[2].

36[1]. And if those who secretly compass death[2], or perjurers, or proved homicides presume so far as to remain anywhere near the king[3], before they have undertaken to make amends both towards church and state, they shall be in danger of losing their (landed) property and all their personal possessions[4], unless they are suppliants for protection.

37[1]. And if anyone plots against the king's life, he shall forfeit his life and all that he possesses, if it is proved against him[2]; and if he seeks and is able to clear himself, he shall do so by means of the most solemn oath[3] or by the triple ordeal in districts under English law, and in those under Danish law in accordance with their constitution[4].

38[1]. And if anyone is guilty of offering obstruction anywhere to the law of Christ or the king, he shall pay either wergeld or fine[2] according to the nature of the offence, and if he offers resistance and so acts as to bring about his own death, no compensation shall be paid for him.

39[1]. And if anyone injures a nun or does violence to a widow, he shall make amends to the utmost of his ability both towards church and state.

40[1]. And constant thought shall be taken in every way how best to determine what is advisable for the public good, and how best to promote true Christianity, and to suppress with all diligence every injustice.

§ 1[1]. For it is only by the suppression of injustice and the love of righteousness in matters both religious and secular that any improvement shall be obtained in the condition of the country.

41[1]. Now we desire likewise earnestly to enjoin upon the servants of God, that above all they carefully take thought for themselves, and by God's help practise celibacy[2], and diligently apply themselves to their books and prayers, and day and night frequently and often call upon Christ, and zealously intercede for all Christian people.

42. Eac we[1] gyt willað myngian georne[2] freonda gehwilcne,
    ealswa us neod is gelome to donne, þæt gehwa hine sylfne
    georne beþence, 7 þæt he fram synnan georne gecyrre 7
    oþrum mannum unrihtes styre[3], 7 þæt he oft 7 gelome hæbbe
    on gemynde þæt mannum is mæst þearf oftost to gemunene,
    þæt is, þæt hy rihtne geleafan anrædlice[2] habban on þone
    soþan God, þe is wealdend 7 wyrhta ealra gesceafta, 7 þæt
    hy rihtne Christendom rihtlice healdan, 7 þæt hy godcundan
    lareawan geornlice hyran 7 Godes larum 7 lagum geornlice[4]
    fylgean, 7 þæt hy Godes cyrican æghwar georne griðian 7
    friþian 7 mid leohte 7 lacum hi gelome gegretan 7 hy sylfe
    þær georne to Christe[5] gebiddan.

43. 7 þæt hy Godes gerihta æghwylce geare mid rihte gelæstan,
    7 freolsa 7 fæstena rihtlice healdan.

44. 7 þæt hy Sunnandaga[6] cypinga 7 folciscra gemota georne
    geswican.

45. 7 þæt hy Godes þeowas symle werian 7 weorðian.

46. 7 þæt hy Godes þearfan frefrian 7 fedan.

47. 7 þæt hy wydewan 7 steopcild to oft ne ahwænan ac georne
    hi gladian.

48. And þæt hi ælþeodige men 7 feorran cumene ne tyrian ne
    tynan.

49. 7 þæt hy oþrum mannum unriht ne beodan ealles to swyþe,
    ac manna gehwylc oþrum beode þæt riht þæt he wille þæt
    man him beode, be þam þe hit mæð sy[7]; 7 þæt is swyþe riht
    lagu.

50. 7 se þe ahwar heonan forð rihte laga wyrde, Godes oþþon
    manna, gebete hit georne swa hwæþer swa hit gebyrige, swa
    mid godcundre bote, swa mid woroldcundre steore.

51. 7 gif for godbotan feohbot ariseð, swa swa wise woroldwitan
    to steore gesettan, þæt gebyreð rihtlice, be biscpa dihte, to

---

[1] *And git we* D.   [2] Om. D.
[3] *stire* 7 *þæt he (he þæt* MS.) *ofer ealle oðre þingc lufige his Drihten* D.
[4] *rihtlice* D.   [5] *to Ch.* om. D.   [6] *Sunnandæges* D.
[7] At this point the extract in D ends.

42. And likewise we desire earnestly to exhort all our friends[1], as there is need for us to do frequently, to take thought diligently for themselves, and eagerly to turn from sins, and to restrain other men from wrong-doing, and frequently and often to have in mind what is of supreme importance for men to remember, namely, that they should have a right belief in the true God, who is the ruler and maker of all created things, and that they should duly keep the true Christian faith, and diligently obey their spiritual teachers, and zealously follow the precepts and ordinances of God, and that they should diligently maintain the security and sanctity of the churches of God[2] everywhere, and frequently visit them with candles[3] and offerings, and themselves there earnestly pray to Christ.

43[1]. And that every year they should duly render their ecclesiastical dues, and duly observe festivals and fasts.

44[1]. And that they should diligently abstain from marketings and public assemblies on Sundays.

45[1]. And that they should always protect and honour the servants of God.

46[1]. And that they should comfort and feed the poor of God.

47[1]. And that they should not be constantly oppressing the widow and the orphan, but that they should diligently cheer them.

48[1]. And that they should not vex[2] or oppress strangers and men come from afar.

49[1]. And that they should not excel in offering injustice to other men, but that every man should, to the best of his ability, show the justice to others that he desires should be shown to him[2]—which is a very just rule[3].

50[1]. And he who henceforth anywhere violates the just[2] decrees of God or of men shall render full compensation in whatever way is fitting, whether by making the amends required by the ecclesiastical authority or by paying the penalty demanded by the secular law.

51. And if monetary compensation is paid as amends for religious offences, in accordance with the penalties fixed by

gebedbigene 7 to þearfena hyþþe 7 to cyricbote 7 to lardome 7 to wæde 7 to wiste þam þe Gode þeowian 7 to bocan 7 to bellan 7 to cyricwædan, 7 næfre to woroldlican idelan glengan, ac for woroldsteoran to godcundan neodan, hwilum be wite, hwilum be wergylde, hwilum be halsfange, hwilum be lahslite, hwilum be are, hwilum be æhte, 7 hwilum be maran, hwilum be læssan.

52. 7 á swa man bið mihtigra her nu for worulde oþþon þurh geþingða hearra on hade, swa sceal he deoppor synna gebetan 7 ælce misdæda deoror agyldan, for þam þe se maga 7 se unmaga ne beoð na gelice, ne ne magon na gelice byrþene ahebban, ne se unhala þe ma þam halum gelice; 7 þy man sceal medmian 7 gescadlice toscadan, ge on godcundan scriftan ge on woroldcundan steoran, ylde 7 geogoþe, welan 7 wædle, hæle 7 unhæle, 7 hada gehwilcne.

§ 1. 7 gif hit geweorþeð, þæt man unwilles oþþe ungewealdes ænig þing misdeð, na bið þæt na gelic þam þe willes 7 gewealdes sylfwilles misdeð; 7 eac se þe nydwyrhta bið þæs þe he misdeð, se bið gebeorhges 7 þy beteran domes symle wyrðe, þe he nydwyrhta wæs þæs þe he worhte.

53. Ælce dæde toscade man wærlice 7 a dom be dæde fadige mid rihte 7 medemige be mæþe for Gode 7 for worolde; 7 miltsige man for Godes ege 7 liþige man georne 7 beorge be dæle þam þe þæs þearf sy; forþam ealle we beþurfan þæt us ure Drihten oft 7 gelome his miltse geunne. Amen.

wise secular authorities[1], it is proper that this should be applied, in accordance with the direction of the bishops, to paying for prayers, and to the maintenance of the indigent, and to the repair of churches, and to education, and to clothing and feeding those who serve God, and to the purchase of books and bells and ecclesiastical vestments[2]. It shall never be applied to the pomps and vanities of the world[3], but payments for the needs of religion shall take the place of payments to the secular authorities—whether [they arise from] fines or wergeld or *healsfang* or *lahslit*, whether they affect landed or personal property, and whether the amounts involved are large or small[4].

52[1]. And always the greater a man's position in this present life or the higher the privileges of his rank, the more fully shall he make amends for his sins, and the more dearly shall he pay for all misdeeds; for the strong and the weak are not alike nor can they bear a like burden, any more than the sick can be treated like the sound. And therefore, in forming a judgment, careful discrimination must be made between age and youth, wealth and poverty, health and sickness, and the various ranks of life, both in the amends imposed by the ecclesiastical authority and in the penalties inflicted by the secular law.

§ 1[1]. And if it happens that a man commits a misdeed, involuntarily or unintentionally, the case is different from that of one who offends of his own freewill, voluntarily and intentionally[2]; and likewise he who is an involuntary agent in his misdeeds should always be entitled to clemency and to better terms, owing to the fact that he acted as an involuntary agent.

53[1]. Careful discrimination shall be made in judging every deed, and the judgment shall always be ordered with justice, according to the nature of the deed, and meted out in proportion, in affairs both religious and secular; and, through the fear of God, mercy and leniency and some measure of forbearance shall be shown towards those who have need of them. For all of us have need that our Lord grant us his mercy frequently and often. Amen.

VII ÆTHELRED

[1][I. Ut de omni caruca detur denarius sanctae Dei ecclesiae, et tainus decimet quicquid habet[2]. II. De ieiunio et feriatione III dierum ante festum sancti Michaelis. III. Quid pro rege et populo omni die sit cantandum. IIII. De reddendis omnibus consuetudinibus sanctae Dei ecclesiae. V. Ne quis vendatur extra patriam. VI. De robaria. VII. De elemosinis et rectitudinibus ecclesiae.]

Hoc[3] instituerunt Æþelredus rex et sapientes eius apud Badam[4].

1. Inprimis, ut unus Deus super omnia diligatur et honoretur, et ut omnes regi suo pareant, sicut antecessores sui melius fecerunt, et cum eo pariter defendant regnum suum.

§ 1. Et constituerunt inprimis Dei misericordiam et auxilium invocare ieiuniis, elemosinis, confessione et abstinentia á malefactis et iniustitia[5].

§ 2. Hoc est ut[6] detur de omni carruca denarius vel denarii valens.

§ 3. Et omnis qui familiam habet efficiat, ut omnis hyremannus suus det unum denarium. Qui[7] si non habeat[8], det dominus eius pro eo; et omnis tainus decimet totum quicquid habet.

2. Et instituimus, ut omnis Christianus qui aetatem habet ieiunet tribus diebus in pane et aqua et herbis crudis[9].

§ 1. Et omnis homo ad confessionem vadat et nudis pedibus ad ecclesiam et peccatis omnibus abrenuntiet emendando, cessando.

§ 2. Et eat omnis presbiter cum populo suo ad processionem tribus diebus nudis pedibus.

§ 2a. Et super hoc cantet omnis presbiter XXX missas et omnis diaconus et clericus XXX psalmos.

---

[1] The table of contents is found in M, Hk, Br but not in T.
[2] *De denario s. e. dando et decimatione thaynorum* Br.
[3] *haec* Br.   [4] *Habam* M, Hk, Br.   [5] *et m. et i. abstinere* Br.
[6] *Et ut* Br; *hoc ut* Hk.   [7] *Quod* Br.   [8] *habet* T.
[9] *bis crudis* M, Br; *erudis* Hk; Br adds *ante festum S. Michaelis.*

VII ÆTHELRED

This is the edict which was drawn up by King Æthelred and his councillors at Bath[1].

1[1]. In the first place, one God shall be loved and honoured above all, and all men shall show obedience to their king in accordance with the best traditions of their ancestors[2], and cooperate with him in defending his kingdom.

§ 1[1]. And they agreed first of all to invoke the mercy and help of God by fasts and almsgiving, by confession, and by abstaining from misdeeds and injustice.

§ 2[1]. From every plough-land[2] a penny or the value of a penny[3] shall be given.

§ 3[1]. And everyone who has a household[2] shall see to it that each of his dependents[3] gives a penny. If anyone is without money, his lord shall give it for him; and every thegn shall render a tithe of all that he has.

2[1]. And we have decreed that every adult Christian shall fast on bread and water and raw herbs[2] for three days[3].

§ 1[1]. And everyone shall go to confession and with bare feet to church, and by making amends and ceasing [from evil] shall renounce all [his] sins.

§ 2[1]. And every priest shall go barefoot in the Procession with his people on the three days.

§ 2a[1]. And in addition every priest shall sing 30 masses, and every deacon and cleric 30 psalms.

§ 2*b.* Et apparetur III diebus corredium uniuscuiusque sine
carne; in cibo et potu, sicut idem comedere deberet, (et)
dividatur hoc totum pauperibus.

§ 3. Et sit omnis servus liber ab opere illis tribus diebus,
quo melius ieiunare possit, et operetur sibimet quod
vult.

§ 3*a.* Hii sunt illi tres dies—dies Lunae, dies Martis et dies
Mercurii proximi ante festum sancti Michaelis.

§ 4. Si quis ieiunium suum infringat, servus corio suo componat, liber pauper reddat XXX denarios et tainus regis
CXX sol.; et dividatur haec pecunia pauperibus.

§ 5. Et sciat omnis presbiter et tungravius et decimales
homines, ut haec elemosina et ieiunium proveniat[1], sicut
in sanctis iurare poterunt.

3. Et praecipimus, ut in omni congregatione cantetur cotidie
communiter pro rege et omni populo suo una missa ad
matutinalem missam quae inscripta est 'contra paganos.'

§ 1. Et ad singulas horas decantet totus conventus extensis
membris in terra psalmum illum: "Domine, quid[2] multi-
plicati sunt," et collectam contra paganos; et hoc fiat
quamdiu necessitas ista nobis est in manibus.

§ 2. Et in omni cenobio et[3] conventu monachorum celebret
omnis presbiter singulatim XXX missas pro rege et omni
populo, et omnis monacus XXX psalteria.

4. Et praecipimus, ut omnis homo super dileccionem Dei et
omnium sanctorum det cyricsceattum[4] et rectam decimam
suam, sicut in diebus antecessorum nostrorum stetit[5],
quando melius stetit[5]—hoc est sicut aratrum peragrabit
per[6] decimam acram.

---

[1] *perv.* H, Hk, Br.   [2] *quî* Br.   [3] *vel* M, Hk, Br.
[4] *scy.* T; *cyris.* M; *syris.* Hk; *cyrisc.* Br.   [5] *fecit* Br.   [6] Om. M, Hk, Br.

§ 2b^1. And everyone shall have his food served during the
three days without meat, and whatever he would have
consumed in food and drink shall be distributed among
the poor.

§ 3[1]. And all slaves shall be exempt from work on those
three days, so that they can fast the better and may
make[2] what they want for themselves.

§ 3a^1. These are the three days—the Monday, Tuesday and
Wednesday immediately preceding the feast of St
Michael[2].

§ 4[1]. In the case of the fast being broken—if it is a slave [who
does so], he shall undergo the lash[2], if it is a poor freeman[3], he shall pay 30 pence, and a thegn of the king's
[shall pay] 120 shillings[4]. And this money shall be
divided among the poor[5].

§ 5[1]. And every priest and the reeve of every village[2] and
the heads of the tithings[3] shall be witnesses that this
alms-giving and fasting is carried out, and shall be able
to swear to it on the holy relics[4].

3[1]. And we decree that in every religious foundation[2] a mass
entitled "Against the heathen" shall be sung daily at
matins, by the whole community, on behalf of the king
and all his people[3].

§ 1. And at the various Hours all the members of the foundation, prostrate on the ground, shall chant the psalm:
"O Lord, how are they multiplied," and the Collect
against the heathen, and this shall be done as long
as the present need continues.

§ 2. And in every foundation and college of monks every
priest severally[1] shall celebrate 30 masses for the king
and the whole nation, and every monk shall repeat
[the psalms from] his psalter 30 times.

4[1]. And we decree that all men, for love of God and all the
saints, shall give their church-dues and their rightful tithes
in accordance with the best rules observed in the days of
our ancestors, namely, [the produce of] every tenth acre
traversed by the plough[2].

§ 1. Et omnis consuetudo reddatur super amicitiam Dei ad matrem ecclesiam cui adiacet.

§ 2. Et nemo auferat Deo quod ad eum[1] pertinet et praedecessores[2] nostri concesserunt ei[3].

5. Et prohibemus ne aliquis[4] extra[5] vendatur. Si quis hoc praesumat, sit praeter benedictionem Dei et omnium sanctorum et praeter omnem Christianitatem, nisi peniteat et emendet, sicut episcopus suus edocebit.

6. Et prohibemus omnem robariam omni homini.

§ 1. Et sit omnis homo dignus iure publico, pauper et dives.

§ 2. Et reddatur omnis robaria, si quis aliquam fecerit, et emendet, sicut prius et postea stetit[6].

§ 3. Et si quis praepositus eam fecerit, duppliciter emendet quod alii iudicaretur.

7. Et reddatur pecunia elemosinae hinc[7] ad festum sancti Michaelis, si alicubi retro[8] sit, per plenam witam.

§ 1. Et omnibus annis deinceps reddantur Dei rectitudines in omnibus rebus quae supradictae sunt per amiciciam Dei et sanctorum omnium, ut Deus omnipotens misericordiam nobis faciat et de hostibus triumphum nobis et pacem indulgeat, quem sedulo deprecemur ut misericordiam eius consequamur et gratiam[9] hic et in futuro[10] requiem sine fine. Amen[11].

[1] *Deum* M, Hk, Br.　　　[2] *praec.* Br.　　　[3] Om. Br.
[4] *quis* M, Hk, Br.　　　[5] *ex. patriam* Br.　　　[6] *stet* Hk; *fecit* Br.
[7] *hic* Br.　　[8] *rectus* T.　　[9] *et gr.* om. Br.　　[10] *-ram* T.　　[11] Om. Br.

§ 1[1]. And all church dues shall be rendered, for love of God, to the mother-church to which they belong.

§ 2. And no-one shall deprive God of what belongs to him and of what our ancestors[1] granted him.

5[1]. And we forbid that anyone be sold out of the country. If anyone dares to do so, he shall be shut out from the blessing of God and of all the Saints, and from all share in the Christian religion, unless he repents and makes amends as his bishop shall direct.

6[1]. And we forbid anyone to commit theft.

§ 1[1]. And all men, whether poor or rich, shall be entitled to the benefit of the law.

§ 2[1]. And if anyone has committed theft, he shall restore all that he has stolen and make amends, as has always[2] been the rule.

§ 3. And if any reeve has committed theft, the compensation paid by him shall be double[1] that prescribed to any other person.

7. And alms-money[1], if it is in arrears, shall be paid between now and Michaelmas[2], under pain of incurring the full penalty[3].

§ 1[1]. And every year in future God's dues shall be rendered in all cases specified above[2], for love of God[3] and all the saints, so that[4] God omnipotent may show mercy towards us and grant us victory over our foes, and peace. Let us zealously entreat Him, that we may obtain His mercy and grace here, and, in the life to come, rest without end. Amen.

VII ÆTHELRED (ANGLO-SAXON)

Ðis man gerædde ða se micele here com to lande.

Ealle we beþurfan þæt we geornlice earnian þæt we Godes miltse 7 his mildheortnesse habban moton 7 þæt we þurh his fultum magon feondum wiðstandan.

1. Nu wille we þæt eal folc to gemænelicre dædbote þrig dagas be hlafe 7 wirtum 7 wætere, þæt is on Monandæg 7 on Tiwesdæg 7 on Wodnesdæg ær Michaeles mæssan.

2. 7 cume manna gehwilc bærefot to circan buton golde 7 glæncgum 7 ga man to scrifte.

   § 1. 7 gan ealle út mid haligdome 7 clipian inweardre heortan georne to Criste.

   § 2. 7 sceote man æghwilce hide pænig oððe pæniges weorð.

   § 3. 7 bringe man þæt to cirican 7 siððan on þreo dæle be scriftes 7 be tunesgerefan gewitnesse.

3. 7 gif hwa þis ne gelæste, ðonne gebete he þæt, swa swa hit gelagod is: bunda mid xxx p̃, þræl mid his hide, þegn mid xxx scill'.

4. 7 swa hwar swa þæt feoh up arise, dæle man on Godes est æghwilcne pænig.

   § 1. 7 ealswa þone mete þe gehwa brucan wolde, gif him þæt fæsten swa geboden nære, dæle man on Godes est georne æfter þam fæstene eal þearfigendum mannum 7 bedridan 7 swa gebrocedum mannum þe swa fæstan ne magon.

5. 7 hiredmanna gehwilc sille pænig to ælmessan oððe his hlaford sille for hine, buton he silf hæbbe, 7 heafodmen teoðian.

   § 1. 7 þeowemen þa ðrig dagas beon weorces gefréode wið ciricsocne 7 wið ðam þe hi þæt fæsten þe lustlicor gefæstan.

VII ÆTHELRED (ANGLO-SAXON)

This edict was drawn up when the great army came to the country.

All of us have need to strive earnestly that we may obtain the mercy and compassion of God and through his help withstand our foes[1].

1[1]. It is our desire that the whole people, as a national penalty, [fast] on bread and herbs and water for three days, namely, on the Monday, Tuesday and Wednesday before Michaelmas.

2[1]. And everyone shall come barefoot to church without gold or ornaments and shall go to confession.

§ 1[1]. And all shall go out with the relics, and from their inmost heart call earnestly upon Christ.

§ 2[1]. And from every hide a penny or the value of a penny shall be given as dues.

§ 3[1]. And it shall be brought to church and afterwards divided in three[2] in the presence of the confessor and the reeve of the village as witnesses.

3[1]. And if anyone does not render this, he shall make amends as has been established by law: a householder shall pay 30 pence, a slave shall undergo the lash, and a thegn shall pay 30 shillings[2].

4. And wherever such payment has to be made[1], every penny shall be distributed[2] for love of God[3].

§ 1[1]. And likewise all the food which each would enjoy, if this fast were not prescribed for him, shall be zealously distributed after the fast, for love of God[2], among the needy and the bed-ridden and the afflicted who cannot fast in this way.

5[1]. And every member of a household shall give a penny as alms, or his lord shall give it for him, if he has nothing himself, and men of position[2] shall pay tithes.

§ 1[1]. And on these three days slaves shall be exempt from work, in order to attend church and keep the fast more willingly.

6. 7 on æghwilcan mynstre singe eal geferræden ætgædere
heora saltere þa ðry dagas.

§ 1. 7 ælc mæssepreost mæssige for urne hlaford 7 for ealle
his þeode.

§ 2. 7 þar to eacan mæssige man æghwilce dæge on ælcan
minstre ane mæssan sinderlice for ðare neode þe us nu
on handa stent, oð þæt hit betere wurðe.

§ 3. 7 æt ælcan tídsange eal hired aþenedum limum ætforan
Godes weofode singe þone sealm: "Domine, quid multi-
plicati sunt" 7 preces 7 col'.

7. 7 ealle gemænelice, gehadode 7 læwede, bugan to Gode
georne 7 geearnian his mildse.

8. 7 æghwilce geare heonon forð gelæste man Godes gerihta
huru rihtlice, wið ðam þe us God ælmihtig gemiltsige 7 us
geunne þæt we ure fynd ofercuman motan.
God ure helpe. Amen.

VIII ÆTHELRED

Anno MXIIII. ab incarnatione Domini nostri Iesu Christi[1].

Þis is an ðara gerædnessa þe Engla cyningc gedihte mid his
witena geþeahte.

1. Þæt is ærest, þæt he wile þæt ealle Godes circan beon fulles
griðes wurðe.

§ 1. And gif æfre ænig man heonan forð Godes ciricgrið swa
abrece þæt he binnon ciricwagum mansleaga wurðe,
þonne sy þæt botleas, 7 ehte his ælc þara þe Godes
freond sy, buton þæt gewurðe þæt he þanon ætberste
7 swa deope friðsocne gesece þæt se cyningc him þurh
þæt feores geunne, wið fulre bote ge wið God ge wið men.

---

[1] *Be cyricgriðe. In nomine Domini* G.

6[1]. And in every religious foundation, on these three days, all the brotherhood in common shall chant [the psalms from] their psalters[2].

§ 1[1]. And every priest shall say mass for our lord and for all his people.

§ 2[1]. And in addition, in every religious foundation, one mass shall be said daily with special reference[2] to the distress with which we are now afflicted[3], until an improvement takes place.

§ 3[1]. And at every service all the brotherhood, prostrate before the altar of God, shall chant the psalm: "O Lord, how are they multiplied" and the Prayers and Collect.

7[1]. And all men with one accord, both clerics and laymen, shall zealously turn to God and obtain his mercy.

8[1]. And every year henceforth the most scrupulous care shall be taken in the payment of God's dues, in order that God Almighty may have mercy upon us and grant us victory over our enemies.

God help us. Amen.

VIII ÆTHELRED

In the year 1014 after the incarnation of our Lord Jesus Christ[1].

This is one of the ordinances[1] which the English king drew up with the advice of his councillors.

1[1]. In the first place, it is his will that all the churches of God be entitled to exercise their right of protection to the full.

§ 1. And if ever anyone henceforth violates the protection of the church[1] of God by committing homicide within its walls, the crime shall not be atoned for by any payment of compensation[2], and everyone who is the friend of God shall pursue[3] the miscreant, unless it happen that he escapes from there and reaches so inviolable a sanctuary[4] that the king[5], because of that, grant him his life, upon condition that he makes full amends both towards God and men.

2. And þæt is þonne ærest, þæt he his agenne wer gesille þam cyninge 7 Christe 7 mid þam hine silfne inlagige to bote.

> § 1. Forðam Cristen cyning is Cristes gespelia[1] on Cristenre þeode, and he sceal Cristes abilgðe wrecan swiðe georne.

3. And gif hit þonne to bote gega 7 se cyngc þæt geþafige, þonne bete man þæt ciricgrið into ðare circan, be þæs[2] cyninges fullan mundbryce, 7 þa mynsterclænsunge begite, swa þarto gebirige, [7 ægþer ge mægbote ge manbote fullice gebete][3], 7 wið God huru þingian[4] georne.

4. And gif [elles][3] be cwicum mannum ciricgrið abrocen beo, betan[5] man georne be þam þe seo dæd sy, sy hit þurh feohtlac, si hit þurh reaflac, si hit þurh unriht hæmed[6], si þurh þæt þæt hit sy.

> § 1. Bete[7] man æfre[2] ærest þone griðbryce into ðare circan be þam þe seo dæd sy 7 be þam þe þare circan mæð sy.

5. Ne syn ealle cyrcan na gelicre mæðe worldlice wirðe, þeah hi godcundlice habban halgunge gelice.

> § 1. Heafodmynstres griðbryce æt botwurðan þingan bete man be cyninges munde, þæt is mid v pundum on Engla lage, and medemran mynstres mid hundtwelftigan scill', þæt is be cyninges wite, and þonne git læssan [þær legerstow þeh sy][3] mid sixtigan scill', and æt feldcircan mid xxx scill'.

---

[1] g. geteald G.   [2] Om. G.   [3] G; om. D.   [4] -ie G.
[5] bete G.   [6] si hit þ. u. h. om. G.   [7] gebete G.

2. And the first condition is, that he shall give his own wergeld[1] to the king and to Christ[2], and by that means obtain the legal right[3] to offer compensation.

§ 1. For a Christian king is Christ's deputy[1] among Christian people, and he must avenge with the utmost diligence offences against Christ.

3. And if it comes to the payment of compensation and the king allows this course, amends for the violation of the protection of the church shall be made by the payment to the church in question of the full fine for breach of the king's "mund,"[1] and the purification of the church shall be carried out as is fitting, [and compensation both to the kin[2] and to the lord[3] of the slain man shall be fully paid], and, above all, supplication shall earnestly be made[4] to God.

4[1]. And if the protection of the church is broken in some other respect, without the taking of life[2], amends shall diligently be made in accordance with the nature of the offence, whether it be fighting or robbery or illicit intercourse[3] or whatever it may be.

§ 1[1]. And in the first instance, amends for breach of its protection shall always be made to the church, in accordance with the nature of the offence and also in proportion to the status[2] of the church.

5[1]. Not all churches are to be regarded as possessing the same status in civil law, though from the side of religion they all possess the same sanctity.

§ 1. Amends for violation of the protection of a principal church[1], in cases in which compensation can be paid[2], shall be made by payment of the fine for breach of the king's "mund," i.e. £5 in districts under English law, and in the case of a church of medium rank, by the payment of 120 shillings[3], i.e. by the fine due to the king (for insubordination)[4], and in the case of one still smaller [where however there is a graveyard][5], by the payment of 60 shillings, and in the case of a country chapel, by the payment of 30 shillings[6].

§ 2. A sceal mid rihte dom æfter dæde 7 medmung be mæþe[1].

6. And be teoðunge se cyng 7 his witan habbað gecoren 7 gecweden, ealswa hit riht is, þæt ðriddan dæl þare teoðunge þe to circan gebyrge ga to ciricbote 7 oðer dæl þam Godes þeowum, þridde Godes þearfum 7 earman þeowetlingan.

7. And wite Cristenra manna gehwilc, þæt he his Drihtene his teoþunge, a swa seo sulh þone teoðan æcer gegá, rihtlice gelæste be Godes miltse 7 be þam fullan wite þe Eadgar cyningc gelagode.

8. Ðæt is: Gif hwa teoþunge rihtlice gelæstan nelle, þonne fare tó þæs cyninges gerefa 7 þæs mynstres mæssepreost— oððe þæs landrican 7 þæs biscopes gerefa—7 niman unþances ðone teoðan dæl to ðam mynstre þe hit to gebirige, 7 tæcan him to ðam nigoðan dæle, 7 todæle man ða eahta dælas on twá, 7 fó se landhlaford to healfum, to healfum se biscop, si hit cyninges man, sy hit þegnes.

9. And sy ælc geoguðe teoðung gelæst be pentecosten be wite, and eorðwestma be emnihte, oððe huru be ealra halgena mæssan.

10. And Romfeoh gelæste man æghwilce geare be Petres mæssan.

§ 1. 7 se þe þæt nelle gelæstan, sille þar to eacan xxx p' 7 gilde þam cyninge cxx scill'.

11. And ciricsceat gelæste man be Martinus mæssan.

§ 1. 7 se þe ðæt ne gelæste, forgilde hine mid twelffealdan 7 þam cyninge cxx scill'.

---

[1] At this point the extract in G ends.

§ 2[1]. Judgment, following the principles of justice, shall always be in accordance with the nature of the deed, and the penalty shall be proportionate to the offence.

6[1]. And with regard to tithes, the king and his councillors have decided and agreed, in accordance with the principles of justice, that a third part of the tithes which belong to the church shall be assigned to the repair of churches, the second portion to the servants of God, and the third portion to God's poor[2] and to poverty-stricken slaves[3].

7[1]. And every Christian man, in order to obtain the mercy of God, shall see to it that he duly renders his tithes to his Lord, namely, in every case, the produce of every tenth acre traversed by the plough, or else he shall incur the full penalty[2] which King Edgar[3] instituted by law.

8[1]. Namely: if anyone refuses to make due rendering of his tithes, the king's reeve and the priest of the church—or the reeve of the lord of the manor[2] and the bishop's reeve—shall go to him and, without his consent, shall take the tenth part for the church to which it belongs, and the next tenth shall be allotted to him, and the eight [remaining] parts shall be divided in two, and the lord of the manor shall take half and the bishop half, whether the man be under the lordship of the king or of a thegn.

9[1]. And every tithe of young livestock shall be rendered by Pentecost, under pain of incurring the fine, and the tithe of the fruits of the earth by the equinox, or at least by the feast of All Saints.

10[1]. And Peter's Pence shall be rendered every year by St Peter's Day.

§ 1[1]. And he who refuses to render it shall give in addition 30 pence, and shall pay 120 shillings to the king.

11[1]. And church dues shall be rendered by Martinmas.

§ 1[1]. And he who fails to do so shall pay them twelve-fold and [give] 120 shillings to the king.

12. Sulhælmessan gebireð þæt man gelæste be wite æghwilce geare, þonne xv niht beoð agan ofer castertid.

§ 1. 7 leohtgescot gelæste man to candelmæssan; dó oftor se ðe wille.

13. And sawlsceat is rihtast þæt man symle gelæste a æt openum græfe.

14. And ealle Godes gerihta firðrige man georne, ealswa hit þearf is.

15. And gif hwa þæt nelle, gewilde man hine to rihte mid worldlicre steore, 7 þæt si gemæne Criste 7 cyninge, ealswa hit iu wæs.

16. And freolsa 7 fæstena be wite healde man rihtlice.

17. And Sunnondaga cypinga forbeode man georne be fullan worldwite.

18. And weofodþéna mæðe medemige man for Godes ege.

19. Gif man mæssepreost tihtlige þe regollice libbe andfealdre spræce, mæssige, gif he durre, 7 ladige hine on ðam husle silf hine silfne.

§ 1. And æt þrifealdre spræce ladige, gif he durre, eac on ðam husle mid twam his gehádan.

20. Gif man diacon tihtlige þe regollice libbe andfealdre spræce, nime twegen his gehádan 7 ladige hine mid þam.

§ 1. And gif man hine tihtlige þryfealdre spræce, nime six his gehádan 7 ladige mid þam 7 beo he silf seofoða.

21. Gif man folciscne mæssepreost mid tihtlan belecge þe regollif næbbe, ladige hine swa swa diacon þe regollife libbe.

12[1]. Plough-alms ought to be rendered every year 15 days after Easter, under pain of incurring the fine.

§ 1[1]. And light-dues shall be rendered at Candlemas; he who so desires may give them more frequently.

13[1]. And it is best that payment for the souls of the dead should always be rendered before the grave is closed.

14[1]. And all God's dues shall be promptly rendered, as the occasion requires.

15[1]. And if anyone refuses to do so, he shall be brought to justice by a civil penalty, and this shall be divided between Christ and the king, in accordance with former custom.

16[1]. And festivals and fasts shall be duly observed, under pain of incurring the fine[2].

17[1]. And Sunday marketings shall be strictly forbidden, under pain of incurring the full civil penalty.

18[1]. And the status of the priesthood[2] shall be respected through the fear of God.

19[1]. If a simple accusation is brought against a priest who lives according to a rule, he shall say mass, if he dares, and by his own asseveration clear himself by the Holy Communion[2].

§ 1. And in the case of a triple accusation he shall also clear himself, if he dares, by the Holy Communion, with two supporters of the same ecclesiastical rank as himself.

20. If a simple accusation is brought against a deacon who lives according to a rule, he shall take two supporters of the same ecclesiastical rank and clear himself with their help.

§ 1. And if a triple accusation is brought against him, he shall take six supporters of the same ecclesiastical rank —himself making a seventh—and clear himself with their help.

21. If an accusation is brought against a secular priest who does not live according to a rule, he shall clear himself in the same way as a deacon who lives according to a rule.

22. Gif man freondleasne weofodþén mid tihtlan belecge, þe adfultum næbbe, gá to corsnǽde 7 þar þonne æt gefare þæt þæt God wille, buton he on husle ladian mote.

23. And gif man gehadodne mid fæhðe belecge 7 secge þæt he wære dǽdbana oððe rædbana, ladige mid his magan þe fæhðe moton mid beran oððe forebetan.

24. And gif he sý mægleas, ladige mid geferan, oððe fæste to corsnǽde 7 þaræt gefare þæt þæt God ræde.

25. And ne þearf ænig mynstermunuc ahwar mid rihte fæhðbote biddan ne fæhðbote betan; he gæð of his mæglage þonne he gebihð to regollage.

26. Gif mæssepreost manslaga wurðe oððe elles mánweorc to swiðe gewurce, þonne þolige he ægðres ge hádes gé éardes 7 wræcnige swa wíde swa papa him scrife 7 dædbete georne.

27. Gif mæssepreost ahwar stande on leasre gewitnesse oððe on mǽnan aðe, oððe þeofa gewita 7 geweorhta beo, þonne sy he aworpen of gehadodra gemanan 7 þolige ægðer ge geferscipes ge freondscipes ge æghwilces wurðscipes, buton he wið God 7 wið men þe deoplicor gebete, fullice swa biscop him tæce, 7 him borh finde þæt he þanan forð æfre swilces geswice.

§ 1. And gif he ladian wille, geladige be dæde mæðe, swa mid þryfealdre, [swa mid anfealdre][1], be þam þe seo dǽd sy.

28. Gif weofodþen be boca tæcincge his agen lif rihtlice fadige, þonne sy he fulles þegnweres 7 weorðscipes wurðe, ge on life ge on legere.

[1] Following Thorpe, cf. I Cn. 5, 4.

22. If an accusation is brought against a minister of the altar who has no friends and no-one to support his oath, he shall go to the ordeal of consecrated bread[1], and shall experience there what is the will of God, unless he is allowed to clear himself by the Holy Communion.

23. And if a man in holy orders is charged with vendetta, and accused of having committed or instigated homicide, he shall clear himself with the help of his kin[1], who must share the vendetta[2] with him or pay compensation for it.

24. And if he has no kin, he shall clear himself with the help of his fellow-ecclesiastics[1], or fast in preparation for the ordeal of consecrated bread, and experience there what God shall decree.

25[1]. And no monk who belongs to a monastery anywhere may lawfully either demand or pay any compensation incurred by vendetta. He leaves the law of his kindred behind when he accepts monastic rule.

26[1]. If a priest commits homicide or perpetrates any other great crime, he shall be deprived of his ecclesiastical office and likewise banished, and shall travel as a pilgrim as far as the Pope appoints for him, and zealously make amends.

27[1]. If a priest anywhere be concerned in false witness or perjury[2], or be the accessory and accomplice of thieves, he shall be cast out from the fellowship of those in holy orders, and shall forfeit both their society and their friendship and every kind of privilege[3], unless he make full amends, both towards God and towards men, to the utmost of his ability, as the bishop shall prescribe for him, and find surety that henceforth he will cease for ever from all such [wrong-doing].
   § 1. And if he seeks to clear himself, he shall do so in proportion to the deed, either by the triple mode of proof, [or by the simple][1], in accordance with the nature of the deed.

28[1]. If a member of the priesthood orders his own life aright, according to the teaching of the canon law[2], he shall be entitled to the full wergeld and privileges of a thegn, both during his life and after his death.

29. And gif he his lif misfadige, wanige his weorðscipe be þam
þe seo dæd sy.

30. Wite, gif he wille, ne gebirað him nan þinge ne to wife ne
to worldwige, gif he Gode wile rihtlice hyran 7 Godes laga
healdan, swa swa his hade gedafenað mid rihte.

31. Ac we læra ð georne 7 luflice biddað, þæt ælces hades men
þam life libban þe heom to gebirige.

§ 1. 7 heonan forð we willað þæt abbodas 7 munecas re-
gollicor libban þonne hi nu ær ðisan on gewunan hæfdon.

32. And se cynge beodeð eallum his gerefan on æghwilcere
stowe, þæt ge þam abbodan æt eallum worldneodum beorgan
swa ge betst magon, 7 be þam þe ge willan Godes oððe
minne freondscipe habban, filstan heora wícneran æghwar
to rihte, þæt heo sylfe magan þe oftor on mynstrum fæste
gewunian 7 regollice libban.

33. And gif man gehadodne oððe ælþeodigne man þurh ænig
þinc forræde æt feo oððe æt feore, oððe hine bænde oððe hine
beate oððe gebismrige on ænige wisan, þonne sceal him
cynge beon for mæg 7 for mundboran, buton he elles oðerne
hæbbe.

34. And bete man ægðer ge him ge þam cynge, swa swa hit
gebirige, be þam þe séo dæd sy, oððe he ða dæde wrece
swiðe deope.

35. Cristenum mannan[1] gebira ð swiðe rihte þæt he Godes
abilgðe wrece swiðe georne.

36. And wise wæran worldwitan þe to godcundan rihtlagan
woroldlaga settan, folce to steore, 7 Criste 7 cyninge ge-
rehtan[2] þa bote þar man swa scolde manega for neode
gewildan to rihte.

37. Ac on þam gemotan, þeah rædlice wurðan on namcuðan
stowan, æfter Eadgares lifdagum, Cristes lage wanodan 7
cyninges laga litledon.

---

[1] -um D.   [2] -rihtan D.

29. And if he misdirects his life, his privileges shall be reduced, according to the nature of the offence.

30. Let him understand, if he will, that it is not seemly for him to have anything to do either with marriage or with worldly strife, if he will duly obey God and observe his laws, as properly befits his estate.

31[1]. But we earnestly enjoin and, with all good-will, beg men of every estate to live such a life as befits them.

   § 1. And henceforth we desire abbots and monks to live more according to a rule than they have been accustomed to do until now.

32. And the king enjoins upon all his reeves in every locality: you shall support the abbots in all their temporal needs as you best can, and if you desire to have God's favour and mine[1], help their stewards everywhere to obtain their rights, so that they themselves may constantly remain secure in their monasteries and live according to their rule.

33[1]. And if an attempt is made to deprive in any way a man in orders or a stranger of either his goods or his life, or if he is bound[2] or beaten or insulted in any way, the king shall act as his kinsman and protector, if he has no other.

34. And compensation according to the nature of the deed shall be paid both to him and to the king, as is fitting, or he (the king) shall avenge the deed to the uttermost.

35[1]. It is the duty most incumbent upon a Christian man that he should avenge offences against God with the utmost diligence.

36[1]. And secular councillors showed wisdom in appointing civil laws to uphold the privileges of religion, for the governance of the people, and in assigning the compensation to Christ and the king, so that[2] thereby many are forced of necessity to submit to justice.

37. But in the assemblies since the days of Edgar, though advisedly they have been held in places of note[1], the laws of Christ have been neglected and the laws of the king disregarded[2].

38. And þa man getwæmde þæt ær wæs gemæne Criste 7 cyningce on worldlicre steore, 7 a hit wearð þe wirse for Gode 7 for worlde; cume nu to bote, gif hit God wille.

39. And git mæg ðeah bot cuman, wille hit man georne on eornost aginnan.

40. And gif man eard wille rihtlice clænsian, þonne mot man smeagan 7 geornlice spirian, hwar ða manfullan wununge habban þe nellað geswican ne for Gode betan, ac swa hwar swa hi man finde, gewilde hi to rihte, þances oððe unðances, oððe hi afirsige mid ealle of earde, buton hi gebugan 7 to rihte gewændan.

41. Gif munuc oððe mæssepreost wiðersaca wurðe mid ealle, he sy amansumod æfre, buton he þe rædlicor gebuge to his þearfe.

42. And se þe Godes utlagan ofer þone andagan, þe se cyngc sette, hæbbe on gewealde, plihte to him sylfum 7 ealre his are wið Cristes gespelian þe Cristendom 7 cynedom healdað 7 wealdað, þa hwile þe þæs God geann.

43. Ac uton don swa us pea[r]f[1] is: uton niman us to bisnan þæt ærran worldwitan to ræde geræddon, Æþelstan 7 Eadmund 7 Eadgar þe nihst wæs, hu hi God weorðodon 7 Godes lage heoldon 7 Godes gafel læstan, þa hwile þe hi leofodon.

§ 1. 7 utan God lufian innewerdre heortan 7 Godes laga gíman, swa wel swa we betst magon.

44. And uton rihtne Cristendom geornlice wurðian 7 ælcne hæðendom mid ealle oferhogian.

§ 1. And uton ænne cynehlaford holdlice healdan, 7 freonda gehwilc mid rihtan getriwðan oðerne lufige 7 healde mid rihte.

¹ þeaf D.

38. And then the [dues from] civil penalties which had previously been shared between[1] Christ and the king were separated, and things have continually gone from bad to worse both in religious and in secular affairs. God grant that there may now be improvement![2]

39[1]. And yet nevertheless improvement can come, if there is the zealous desire to begin it in earnest.

40[1]. And if the land is to be thoroughly purified, inquiry and search must be diligently made for the dwelling-places of the wicked who will not abstain [from evil] or make amends in the sight of God, and wherever they are found they shall be brought to justice, willingly or unwillingly, or they shall be utterly driven from the land, unless they submit and amend their ways.

41[1]. If a monk or a priest becomes an utter apostate, he shall be excommunicated for ever, unless he is wise enough to return to his duty.

42[1]. And he who keeps under his protection an excommunicated man[2], beyond the term fixed by the king, shall be in danger of forfeiting his life and all his property to the deputies of Christ[3], who shall be the defenders and upholders of the Christian religion and the royal authority[4], as long as God shall permit.

43. But let us do what is our duty, let us take as our example what the secular authorities of old wisely decreed—Æthelstan and Edmund[1] and Edgar[2], who came last—how they honoured God and kept his law[3] and rendered tribute to him, as long as they lived.

§ 1[1]. And let us love God from our inmost heart and observe his laws to the best of our ability.

44[1]. And let us zealously honour the true Christian religion and utterly despise all heathen practices.

§ 1[1]. And let us loyally support one royal lord, and let each of our friends[2] love the other with true fidelity and treat him justly.

IX ÆTHELRED

(*Incip.*)[1] Ðis is sio gerædnes þe Æþelred cyning and ealle his witan æt Wudustoce geræddan.

1. An ærest, þæt we ealle to Gode ælmihtigan georne gebugan 7 his bebodu healdan 7 unrihtes ealle geswican.

(*Expl.*)[1] An[d][2] uton ænne God lufian and weorðian and ænne Cristendom ealle heald[an][3] 7 ælcne hæþendom mid ealle aweorpan. Uton ænne cynehlaford holdliche...(*desunt reliqua.*)[1]

X ÆTHELRED

An is ece Godd wealdend 7 wyrhta ealra gesceafta; 7 on þæs naman weorðunge ic, Æðelred cyning, ærest smeade, hu ic Cristendom æfre mihte 7 rihtne cynedom fyrmest aræran, 7 hu ic mihte þearflicast me sylfum gerædan for Gode 7 for worolde 7 eallum minum leodscype rihtlicast lagian þa þing to þearfe þe we scýlan healdan.

§ 1. Mearn to gemynde oft 7 gelome þe godcunde lara 7 wislice woroldlaga Cristendom fyrðriað 7 cynedom micliað, folce gefremiað 7 weorðscypes wealdað, sibbiað 7 sehtað 7 sace twæmað 7 þeode þeawas ealle gebetað.

§ 2. Nu wille ic georne æfter þam spyrian, hu we lara 7 laga betst magan healdan 7 æghwylce unlaga swyþost aweorpan.

§ 3. 7 þis is seo gerædnes þe we willað healdan, swa swa we æt Eanham fæste gecwædon.

---

[1] Wanley.   [2] *An.*   [3] *·c.*

IX ÆTHELRED

This is the ordinance which King Æthelred and all his councillors have determined upon at Woodstock[1].

1[1]. In the first place, we shall all zealously turn to God Almighty and keep his commandments and all cease from evil....

And let us love and honour one God and all uphold[1] one Christian faith and utterly renounce all heathen practices. Let us loyally[1] [support] one royal lord[2]....

X ÆTHELRED

The eternal God alone is the ruler and maker of all created things[1], and in honour of his name I, King Æthelred, have been considering first of all how I could best promote Christianity[2] and the just interests of the royal authority, and how, in affairs both religious and secular, I could determine with the greatest profit to myself[3], and ordain most justly[4], for the advantage of all my subjects, the conditions which we ought to observe.

§ 1[1]. Frequently and often it has come into my mind that sacred precepts and wise secular decrees promote Christianity and strengthen royal authority, further public interests and are the source of honour, bring about peace and reconciliation, put an end to strife and improve the whole character of the nation.

§ 2. Now I desire zealously to search out how we may best uphold precepts and laws and most fully renounce all unjust practices[1].

§ 3. And this is the ordinance which we desire to observe in accordance with what we have firmly decreed at Enham[1].

1. Ðæt is þonne ærest, þæt we ealle fram synnan georne gecyrran 7 ure misdæda geornlice betan 7 ænne God æfre lufian 7 weorðian 7 ænne Christendom georne healdan 7 ælcne hæðendom mid ealle aweorpan.

2. 7 witena geræðnes is, þæt man rihte laga upp arære 7 ælce unlaga georne afylle, 7 þæt man læte beon æghwylcne man rihtes wyrðe.

§ 1. 7 þæt man frið 7 freondscype rihtlice healde for Gode 7 for worolde.

1¹. The first provision is, that all of us zealously turn from sins and zealously make amends for our misdeeds, and love and honour for all time one God, and zealously uphold one Christian faith, and utterly renounce all heathen practices.

2¹. And the decree of the councillors is, that justice be promoted and every injustice zealously suppressed, and that every man be allowed the benefit of the law.

§ 1. And that peace and goodwill be duly maintained in matters both religious and secular.

THE LAWS OF CANUTE

THE LAWS OF CANUTE

Two proclamations and one long code of laws issued by Canute have been preserved. The latter falls into two parts, generally distinguished as I and II Canute, the first of which deals with ecclesiastical affairs, the second with secular (cf. II, III Edgar).

The first Proclamation seems to have been issued early in 1020 (see Notes), and is addressed to all his subjects in England. It contains interesting references to recent events, *e.g.* the receipt of letters and injunctions from the Pope (cap. 3), the removal of the menace of hostility from Denmark, for which Canute takes full credit to himself (cap. 5), and the general acceptance of the laws of Edgar at Oxford (cap. 13). It marks therefore an important stage in the history of the country. The wars, discord and unrest of the preceding years are at an end, and just government is assured for the future. The homiletic tone of the whole proclamation recalls the Laws of Æthelred, and may be due to the influence of Wulfstan of York (see Notes).

The second Proclamation, prepared by Canute on his way from Rome to Denmark, belongs to the year 1027 (see cap. 3 and Note). Historically it is of great importance for the information it supplies regarding Canute's movements in 1027 (see caps. 13, 14), his position in relation to the Pope and the princes of Western Europe (cap. 5), and his diplomatic successes abroad (caps. 6, 7). His instructions to his officials to maintain justice and to secure full payment of church dues contain nothing new. In both Proclamations the statement of his resolution to rule justly rings sincere (1020, cap. 2; 1027, cap. 10).

Canute's Code of laws was issued one Christmas at Winchester (see Preamble). The year is not stated and cannot be exactly determined, but a date later than 1018, when the assembly met at Oxford and swore to uphold the laws of Edgar, seems most likely. The fact that Canute calls himself King of Denmark further supports this supposition (see 1020, cap. 5 and Note). The years 1019, 1026 and 1028 are definitely excluded, because in each of these Canute was absent from England at Christmas (see Steenstrup, *Normannerne*, III. 312, 409). This leaves as possible the years 1020–1025, 1027, 1029–1034. The statement in the heading of MS D, that the code was drawn up immediately after the establishment of peace between Danes and English, would indicate an early date, but, as it does not appear in any of the other MSS, and as D otherwise is fragmentary and untrustworthy, it is probably not authentic (see Liebermann, III. p. 194). In one MS class (A, *Consiliatio Cnuti*) the title "King of Norway" is also found but may have been added by a scribe (see 1027, Preamble and Note). From the statement of Wm. of Malmesbury (*Gesta Regum*, § 183, Rolls Series, p. 224) it would seem that the laws were not promulgated till after Canute's return from Rome. The fact that no reference occurs in either of his proclamations to earlier enactments of his own, and that certain points brought forward there are dealt with more fully in the Laws (cf. 1027, cap. 16 and I Cn. 8–14) seems to confirm this statement. The years most likely therefore are 1027, 1029–34 (see Liebermann, III. p. 194).

Canute's Code of laws is notably comprehensive. It shows no marked originality, however, as a large proportion of its injunctions and regulations are drawn from homilies and penitentials and from earlier laws (especially those of Edgar and Æthelred). In arrangement the Code shows little advance on those of Canute's predecessors. Repetitions are frequent, but in general the style is clear and straightforward. Especially interesting are the sections giving detailed accounts of the dues to which the king was entitled in Wessex, Mercia and the Danelaw (II Cn. caps. 12–15), and of the grading of heriots (II Cn. caps. 70–72, 1). In both cases probably, to judge from the evidence of earlier and contemporary documents, the regulations here definitely expressed for the first time in a code of laws had long been observed in practice.

The only MS copy of the Proclamation of 1020 dates from about 1050 and is preserved in the Minster Library at York. The Proclamation of 1027 has been preserved only in a Latin translation and is found in Florence of Worcester, ed. Thorpe, I. p. 185 ff. (which I have collated with MS Oxford Corpus 157, p. 329), and Wm. of Malmesbury, *Gesta Reg.* Lib. II. § 183.

I, II Canute is found complete in MSS G and A and in Lambarde's edition. Some leaves of MS B containing caps. 1–14, 2 have been lost but from that point the code is complete. Fragments appear in MS D (see Notes). Three Latin translations are also extant, namely, in the Quadripartitus, the Instituta Cnuti and the Consiliatio Cnuti. For an account of the various MSS and their relationship see Liebermann, III. p. 192 f. The following text of I and II Canute has been taken from B, the missing clauses of I being supplied from G.

CANUTE'S PROCLAMATION OF 1020

1. Cnut cyning gret his arcebiscopas 7 his leodbiscopas 7 Þurcyl eorl 7 ealle his eorlas 7 ealne his þeodscype, twelf-hynde 7 twyhynde, gehadode 7 læwede, on Englalande freondlice.

2. 7 ic cyðe eow þæt ic wylle beon hold hlaford 7 unswicende to Godes gerihtum 7 to rihtre woroldlage.

3. Ic nam me to gemynde þa gewritu 7 þa word þe se arce-biscop Lyfing me fram þam papan brohte of Rome, þæt ic scolde æghwær Godes lof upp aræran 7 unriht alecgan 7 full frið wyrcean be ðære mihte þe me God syllan wolde.

4. Nu ne wandode ic na minum sceattum, þa hwile þe eow unfrið on handa stod; nu ic mid Godes fultume þæt tot-wæmde mid minum scattum.

5. Þa cydde man me þæt us mara hearm to fundode þonne us wel licode; 7 þa for ic me sylf, mid þam mannum þe me mid foron, into Denmearcon þe eow mæst hearm of com; 7 þæt hæbbe [ic][1] mid Godes fultume forene forfangen, þæt eow næfre heonon forð þanon nan unfrið to ne cymð, þa hwile þe ge mé rihtlice healdað 7 min lif byð.

6. Nu ðancige ic Gode ælmihtigum his fultumes 7 his mild-heortnesse, þæt ic þa myclan hearmas þe us to fundedon swa gelogod hæbbe, þæt we ne þurfon þanon nenes hearmes us asittan, ac us to fullan fultume 7 to ahreddingge, gyf us neod byð.

7. Nu wylle ic þæt we ealle eadmodlice Gode ælmihtigum þancian þære mildheortnesse þe he us to fultume gedon hæfð.

[1] Not in MS.

CANUTE'S PROCLAMATION OF 1020

1. King Canute[1] sends friendly greetings[2] to his archbishops[3] and his diocesan bishops and Earl Thurkil[4] and all his earls[5] and all his subjects in England, nobles and commoners, ecclesiastics and laymen.

2. And I declare to you that I will be a gracious lord[1], and will not fail to support the rights of the church[2] and just secular law.

3. I have taken cognisance of the written[1] and verbal injunctions which Archbishop Lyfing brought me from Rome from the Pope[2], namely, that I should everywhere magnify the glory of God and suppress injustice and establish perfect security through the power which God has been pleased to grant me.

4. Recently I did not spare my money when hostility[1] was threatening you, and now, with the help of God, I have averted[2] it with my money.

5. When I was informed that we were threatened with danger greater than we could regard with equanimity, I went[1] in person, with those who accompanied me, to Denmark[2], which was the chief source of danger to you, and, with the help of God, I have taken measures to prevent hostility ever from this time forth coming upon you from that quarter, as long as you support me loyally and my life lasts[3].

6. Now I thank God Almighty for his help and his mercy, that I have disposed of the great dangers which threatened us, with the result that we need not expect any danger from that quarter, but rather [that they will grant] us abundant help and deliverance, if we need it.

7. Now it is my desire that we all humbly thank God Almighty for the mercy which he has shown in aiding us[1].

8. Nu bidde ic mine arcebiscopas 7 calle mine leodbiscopas,
    þæt hy calle neodfulle beon ymbe Godes gerihta, ælc on his
    ende þe heom betæht is; 7 eac minum ealdormannum ic
    beode, þæt hy fylstan þam biscopum to Godes gerihtum 7
    to minum kynescype 7 to ealles folces þearfe.

9. Gif hwa swa dyrstig sy, gehadod oððe læwede, Denisc oððe
    Englisc, þæt ongean Godes lage ga 7 ongean minne cynes-
    cype oððe ongean woroldriht, 7 nelle betan 7 geswican æfter
    minra biscopa tæcinge, þonne bidde ic Þurcyl eorl 7 eac
    beode, þæt he ðæne unrihtwisan to rihte gebige, gyf he mæge.

10. Gyf he ne mæge, þonne wille ic mid uncer begra cræfte þæt
    he hine on earde adwæsce oððe ut of earde adræfe, sy he
    betera sy he wyrsa.

11. 7 eac ic beode eallum minum gerefum, be minum freond-
    scype 7 be eallum þam þe hi agon 7 be heora agenum life,
    þæt hy æghwær min folc rihtlice healdan 7 rihte domas
    deman be ðære scira biscopa gewitnesse, 7 swylce mild-
    heortnesse þæron don swylce þære scire biscope riht þince
    7 se man acuman mæge.

12. 7 gyf hwa þeof friðige oððe forena forlicge, sy he emscyldig
    wið me þam ðe þeof scolde, buton he hine mid fulre lade
    wið me geclænsian mæge.

13. 7 ic wylle þæt eal þeodscype, gehadode 7 læwede, fæstlice
    Eadgares lage healde þe ealle men habbað gecoren 7 to
    gesworen on Oxenaforda.

14. For ðam þe ealle biscopas secgað þæt hit swyþe deop wið
    God to betanne þæt man aðas oððe wedd tobrece.

8. Now I pray my archbishops and all my diocesan bishops to be zealous with regard to the rights of the church[1]—each one in the district which is entrusted to him[2]; and likewise I enjoin upon my ealdormen[3] to support the bishops in furthering the rights of the church[1] and my royal authority and the well-being of the whole nation.

9. If anyone, whether a man in orders or a layman, a Dane or an Englishman[1], is so presumptuous as to defy the law of God and my royal authority or secular law, and will not make amends and desist from so doing, according to the instruction given by my bishops[2], then I pray and likewise enjoin upon Earl Thurkil to bring the evil-doer to justice, if he can.

10. If he cannot, it is my will that he should make use of both his own resources and mine for the purpose of driving him out of the country or crushing him, if he remains in the country, whether he be of high[1] or humble station.

11[1]. And likewise I enjoin upon all my reeves, under pain of forfeiting my friendship and all that they possess and their own lives, to govern my people justly everywhere, and to pronounce just judgments with the cognisance of the bishops of the dioceses[2], and to inflict such mitigated penalties[3] as the bishop may approve and the man himself may be able to bear.

12. And if anyone protects a thief or takes action[1] on his behalf, he shall incur the same penalty at my hands as the thief was liable to, unless he can clear himself to my satisfaction with a full oath of exculpation[2].

13[1]. And it is my will that the whole nation, ecclesiastics and laymen, shall steadfastly keep the law of Edgar to which all have given their adherence under oath at Oxford.

14. For all the bishops declare that very severe amends must be made to God for the violation of oaths or pledges.

15. 7 eac hy us furðor lærað, þæt we sceolon eallan mægene 7 eallon myhton þone ecan mildan God inlice secan, lufian 7 weorðian 7 ælc unriht ascunian—ðæt synd mægslagan 7 morðslagan 7 mansworan 7 wiccean 7 wælcyrian 7 æwbrecan 7 syblegeru.

16. 7 eac we beodað on Godes ælmihtiges naman 7 on ealra his haligra, þæt nan man swa dyrstig ne sy, þæt on gehadodre nunnan oððe on mynecenan gewifige.

17. 7 gyf hit hwa gedon hæbbe, beo he utlah wið God 7 amansumod fram eallum Cristendome 7 wið þone cyning scyldig ealles þæs þe he age, buton he ðe raðor geswice 7 þe deopplicor gebete wið God.

18. 7 gyt we furðor maniað, þæt man Sunnandæges freols mid eallum mægene healde 7 weorðige fram Sæternesdæges none oð Monandæges lyhtinge, 7 nan man swa dyrstig ne sy, þæt he aðor oððe cypinge wyrce oððe ænig mot gesæce [on][1] þam halgan dæge.

19. 7 ealle men, earme 7 eadige, heora cyrcan secean 7 for heora synnum þingian 7 ælc beboden fæstan geornlice healdan 7 þa halgan georne weorðian þe us mæssepreostas beodan sceolan.

20. Þæt we magan 7 moton ealle samod, þurh þæs ecean Godes mildheortnesse 7 his halgena þingrædene, to heofena rices myrhðe becuman 7 mid him wunian þe leofað 7 rihxað a butan ende. Amen.

[1] Not in MS.

15. And likewise they teach us further that, with all our might and with all our strength, we should fervently seek, love and honour the eternal, merciful God, and put away from us every form of unrighteousness, such as [the deeds of] parricides[1], murderers, perjurers, witches, sorceresses[2] and adulterers, and incestuous deeds.

16[1]. And likewise we enjoin, in the name of God Almighty and of all his Saints, that no man be so presumptuous as to take to wife a professed nun or a woman who has taken religious vows.

17. And if anyone has done so, he shall be an outcast before God and cut off from the whole community of Christians, and he shall forfeit to the king all that he has, unless he desists [from the unhallowed wedlock] as quickly as possible, and makes amends towards God to the utmost.

18. And further still we admonish all men to keep and observe the Sunday festival[1] with all their might from noon on Saturday till dawn on Monday, and no man shall be so presumptuous as either to trade[2] or to attend any assembly[2] on the holy day.

19. And all men, both rich and poor, shall attend their churches[1] and make supplication for their sins, and zealously keep every prescribed fast[2], and diligently celebrate the saints-days[3] which the priests enjoin upon us[4].

20. So that, through the mercy of the eternal God and the intercession of his saints, we may all together have power and permission to attain to the joy of the kingdom of Heaven[1] and to dwell with Him who liveth and reigneth for ever without end. Amen.

CANUTE'S PROCLAMATION OF 1027

Canutus[1], rex totius Angliae et Denemarciae[2] et Norreganorum[3] et partis Suanorum[4], Æthelnotho[5] metropolitano et Alfrico Eboracensi archiepiscopo[6] omnibusque episcopis et primatibus et toti genti Anglorum tam nobilibus quam plebeiis, salutem.

1. Notifico vobis me noviter isse Romam, oratum pro redemptione peccaminum meorum et pro salute regnorum quique meo subiacent regimini populorum.

2. Hanc quidem profectionem Deo iam olim devoveram, sed pro negotiis regni et causis impedientibus huc usque perficere non poteram.

3. Nunc autem ipsi Deo meo omnipotenti valde humiliter gratias ago, qui[7] mihi[6] concessit in vita mea sanctos[8] apostolos suos[6] Petrum et Paulum et omne sanctuarium quod intra[9] urbem Romam aut extra addiscere potui expetere, et secundum desiderium meum praesentialiter venerari et adorare.

4. Ob id ergo maxime[10] hoc patravi, quia a sapientibus didici sanctum Petrum apostolum magnam potestatem a Domino[11] accepisse ligandi atque[12] solvendi clavigerumque esse coelestis regni, et ideo specialius[13] eius patrocinium apud Deum[14] diligenter[6] expetere valde utile duxi.

5. Sit autem vobis notum, quia magna congregatio nobilium in ipsa pascali solennitate ibi cum domino papa Iohanne et imperatore Cuonrado[15] erat, scilicet omnes principes gentium a monte Gargano usque ad istud proximum mare, qui omnes me et honorifice suscepere et donis pretiosis honoravere[16]; maxime autem ab imperatore donis variis et muneribus pretiosis honoratus sum, tam in vasis aureis et argenteis quam in palliis et vestibus valde pretiosis.

---

[1] *Cnuto* Ma.   [2] *-marchiae* Ma.   [3] *-giae* Ma.
[4] *Swavorum* Ma.   [5] *Aiel., Ail., Al.* Ma; *Athel.* Ox.   [6] *Om.* Ma.
[7] *quod* Ma.   [8] *beatos* Ma.   [9] *infra* Ox.   [10] *Et ideo max.* Ma.
[11] *Deo* Ox.   [12] *et* Ma.   [13] *-liter* Ma.   [14] *Dominum* Th.
[15] *Con.* Ma.   [16] *magnificis d. h.* Ma.

CANUTE'S PROCLAMATION OF 1027

Canute, King of all England and Denmark and of Norway[1] and part of Sweden[2], to Æthelnoth the Metropolitan[3], and to Ælfric, Archbishop of York[4], and to all the bishops and notables and the whole of the English nation, both nobles and commoners[5], greeting.

1. I make known to you that I have lately been to Rome to pray for the redemption of my sins and for the security of the realms and the peoples who are subject to my rule.

2. Long ago I had vowed this journey to God, but, on account of affairs of State and other delays[1], I had not been able to perform it until now.

3. But now very humbly I render thanks to God Almighty, who has permitted me during my life-time to visit his holy apostles, Peter and Paul, and all the sacred places of which I could learn, either within or without the city of Rome, and to worship and adore them in person there in accordance with my desire.

4. My chief reason for doing this was, that I learned from the wise that the holy apostle Peter[1] had received from the Lord great power both to bind and to release, and was the keeper of the keys of the kingdom of Heaven. For this reason, in particular, I thought it exceedingly advantageous to seek diligently to obtain his favour before God.

5. Now be it known to you that there was a great assembly of nobles there at the celebration of Easter with my lord the Pope John and the Emperor Conrad[1], namely, all the princes of the nations from Mount Garganus[2] to the sea which is nearest [to us][3], all of whom received me graciously and honoured me with costly gifts; but chiefly was I honoured by the Emperor[4] with various gifts and costly presents, both vessels of gold and silver and mantles and very costly robes.

6. Locutus sum igitur cum ipso imperatore et domino papa et
   principibus qui ibi erant de necessitatibus totius populi
   universi regni[1] mei, tam Anglorum quam Danorum[2], ut eis
   concederetur lex aequior et pax securior in via Romam
   adeundi, et ne tot clausuris per viam artentur[3] et propter
   thelon[4] iniustum fatigentur; annuitque postulatis imperator
   et Rodulfus[5] rex qui maxime ipsarum clausurarum domi-
   natur, cunctique principes edictis firmaverunt, ut homines
   mei, tam mercatores quam alii orandi causa[6] viatores,
   absque omni angaria clausurarum et theloneariorum[7] firma
   pace et iusta lege securi[8] Romam eant et redeant.

7. Conquestus sum iterum coram domino papa et mihi valde
   displicere causabar[9], quod mei archiepiscopi in tantum
   angariabantur immensitate pecuniarum quae ab eis expete-
   batur[10], dum pro pallio accipiendo secundum[11] morem
   apostolicam sedem expeterent; decretumque est ne id
   deinceps fiat.

8. Cuncta enim[12] quae a domino papa et ab ipso imperatore et
   a rege Rodulfo[13] caeterisque principibus, per quorum terras
   nobis transitus est ad Romam, pro meae gentis utilitate
   postulabam, libentissime[14] annueruntetconcessa sacramento
   etiam firmaverunt sub testimonio quattuor archiepisco-
   porum et viginti episcoporum et innumerae multitudinis
   ducum et nobilium qui ibi aderant[15].

9. Quapropter Deo omnipotenti gratias magnificas reddo, quia
   omnia, quae desideraveram prout mente decreveram, pros-
   pere perfeci votisque meis ad velle satisfeci.

10. Nunc itaque notum sit omnibus vobis[16], quia ipsi Deo
    omnipotenti[17] supplex devovi vitam meam amodo in omnibus
    iustificare, et regna mihi subdita populosque iuste et pie
    regere aequumque iudicium per omnia[18] observare; et si quid

---

[1] *u. r.* om. Ma.   [2] *Angli q. Dani* Ma.   [3] *arct.* Ma.
[4] *in. theloneum* Ma.   [5] *Rodbertus* Ox.   [6] *gratia* Ma.
[7] *-neorum cum f.* Ma.   [8] *et i. l. s.* om. Ma.   [9] *dixi* Ma.
[10] *-bantur* Ma.   [11] *-ndo* Ox.   [12] *ea* Th.
[13] *Rodberto* Ox.   [14] *-nter* Ma.   [15] *quae aderat* Ma.
[16] *o. v.* om. Ma.   [17] Om. Ma.   [18] *omnes* Ox. & most MSS of Ma.

6. I therefore spoke with the Emperor himself, and with my lord the Pope, and with the princes who were present, about the needs of the people throughout my kingdom, both English and Danes, that more just regulations should be accorded them and greater security in their journeys to Rome[1], and that they should not be hindered by so many barriers[2] on their way and harassed by unjust tolls. And the Emperor agreed to my demands, and [so did] King Rudolf[3], in whose dominion lie most of these barriers, and all the princes confirmed by edict[4], that my subjects, both merchants and others travelling in the cause of devotion, should go and come to and from Rome in assured peace and under just regulations, free from all the hindrances caused by barriers and tolls.

7. I complained again in the presence of my lord the Pope, and said how greatly it displeased me, that my Archbishops were so much straitened by the vast sums of money exacted from them when, according to usage, they visited the Apostolic See to receive their pall. And it was decreed that henceforth such exactions should not be made.

8. Indeed, to all the demands which I made, for the benefit of my people, to my lord the Pope and the Emperor and King Rudolf and the other princes, through whose territories lies our way to Rome, they readily agreed, and likewise confirmed their concessions by oath, with the witness of four archbishops and twenty bishops and an innumerable multitude of princes and nobles who were present.

9. Therefore, I render supreme thanks to Almighty God, because, in accordance with my intention, I have successfully accomplished all that I had desired, and have fulfilled my vows in accordance with my wish.

10. Now, therefore, be it known to all of you that, as a suppliant to God Almighty, I have vowed henceforth to regulate my life in all things, and to rule the kingdoms and peoples subject to me justly and uprightly, and to maintain equity in all things, and I purpose henceforth, with the help of

per meae iuventutis intemperantiam aut negligentiam
hactenus praeter id quod iustum erat actum est, totum Deo
auxiliante deinceps[1] dispono emendare.

11. Idcirco obtestor et praecipio meis consiliariis quibus regni
consilia credidi, ne ullo modo aut propter meum timorem
aut alicuius potentis personae favorem aliquam iniustitiam
amodo consentiant vel patiantur[2] pullulare in omni regno
meo.

12. Praecipio etiam omnibus vicecomitibus et praepositis universi regni mei, sicut meam amicitiam aut suam salutem
habere volunt, ut nulli homini, nec diviti nec pauperi, vim
iniustam inferant, sed omnibus, tam nobilibus quam igno-
bilibus, et divitibus et pauperibus[3] sit fas iusta lege potiundi,
a qua nec propter favorem regium aut[4] alicuius potentis
personam nec propter mihi congregandam[5] pecuniam ullo
modo devietur[6], quia nulla mihi necessitas est ut iniqua
exactione mihi pecunia congregetur[7].

13. Ego itaque vobis[8] notum fieri volo, quod eadem via qua
exivi regrediens, Danemarciam eo[9], pacem et firmum
pactum omnium Danorum consilio cum eis gentibus et
populis compositurus qui nos[10] et regno et vita privare, si
eis possibile esset, volebant; sed non poterant[11], Deo scilicet
virtutem eorum destruente, qui nos sua benigna[12] pietate
in regno et honore conservet, omniumque inimicorum nostrorum potentiam et fortitudinem deinceps dissipet et[13]
adnichilet!

14. Composita denique pace cum gentibus quae in circuitu
nostro sunt, dispositoque et pacato omni regno nostro hic
in oriente, ita ut a nulla parte bellum aut inimicitias ali-
quorum timere habeamus, quam citius hac aestate appa-
ratum navigii procurare[14] potero, Angliam venire dispono.

[1] Om. Ma.   [2] *faciant* Ma.   [3] *et d. et p.* om. Ma.   [4] *nec propter al.* Ma.
[5] *congerendam* Ma.   [6] *devient.* Ma.   [7] *congeratur* Ma.
[8] *quod v. n. f. volo, ea.* Fl; *n. v.* Ma.   [9] *vado* Ma.
[10] *comp. cum eis g. quae nos* Ma.   [11] *potuerunt* Ma.
[12] *benignitate* Ma   [13] *et f. d. d. et* om. Ma.   [14] *habere* Ma.

God, to amend whatever has hitherto been done contrary to what is right, through the intemperance of youth[1] or through negligence.

11[1]. I therefore entreat and enjoin upon all my counsellors, to whom I have entrusted the administration of the kingdom, that they shall in no way, whether through fear of me or to gain the favour of any powerful person, henceforth countenance or suffer any form of injustice to flourish in any part of my kingdom.

12[1]. I enjoin likewise upon all the sheriffs[2] and reeves throughout my kingdom that, as they desire to retain my friendship[3] and their own security, they employ no unjust force towards any man, either rich or poor[4], but that all, both nobles and commoners, rich and poor, shall have the right of just possession, which shall not be infringed upon in any way, either for the sake of obtaining the favour of the king or of gratifying any powerful person or of collecting money for me[5]; for I have no need that money should be collected for me by any unjust exactions.

13. I therefore wish to make known to you that, returning by the same way as I went, I am going to Denmark, in order, with the counsel of all the Danes, to make firm and lasting peace with those nations and peoples[1] who, had it been in their power, would have deprived us of both our kingdom and our life; but they were not able to do so, since their strength was destroyed by God. May He, in His loving-kindness, preserve us in authority and in honour, and henceforth confound and bring to naught the power and strength of all our enemies.

14[1]. Then, when peace has been established with the nations round about us, and when all our realm here in the east has been regulated and pacified, so that we need have no fear of war or hostilities on any side, I propose to come to England this summer, as soon as I can have a fleet equipped.

15. Hanc autem epistolam idcirco[1] praemisi, ut de mea prosperitate omnis populus regni mei laetificetur, quia, ut vos ipsi scitis, nunquam memet ipsum nec meum laborem abstinui nec adhuc abstinebo impendere pro omnis populi mei necessaria utilitate.

16. Nunc igitur praecipio et[2] obtestor omnes meos episcopos et regni praepositos, per fidem quam Deo et mihi debetis, quatinus faciatis ut, antequam ego[3] Angliam veniam, omnia[4] debita quae Deo[3] secundum legem antiquam debemus, sint persoluta, scilicet elemosinae[5] pro aratris et decimae animalium ipsius anni[6] procreatorum et denarii quos Romae[7] ad Sanctum Petrum debemus[8], sive ex urbibus sive ex villis, et mediante Augusto decimae frugum et in festivitate Sancti Martini primitiae seminum ad ecclesiam sub cuius parrochia quisque deget[9], quae Anglice ciricsceatt nominantur[10].

17. Haec et his similia si, dum venero[11], non erunt persoluta, regia exactio[12] secundum leges in quem culpa cadit, districte absque venia comparabit. Valete[3].

---

[1] *iam* Ma.   [2] *p. et* om. Ma.   [3] Om. Ma.   [4] *omnium* Ma.
[5] *-na* Ma.   [6] *ipso anno* Ma.   [7] *Romam* Ma.   [8] *debetis* Ma.
[9] *degit* Ma, one MS of Fl.   [10] *-atur* Ma.   [11] *Haec et alia si, cum ven.* Ma.
[12] *-ione* Ox, Ma.

15. But I have sent this letter in advance, that all the people in my kingdom may rejoice in my success, because, as you yourselves know, I have never spared—nor will I in the future spare—to devote myself[1] and my labours to secure what is necessary for the well-being of all my people.

16. Now, therefore, I enjoin upon and beseech all you my bishops and the reeves of the kingdom, by the fealty which you owe to God and to me, to bring it to pass that, before I come to England, full payment has been made of all the debts which, according to old-established law[1], we owe to God, namely, plough-alms, and the tithe of animals born during the year, and the pence which we owe to St Peter at Rome, both from towns and villages, and, in the middle of August[2], the tithe of fruits, and at the feast of St Martin the first-fruits of the crops[3] (called in English "ciricsceatt") which each one owes to the church of the parish in which he lives.

17. If, when I come, these and other similar dues have not been paid, they shall be exacted by the royal officials[1] in accordance with the laws, sternly and without remission[2], from him who is found to be in fault.

I CANUTE

[Ðis is seo gerednes, þe Cnut cyning, ealles Englalandes
cyningc 7 Dena cyningc 7 Norþrigena cyningc, gerædde, 7 his
witan, Gode to lofe 7 him sylfum to cynescipe 7 to þearfe, rade
swa hwæðer swa man wille.][1]

[2]Ðis is seo gerædnys þe Cnut ciningc, ealles Englalandes
ciningc 7 Dena cining[3], mid his witena geþeahte gerædde, Gode
to lofe 7 him sylfum to cynescipe 7 [folce][4] to þearfe; 7 þæt
wæs on ðære halgan midewintres tide on Winceastre.

1. Ðæt is þonne ærest[5], þæt hi ofer ealle oþre þingc ænne God
   æfre woldan lufian 7 wurþian[6] 7 ænne Cristendom anrædlice
   healdan and Cnut cingc lufian[7] mid rihtan[8] getrywþan.

2. And [uton][9] Godes cyrican griðian 7 friðian 7 gelomlice
   secean saulum to hæle 7[10] us sylfum to þearfe.

   § 1. Ælc cyrice is mid rihte on Cristes agenan griðe 7 ælc
   Cristen man ah mycele þearfe þæt he on þam griðe
   mycele mæðe wite, forðam Godes grið is ealra griða selost
   to geearnigenne 7 geornost to healdenne, 7 þær nehst
   cininges.

   § 2. Þonne is swiðe rihtlic, þæt Godes ciricgrið binnon
   wagum 7 Cristenes ciningces handgrið stande æfre[11]
   unwemme[12]; 7 se ðe aðor fulbrece þolige landes 7 lifes,
   butan [him][13] se ciningc gearian wille.

---

[1] A; *In nomine Domini. Ðis is seo gerædnes þe witan geræddon 7 be manegum
godum bisnum asmeadon; and þæt wæs geworden sona swa Cnút cyngc mid his
witena geþeahte frið 7 freondscipe betweox Denum 7 Englum fullice gefæstnode
7 heora ærran saca ealle getwæmde* D.

[2] G; no preamble in D.   [3] *ealles...cining* om. A.

[4] *folc* Ld, om. G, A.   [5] G, A; *þonne is þæt ærest þæt witan geræddan* D.

[6] *7 w.* om. Ld; *æ. G. æ. wurðodon* D.   [7] *wurþian* Ld.

[8] *7 miá trywðan 7 Eadgares lagan geornlice folgian. And hig gecwædan þæt hi
furðor on æmtan smeagan woldan þeode þearfe mid Godes fylste swa hi betst mihton.
Nu wille we swutelian hwæt us mæg to ræde for Gode 7 for worlde, gime se þe
wille. Uton swiþe georne fram sinnan acirran 7 ure misdæda geornlice betan 7
ænne God rihtlice lufian 7 wurðian 7 ænne Cristendom anrædlice healdan 7 ælcne
hæðendom georne forbugan* D.

[9] D; *witan* A; om. G.   [10] *s. to h.* 7 om. D, A.   [11] *efen* D, A.

[12] II Cn. 1–7 follows in D.   [13] A, Ld, om. G.

I CANUTE

[This is the ordinance[1] which King Canute, King of all England and of the Danes and the Norwegians, determined upon, together with his Councillors, to the praise of God and for the furtherance of his own royal authority and for his own benefit—let each man decide which course he will adopt[2].]

This is the ordinance which King Canute, King of all England and King of the Danes, determined upon with the advice of his Councillors, to the glory of God and for the furtherance of his own royal authority and for his [people's][1] benefit; and that was during the holy Christmas[2] season at Winchester[3].

1. The first provision is, that above all else they would ever love and honour one God, and unanimously uphold one Christian faith[1], and love King Canute[2] with due fidelity.

2[1]. And let us maintain the security and sanctity of the churches of God[2], and frequently attend[3] them for the salvation of our souls and our own benefit[4].

§ 1[1]. Every church is rightly in the protection of Christ himself, and it is the special duty of every Christian man to show great respect for that protection, for the protection of God is of all kinds of protection most especially to be sought after and most zealously to be upheld, and next to that the protection of the king.

§ 2[1]. Therefore it is very right and proper that the protection given by the church of God within its walls, and the protection granted by a Christian king in person should always remain inviolate; and he who violates[2] either of them shall lose both land and life[3], unless the king[4] is willing to pardon him.

§ 3. And gyf æfre ænig mann heonon forð Godes cyricgrið
swa abrece þæt he binnon ciricwagum mannslaga
weorþe, þonne sig[1] þæt botleas, 7 ehte his ælc þæra þe
Godes freond sig, butan þæt geweorðe þæt he þanon
ætberste 7 swa deope friðsocne gesece, þæt se cyningc
him þurh ðæt feores geunne wiþ fulre bote ge wið God
ge wið menn.

§ 4. And þæt is þonne ærest, þæt he his agene wer Criste
7 þam cyningce gesylle 7 mid þam hine sylfne inlagie
to bote.

§ 5. 7 gif hit þonne to bote gegá 7 se cyningc þæt geþafige,
þonne bete man þæt cyricgrið into þære cyricean be
ciningces fullan mundbryce, 7 þa my[n]sterclænsunge[2]
begyte swa þærto gebyrige, 7 ægþer ge mægbote ge
manbote fullice gebete, 7 wið God[3] huru þingie georne.

3. And gyf elles be cwicum mannum[4] ciricgrið abrocen sy,
bete man georne be þam þe seo dæd sy, sy hit þurh feohtlac,
si hit þurh reaflac, sig þurh þæt he hi[t][5] sy.

3a. Bete man ærest þone[6] griðbryce into þære cyrican be þam
þe seo dæd sy 7 be þam þe ðære cyricean mæð sy.

§ 1. Ne synd ealle cyricean na gelicre mæðe woruldlice
wurðscipes[7] wyrðe, þeah hig godcundlice habban hal-
[g]unge[8] gelice.

§ 2. Heafodmynstres[9] griðbryce is æt botwyrþum þingum
be cingces munde, þæt is mid v pundum on Engla lage,
(7 on Centlande æt þam mundbryce v pund þam cingce

---

[1] *is* A, Ld.   [2] *myst.* G; *þas mynstres clansunge* A, Ld.
[3] *Gode* A, Ld.   [4] *b. c. m.* om. Ld.   [5] *hi* G.   [6] *þonne* A, Ld.
[7] Om. A, Ld.   [8] A; *halsunge* G.   [9] *heafodcyricum* Ld.

§ 3[1]. And if ever anyone henceforth violates the protection of the church of God by committing homicide within its walls, that crime shall not be atoned for by any payment of compensation, and everyone who is the friend of God shall pursue the miscreant, unless it happen that he escapes from there and reaches so inviolable a sanctuary[2] that the king, because of that, grants him his life, upon condition that he makes full amends both towards God and towards men.

§ 4[1]. And the first condition is, that he shall give his own wergeld to Christ and to the king and by that means obtain the legal right to offer compensation.

§ 5. And if it comes to the payment of compensation, and the king allows this course, amends for the violation of the protection of the church shall be made by the payment to the church in question of the full fine for breach of the king's *mund*, and the purification of the church shall be carried out as is fitting, and compensation both to the kin and to the lord of the slain man shall be fully paid, and above all supplication shall earnestly be made to God.

3[1]. And if the protection of the church is broken in some other respect, without the taking of life, amends shall diligently be made in accordance with the nature of the offence, whether it be fighting or robbery or whatever it may be.

3*a*. In the first instance, amends for breach of its protection shall be made to the church, in accordance with the nature of the offence and also in proportion to the status of the church.

§ 1[1]. Not all churches are to be regarded as possessing the same status in civil law, though from the side of religion they all possess the same sanctity.

§ 2. Amends for violation of the protection of a principal church[1], in cases in which compensation can be paid, shall be made by payment of the fine for breach of the king's *mund*, *i.e.* £5 in districts under English law, (and in Kent[2] for breach of the *mund*, £5 to the king and

7 þreo þam arcebiscope)[1], 7 medemran mynstres mid cxx scill', þæt is be cingces wite, 7 þonne gyt læssan þær lytel þeowdom sig 7 legerstow þeah sig, mid LX scill', and feldcyricean þær legerstow ne sig mid xxx scyll'.

4. Eallum Cristenum mannum gebyrað swiþe rihte, þæt hig haligdom 7 hadas 7 gehalgode Godes hus æfre swiþe georne griðian 7 friðian, 7 þæt hi hada gehwylcne weorðian be mæðe.

§ 1. Forþam, understande se ðe[2] cunne, mycel is 7 mære þæt sacerd ah to donne folce to þearfe, gif he his Drihtne gecwemeð mid rihte.

§ 2. Mycel is seo halsung 7 mære is seo halgung þe[3] deofla afyrsað 7 on fleame gebringeð, swa oft swa[4] man fullað oððe husel halgað; 7 halige[5] englas þær abutan[5] hwearfiað 7 þa dæda beweardiað 7 þurh Godes mihta þam sacerdon fylstað, swa oft swa hig Criste ðeniað mid rihte.

§ 3. 7 swa hi doð symle, swa oft swa hig geornlice inweardre heortan clypiað to Criste 7 for folces neode þingiað georne, 7 þi man sceal for Godes ege mæðe on hade gecnawan mid gesceade.

5. And gyf hit geweorðe þæt man mid tyhtlan 7 mid uncræftum sacerd belecge þe regollice libbe, 7 he hine sylfne wite þæs clænne, mæssige, gyf he durre, 7 ladige on þam husle he ana[6] hine sylfne æt anfealdre spæce.

5a. 7 æt þryfealdre spæce ladige he[5], gyf he durre, eac on þam husle mid twam his gehádan.

---

[1] 7 *on...arcebiscope* only in G.   [2] *wylle oðð* A; *wille oððe* Ld.
[3] *þe he d. afyrseð* A, Ld.   [4] *he man* A, Ld.   [5] Om. A, Ld.
[6] *sylf* A; *sylfe* Ld instead of *h. a.*

£3[3] to the Archbishop), and in the case of a church of medium rank[4], by the payment of 120 shillings, *i.e.* by the fine due to the king (for insubordination), and in the case of one still smaller where there is little divine service but where, however, there is a graveyard, by the payment of 60 shillings, and in the case of a country chapel where there is no graveyard, by the payment of 30 shillings.

4[1]. It very justly befits all Christian men to maintain very zealously at all times the security and sanctity of holy things[2], and of the members of the clergy, and of the consecrated houses of God, and to honour each member of the clergy according to his rank.

§ 1[1]. Because—let him understand who can—great and wonderful are the things which a priest is able to do for the benefit of the people, if he is duly pleasing to his Lord.

§ 2. Great is the exorcising and wonderful is the hallowing[1] through which he drives away devils and puts them to flight, as often as he baptises anyone or hallows the Eucharist; and holy angels[2] hover round there and protect these acts, and, through the power of God, help the priests as often as they serve Christ as they ought.

§ 3. And that they always do as often as they earnestly call upon Christ from their inmost heart, and zealously make intercession for the needs of the people[1], and therefore the various ranks in holy orders must be recognised and distinguished for the fear of God.

5[1]. And if it happens that an accusation and a charge of evil practices[2] is brought against a priest who lives according to a rule, and he knows himself to be guiltless of the charge, he shall say Mass, if he dares, and by his own asseveration clear himself by the Holy Communion in the case of a simple accusation.

5a. And in the case of a triple accusation he shall also clear himself, if he dares, by the Holy Communion with two supporters of the same ecclesiastical rank as himself.

§ 1. Gif man deacon tihtlige þe regollice libbe anfealdre spæce, nime twegen his gehadan 7 ladige hine mid þam.

§ 1*a*. 7 gyf man hine tihtlige þryfealdre spæce, nime vi his gehadan 7 ladige hine mid ðam 7 beo he sylf seofeþa.

§ 2. Gif man folciscne mæssepreost mid tihtlan belecge ðe regollif næbbe, ladige hine swa diacon þe regollife libbe.

§ 2*a*. And gyf man freondleasne weofodþen mid tihtlan belecge, þe aðfultum næbbe, ga to corsnǽde 7 þær þonne æt gefare þæt þæt God wylle, buton he on husle geladian mote.

§ 2*b*. And gyf man gehadodne mid fæhþe belecge 7 secge þæt he wære dædbana oððe rædbana, ladige mid his magum þe fæhðe moton mid beran oððe forebetan.

§ 2*c*. 7 gyf he sig[1] mægleas, ladige[2] mid geferan oððe on fæsten fó, gif he þæt þurfe, 7 ga to corsnæde 7 þæræt gefare swa swa God ræde.

§ 2*d*. And na þearf ænig mynstermunuc ahwær mid rihte fæhðbote biddan ne fæhþbote betan; he gæð of his mægðlage, þonne he gebyhð to regollage.

§ 3. And gyf mæssepreost æfre ahwær stande on leasre gewitnesse oððe on mænan aðe oððe ðeofa gewita oððe gewyrhta beo, þonne sy he aworpen of gehadodra gemanan 7 þolige ægþer ge geferscipes ge freondscipes ge æghwylces weorðscipes, butan he wið God 7 wið menn þe deoplicor gebete, swa bisceop him tæce, 7 him borh finde þæt he þanon forð æfre swylces geswice.

---

[1] *hi is* A, Ld.   [2] *l. hine* A, Ld.

§ 1. If a simple accusation is brought against a deacon who lives according to a rule, he shall take two supporters of the same ecclesiastical rank and clear himself with their help.

§ 1a. And if a triple accusation is brought against him, he shall take six supporters of the same ecclesiastical rank —himself being a seventh—and clear himself with their help.

§ 2. If an accusation is brought against a secular priest who does not live according to a rule, he shall clear himself in the same way as a deacon who lives according to a rule.

§ 2a. And if an accusation is brought against a member of the priesthood who has no friends and no-one to support his oath, he shall go to the ordeal of consecrated bread, and shall experience there what is the will of God, unless he is allowed to clear himself by the Holy Communion.

§ 2b. And if a man in holy orders is charged with vendetta and accused of having committed or instigated homicide, he shall clear himself with the help of his kin, who must share the vendetta with him or pay compensation for it.

§ 2c. And if he has no kindred, he shall clear himself with the help of his fellow-ecclesiastics, or have recourse to fasting, if he must, and go to the ordeal of consecrated bread, and experience there what God shall decree.

§ 2d. And no monk who belongs to a monastery anywhere may lawfully either demand or pay any compensation incurred by vendetta. He leaves the law of his kindred behind when he accepts monastic rule.

§ 3¹. And if a priest anywhere be concerned in false witness or perjury, or be the accessory and accomplice of thieves, he shall be cast out from the fellowship of those in holy orders and shall forfeit both their society and their friendship and every kind of privilege, unless he make amends, both towards God and towards men, to the utmost of his ability, as the bishop shall prescribe for him, and find surety that henceforth he will cease for ever from all such ⌈wrong-doing⌉.

§ 4. 7 gyf he ladian[1] wille, geladige þonne be dæde mæðe, swa mid þryfealdre swa mid anfealdre[2] lade, be ðam þe seo dæd sy.

6. And[3] we wyllað þæt ælces hades menn georne gebugan ælc to þam rihte þe him to gebyrige.

6a. 7 huruþinga Godes þeowas—bisceopas 7 abbodas, munecas 7 mynecena, canonicas 7 nunnan—to rihte gebugan 7 regollice libban 7 dæges 7 nihtes oft 7 gelome clypian to Criste 7 for eall Cristen folc þingian georne.

§ 1. 7 ealle Godes þeowas we biddað 7 lærað 7 huruþinga sacerdas, þæt hi Gode hyran 7 clænnesse lufian 7 beorgan heom sylfum wið Godes yrre 7 wið ðone weallendan brýne þe weallað on helle,

§ 2. Fullgeorne hig[4] witan þæt hig nagon mid rihte þurh hæmedþingc wifes gemanan.

§ 2a. 7 se ðe þæs geswican wille 7 clænnesse healdan, hæbbe he Godes miltse 7 to woruldwurðscipe si he þegenlage wyrðe.

§ 3. And æghwylc Cristen mann eac for his Drihtenes ege unrihthæmed georne forbuge 7 godcunde lage rihtlice healde.

7. And we lærað 7 biddað 7 on Godes naman beodað, þæt ænig Cristen mann binnon vi manna sibfæce[5] on his agenum cynne æfre ne gewifie[6], ne on his mæges lafe þe swa neahsib wære, ne on þæs[7] wifes nedmagon þe he sylf ær hæfde;

§ 1. ne on his gefæderan, ne on gehalgodre nunnan, ne on ælætan ænig Cristen mann æfre ne gewifige[8];

§ 2. ne ænige forligru ahwar ne begange;

§ 3. ne na má wifa þonne án hæbbe[9] 7 þæt beo his beweddode wif[10], 7[11] beo be þære anre, þa hwile þe heo libbe[12], se ðe wyle Godes lage giman mid rihte 7 wið hellebryne beorhgan his sawle[13].

---

[1] h. hine l. A, Ld.   [2] s. m. a. om. A; þrifeald lade swa be Ld.
[3] And witena gerædnes is þæt hi w. D.   [4] we D.   [5] sibba fæce A, Ld.
[6] wifige D.   [7] his A, Ld.   [8] n. wifige afre A; n. w. æfre D, Ld.
[9] ne...h. om. A.   [10] 7...wif om. D, A.   [11] ac D, A.
[12] The scribe of G has added by mistake: þus scyldon æfre ge.
[13] Here follows VI Atr. 16 in D.

§ 4. And if he seeks to clear himself, he shall do so in proportion to the deed, either by the triple mode of proof or by the simple, in accordance with the nature of the deed.

6[1]. And we desire that men of every estate[2] readily submit to the duty which befits them.

6a[1]. And most of all the servants of God—bishops and abbots, monks and nuns, canons and women under religious vows— shall submit to their duty and live according to their rule, and day and night frequently and often call upon Christ, and zealously intercede for all Christian people.

§ 1[1]. And we pray and enjoin all the servants of God, and priests above all, to obey God and practice celibacy and guard themselves[2] from the wrath of God and from the raging fire which blazes in hell[3].

§ 2[1]. They know full well that they have no right to marry.

§ 2a. And he who will turn from marriage and observe celibacy shall obtain the favour of God, and as worldly honour he shall enjoy the privileges of a thegn[1].

§ 3[1]. All Christian men likewise through the fear of God[2] shall strictly avoid illicit unions[3] and duly observe the laws of the church.

7[1]. And we instruct and pray and enjoin, in the name of God, that no Christian man shall ever marry among his own kin within six degrees of relationship, or with the widow of a man as nearly related to him as that, or with a near relative of his first wife's.

§ 1. And no Christian man shall ever marry his god-mother[1] or a professed nun or a divorced woman.

§ 2[1]. And he shall never commit adultery anywhere.

§ 3. And he shall have no more wives than one, and that shall be his wedded wife[1], and he who seeks to observe God's law aright and to save his soul from hell-fire shall remain with the one as long as she lives[2].

8. And gelæste mann Godes gerihta æghwylce geare rihtlice georne.

　§ 1. Þæt is sulhælmesse xv niht ofer Eastran 7 geoguþe teoðunge be Pentecosten 7 eorðwæstma be Ealra halgena mæssan.

　§ 2. 7 gyf hwa þonne þa teoþunge gelæstan nelle swa we gecweden habbað, þæt is se teoða æcer ealswa seo sulh hit gegá[1], þonne fare þæs cingces gerefa to 7 þæs bisceopes 7 þæs landrican 7 þæs mynstres mæssepreost 7 nim[an][2] unþances ðone[3] teoðan dæl to þam mynstre þe hit to gebyrige, 7 tæcan him to þam nigoðan dæle, 7 todæle mann þa eahta dælas on twa, 7 fo se landhlaford to healfum, to healfum se bisceop, si hit ciningces mann, se hit þegnes.

9. And Romfeoh be Petres mæssan.

　§ 1. 7 se ðe ofer þæne dæg hit healde, agyfe þam bisceope þæne penig 7 þærto xxx[4] 7 þam cingce cxx[5] scyll'.

10. And cyricsceat to Martines mæssan.

　§ 1. 7 se þe hine ofer þæne dæg healde agyfe hine þam bisceope 7 forgylde hine xi siðan 7 ðam cingce cxx[5] scyll'.

11. Gyf hwa þonne þegna[6] sig þe on his boclande cyrican hæbbe þe legerstow on sig, gesylle þone[7] þriddan dæl his agenre teoþunge into his cyrican.

　§ 1. And[8] gyf hwa cyricean hæbbe þe legerstow on ne sig, do he of ðam nigon dælum his preoste þæt þæt he wylle.

　§ 2. 7 gá ælc cyricsceat into þam ealdan mynstre be ælcon frigan heorðe.

12. And leohtgesceot þriwa on geare: ærest on Easteræfen healfpenigwurð wexes æt ælcere híde 7 eft on[9] Ealra halgena mæssan eallswa mycel [7 eft[10] to þæm (æfene)[11] sanctan Marian clænsunge ealswa].

---

[1] gegað A, Ld.　　　[2] A, Ld; nime G.　　　[3] þonne A, Ld.
[4] penega A; pening Ld.　　[5] twa hundred 7 twentig scill' A; 220 scill. Ld.
[6] þegen A, Ld.　　[7] þonne A.　　[8] Om. A, Ld.　　[9] to A, Ld.
[10] 7 eft...ealswa Ld and in the margin of G in handwriting of 16th cent.
[11] Following Liebermann.

8[1]. And ecclesiastical dues shall be promptly and duly rendered every year.

§ 1. Namely, plough-alms 15 days after Easter, and the tithe of young animals at Pentecost, and [the tithe] of the fruits of the earth at All Saints.

§ 2[1]. And if anyone refuses to render his tithes as we have decreed, namely, the produce of every tenth acre traversed by the plough, then the king's reeve and the bishop's and the reeve of the lord of the manor and the priest of the church shall go, and, without his consent, take the tenth part for the church to which it is due, and shall assign the next tenth to him, and the eight [remaining] parts shall be divided in two, and the lord of the manor shall take half and the bishop half, whether the man be under the lordship of the king or of a thegn.

9[1]. And Peter's Pence [shall be rendered] by St Peter's Day[2].

§ 1[1]. And he who withholds it beyond that date shall give the bishop the penny and 30 pence in addition, and 120 shillings[2] to the king.

10. And church dues [shall be rendered] at Martinmas.

§ 1[1]. And he who withholds them beyond that date shall give them up to the bishop, and repeat the payment eleven times, and [pay] 120 shillings to the king.

11[1]. If, however, there is any thegn who, on the land which he holds by title deed[2], has a church to which a graveyard is attached, he shall give the third part of his own tithes to his church.

§ 1. If anyone has a church to which no graveyard is attached, he shall give his priest whatever he desires from the nine [remaining] parts.

§ 2. And all the church dues from every free household shall go to the old parish church.

12[1]. And light dues [shall be paid] three times a year: first a halfpennyworth of wax from every hide on Easter Eve, and as much afterwards at the feast of All Saints, [and as much afterwards at the Feast of the Purification of St Mary][2].

13. And sawlsceat is rihtast þæt man symle gelæste á æt openum græfe.

   § 1. And gyf man ǽnig líc of rihtscriftscire elles hwær lecge, gelæste man þone sawlsceat swa þeah into þam mynstre þe hit to hyrde.

14. And ealle Godes gerihta fyrðrige[1] man georne, ealswa hit þearf is.

   § 1. And freolsa 7 fæstena healde mon rihtlice[2].

   § 2. 7 healde man[2] ælces Sunnandæges freolsunge fram Sæternesdæges none oð Monandæges lihtingce 7 ælcne oðerne mæssedæg[3] swa he beboden beo.

15. 7 Sunnandæges[4] cypinge we forbeodað eac eornostlice 7 ælc folcgemót, buton hit for mycelre nydðearfe sy.

   § 1. And huntaðfara 7 ealra woruldlica weorca on ðam halgan dæge geswican[5] man georne.

16. Be fæstene[6].

   Þæt man ælc beboden fæsten healde, sy hit ymbrenfæsten, sy hit lenctenfæsten, sy elles oðer fæsten, mid ealr[e][7] geor[n]fulnysse[8].

16a. And to Sancta Marian mæssan ælcere 7 to ælces apostoles mæssan fæstan[9], buton Philippi et Jacobi[10] we ne beodað nan fæsten for ðan eastorlicon freolse, 7 ælce[s][11] Frígdæges fæston[12], buton hit freols sy.

   § 1. 7 na ðearf man na fæsten[13] fram Eastron oð Pentecosten, buton hwa gescrifen sy oððe he elles fæsten[13] wylle, 7[14] of middanwintre oð octabas Epiphanie[15].

17. We forbeodað ordal 7 aðas freolsdagum 7 ymbrendagum 7 lenctendagum [7 rihtfæstendagum][16] 7 fram Aduentum Domini oð(ðe)[17] se eahteoða dæg agán sy ofer Twelftadæg[18] 7 fram Septuagessima oþ(þe)[17] fiftyne niht ofer Eastron.

---

[1] friðige A, Ld.   [2] r.—man om. A, Ld.
[3] At this point (with the word mæssedæg) B begins and is used here for the remainder of I Cn.
[4] -daga G; -dæga A, Ld.   [5] -swicæ G; -swice A, Ld.
[6] The rubrics in this code are found in B only.   [7] G, A; -ra B.
[8] georf. B.   [9] fæste man G; fæsten A, Ld.
[10] b. to P. et J. mæssan w. G.   [11] G, A; ælce B.   [12] -en G, A, Ld.
[13] fæstan G.   [14] eallswa G.
[15] Epiphanige, þæt is seofen niht ofer Twelftan mæssedæge G.
[16] G, A, Ld; om. B.   [17] oððe B; oð G, A, Ld.   [18] Twelftan mæssedæge G.

13[1]. And it is best that payment for the souls of the dead should always be rendered before the grave is closed.

§ 1. And if a body is buried elsewhere than in the parish to which it properly belongs, the payment shall nevertheless be made to the church to which the deceased belonged.

14. And all God's dues shall be promptly rendered[1], as the occasion requires.

§ 1[1]. And festivals and fasts shall be duly observed.

§ 2[1]. And the festival of every Sunday shall be observed from noon on Saturday till dawn on Monday, and every other feast-day as has been prescribed[2].

15[1]. And likewise we strictly forbid Sunday trade and all public gatherings, unless in cases of great necessity.

§ 1. And hunting and all secular occupations shall be strictly abstained from on the holy day.

16[1]. Concerning fasts.

And every prescribed fast shall be observed with all diligence, whether it be the fast of the Ember Days, or the Lent fast, or any other fast.

16a[1]. And at all the festivals of St Mary and at the festival of every apostle a fast [shall be observed]—except at the festival of St Philip and St James when we do not enjoin a fast because of the Easter festival—and a fast [shall be observed] every Friday, unless it be a festival.

§ 1. And no man need fast from Easter till Pentecost— unless it has been prescribed to him[1] as a penance or he desires to fast for some other reason—or from Christmas to the Octave of Epiphany[2].

17[1]. And we forbid ordeals and oaths during festivals and the Ember Days and days in Lent, and on legally appointed fast days, and from the Advent till the eighth day after Twelfth Night, and from the Septuagesima till fifteen days after Easter.

§ 1. 7 sancte Eadwardes mæssedæg witan habbað gecoren
þæt man freolsian sceal ofer eall Englaland[1] on quinta-
decima kalendas Aprilis 7 sancte Dunstanes mæssedæg
on xiiii kl. Iunii[2].

§ 2. 7 beo ðam halgum tidum eallum Cristenum mannum,
ealswa hit riht is, sib 7 sóm gemǽne 7 ælc sacu[3]
totwæmed.

§ 3. 7 gyf hwá oðrum scyle borh oððe bote æt woruldlicum
ðingum, gelæste hít him georne ǽr oððe æfter.

18. We wyllað[4] 7 we biddað for God[e]s[5] lufan, þæt ælc Cristen
man understande georne his agene ðearfe.

18a. Forðam ealle we sceolan ænne timan gebidan, þæt[6] us wære
leofra ðonne all[7] þæt on middanearde is, ðæ[t][8] we aworhton[9],
ða hwile ðe we mihton, georne Godes willan.

18b. Ac we ðonne sceolon habban anfeald lean ðæs ðe we on
life ær geworhton; wa ðam ðonne ðe ær geærnode hellewíte!

§ 1. Be scrifte.
Ac uton swiðe georne fram synnum gecyrran 7 ure ælc
his misdǽda urum scriftum geornlice andettan 7 æfre
geswican[10] 7 geornlice betan.

§ 2. 7 ure ælc oðrum beode þæt we wyllan þæt man us
beode; þæt is[11] rihtlic dóm 7 Gode swiðe gecwéme; 7 se
bið swiðe gesæli[12] ðe ðæne dóm gehealt.

§ 3. Forþan Gód ælmihtig us ealle geworhte 7 eft deopum
ceape[13] gebohte, þæt is mid his agenum blode[14] ðe hé
for us eallum ageat[15].

19. Gehwylc[16] Cristen man dó, swa him ðearf is: gyme his
Cristendom[17] georne 7 gearwie hine eac to huselgange huru
ðriwa on geare gehwá hine sylfne [s]e[18] ðe his agene ðearfe
wille understandan, swa swa heom ðearf si.

---

[1] Engl. þæt is on þam feowerteoðan dæge on Martige, xviiii (changed later to
xv) kl. Ap. G.
[2] Iun. þæt ys on þam þreotteoðan dæge þe byð on Mæge G.
[3] facn Ld.   [4] w. w. only in B.   [5] G, A; Godas B.
[6] þonne G, A, Ld.   [7] Added in 16th cent. in B.
[8] ðær B, G; þ A, Ld.   [9] á worhtan (-ton) G, Ld.   [10] swican A.
[11] þis A instead of þ. is.   [12] (ge)sælig G, A, Ld.   [13] -pum A.
[14] life G, A, Ld.   [15] sealde G, A, Ld.   [16] ac g. G; ac æghwilc A; 7 æyh. Ld.
[17] -domes G, Ld; -domes á. A.   [18] ðe B; om. G, A, Ld.

§ 1[1]. And the authorities have decided that St Edward's festival shall be celebrated throughout England on the 18th of March, and St Dunstan's festival on the 19th of May.

§ 2[1]. And at the holy festivals, as is fitting, there shall be peace and concord among all Christian men, and every dispute shall be laid aside.

§ 3. And if anyone owes another a debt or compensation in connection with secular matters, he shall render it to him readily either before or after [the festival].

18. We desire and we pray, for the love of God, that every Christian man should readily understand what is for his own good.

18a[1]. For we shall all arrive at a time when we shall wish, above all else in the world, that we had zealously done the will of God, as long as we could.

18b[1]. But we shall then receive simply[2] the reward for what we have done in our lifetime. Woe then to him who has earned the torment of hell![3]

§ 1[1]. Concerning confession.

But let us very zealously turn from sins, and let us all readily confess our misdeeds to our confessors, and altogether cease [from evil], and zealously make amends.

§ 2[1]. And each of us shall treat others as we desire ourselves to be treated; that is a just maxim and very pleasing to God; and he who upholds that maxim shall be greatly blessed.

§ 3. For God Almighty made us all, and afterwards bought us at a great price[1], namely, with his own blood which he shed for us all.

19[1]. Every Christian man shall do as is his duty: he shall pay zealous regard to his Christian profession and shall likewise prepare himself for the sacrament at least three times a year, if he seeks to understand, as he ought, what is for his own good.

§ 1. 7 word 7[1] weorc freonda gehwylc fadige mid rihte 7 að 7 wed wærlice healde.

§ 2. 7 æghwylc unriht aworpe man georne of ðisson earde, ðæs ðe man don mæge.

§ 3. 7 lufie man[2] Godes riht heonan forð georne wordes 7 dæde; ðonne wurð us eallum Godes miltse ðe gearwre.

20. Uton don eac georne[2] swá we gyt læran wyllað; uton beon á urum hlaforde holde 7 getréowe 7 æfre eallum mihtum his wurðscipe ræran 7 his willan gewyrcean.

§ 1. Forðam eall þæt we æfre for rihthlafordhylde doð, eall we doð hit us sylfum to mycelre ðearfe, forðam ðam[3] bið witodlice[2] God hold ðe biþ his hlaforde rihtlice[2] hold[4].

§ 2. 7 eac ah laforda gehwylc ðæs formyccle ðearfe þæt he his men rihtlice healde.

21. 7 ealle Cristene men we lǽrað swiðe georne, þæt hí inweardre[5] heortan æfre God lufian 7 rihtne Cristendóm geornlice healdan 7 godcundan lareowan geornlice hyran 7 Godes lara 7 laga smeagan 7 spyrian oft 7 gelóme, heom sylfum to ðearfe.

22. We lærað þæt ælc Cristen man geleornige þæt he cunne huru rihtne geleafan ariht[6] understandan 7 Pater noster 7 Credan[7] geleornian.

§ 1. Forðam mid ðam oðrum [sceal ælc Cristen mann hine to Gode gebiddan 7 mid þam oðrum][8] geswytelian rihtne gehleafan.

§ 2. Crist sylf sang Pater noster ærest 7 þæt gebed his leorni[n]gcnihtum[9] teahte.

§ 3. 7 on þam godcunda[n][10] gebede syn[11] seofen gebedu mid ðam se ðe hit inweardlice gesingð he geærndað to Gode sylfum ymbe æfre ælce neode ðe man beðearf aðor oððe for ðissum life oððe for ðam toweardan.

[1] *ac* later changed to 7 B. [2] Om. A.
[3] Om. G.   [4] *ðe—hold* om. Ld. [5] *inweardlice* A; *-lic* Ld.
[6] 7 *ariht* B, G.   [7] *Credo* A, Ld.
[8] G, A; om. B and *we ssculan us gebiddan* 7 *mid þam credan* added in later handwriting in the margin.
[9] *leornig.* B.   [10] G, A; *-am* B, Ld.   [11] Changed later to *synd*.

§ 1[1]. And everyone of our friends[2] shall order his words and deeds aright, and strictly abide by his oath and pledge.

§ 2[1]. And every injustice shall be zealously cast out from this land, as far as it is possible to do so.

§ 3[1]. And God's law shall henceforth be zealously cherished in word and in deed; then the mercy of God will be granted the more readily to us all.

20[1]. Let us likewise zealously carry out what we further desire to enjoin: let us ever be faithful and true[2] to our lord, and always, with all our might, promote his honour and carry out his will.

§ 1. For all that we ever do, through just fidelity to our lord, we do to our own great advantage, for truly God shall be gracious to him who is justly faithful to his lord.

§ 2[1]. And likewise it is the great[2] duty of every lord to treat his men justly.

21[1]. And very zealously we enjoin upon all Christian men that ever, from their inmost hearts, they love God and zealously uphold the true Christian faith, and eagerly obey their spiritual teachers, and frequently and often ponder over and inquire into the precepts and laws of God for their own advantage.

22[1]. We enjoin that every Christian man apply himself[2] until he can at least understand aright the true belief, and learn the Pater Noster and the Creed.

§ 1. For with the first every Christian man shall pray to God, and with the second declare the true belief.

§ 2. Christ himself first recited the Pater Noster and taught the prayer to his disciples.

§ 3. And in that sacred prayer there are seven petitions[1], and he who recites it from the depths of his heart inwardly makes supplication thereby to God himself for everything of which a man has need, both for this life and for the life to come.

§ 4. Ac hu mæg ðonne æfre ænig man hine inweardlice to Gode gebiddan, buton he on God hæbbe inwardlice rihtne geleafan?[1]

§ 5. Forðam he nah æfter forðsiðe mid Cristenra[2] gemána[n][3] on gehalgodan restan oððe her on life husles beon wyrðe[4].

§ 6. Ne[5] he ne bið wel Cristen ðe þæt geleornian nyle[6], ne he nah mid rihte oðres mannes to onfonne æt fulluhte ne æt bisceopes hánda ðe má, ær he hit geleornige þæt he hit wel cunne.

23. Godlar.

We læraÐ þæt man wið healice synne 7 wið deoflice dæda scylde[7] swiðe georne on æghwylcne timan, 7 bete swiðe georne be his scriftes geðeahte se ðe ðurh deofles scyfe on synne befealle.

24. 7 we læraÐ þæt man wið fulne galscipe 7 wið unrihthǽmed 7 wið æghwylce ǽwbryce warnian georne[8].

25. 7 we læraÐ eac georne manna gehwylcne, þæt he Godes ege hæbbe symble on his gemynde, 7 dæges 7 nihtes forhtige for synnum, Domesdæg[9] ondrǽde 7 for helle agrise, 7 æfre him gehénde endedæges[10] wene.

26. Bisceopas syndon bydelas 7 Godes larðeowas[11] 7 hy scylan bodian 7 bisnian georne godcunde ðéarfe, gyme se ðe wylle.

§ 1. Forðam wace se hyrde bi[ð][12] funden to hyrde ðe nele ða heorde ðe he healdan scéal mid hréame bewerian, buton he elles[13] mǽge, gyf ðær hwylc ðeodsceaða sceaðian onginneð.

§ 2. Nis nan swa yfel sceaða swa is deofol sylf; he bið a ymbe þæt án, hu he mæge on mannum[14] sawlum mæst gesceaðian.

---

[1] b. he h. inweardlice soðe lufe 7 r. g. to Gode G.
[2] Cristene A; Crisne Ld; Cristenra manna G.   [3] G, A, Ld; -na B.
[4] gemanan ne on gehalgedan lictune to restene ne he nah þæs halgan husles to onfonne her on life G.
[5] þe A.   [6] nolde A, Ld.   [7] Corrected from earlier scyle B.
[8] warnige symle G; wærnige s. A, Ld.   [9] Domdæg G, A, Ld.
[10] endes dæges A, Ld.   [11] Godes lage lareowas (-æs) G, A; laga larewæs Ld.
[12] bid B.   [13] helles B.   [14] manna G.

§ 4[1]. But how then can any man ever pray from the depths of his heart to God, unless he have true belief in God in the depths of his heart?

§ 5[1]. Verily, after his death he cannot rest in a hallowed grave[2] among Christians or here in this life be entitled to receive the sacrament.

§ 6. He is not a true Christian who refuses to learn it, nor may he lawfully stand sponsor to another man at baptism, and as little at confirmation, until he learns it and knows it well.

23[1]. Divine Precepts.
We enjoin that grievous sins and devilish deeds[2] be very zealously guarded against at all times. He who, through the instigation of the devil, falls into sin shall very zealously make amends according to his confessor's advice.

24[1]. And we enjoin that foul lasciviousness and illicit unions[2] and every [kind of] adultery be zealously abhorred.

25[1]. And likewise we earnestly enjoin all men to have the fear of God constantly in their hearts, and day and night to be in terror of sin, dreading the Day of Judgment and shuddering at the thought of hell, and ever expecting their last day to be close at hand.

26[1]. The bishops are God's heralds and teachers[2], and they shall proclaim and zealously give example of our duty towards God—let him who will take heed.

§ 1[1]. For a shepherd[2] will be considered failing in his trust, if he will not provide for the safety of the flock, which is committed to his keeping, by raising the alarm, if he cannot do anything else, when any spoiler proceeds to harm it.

§ 2. There is no spoiler so evil as is the devil himself; he is ever concerned with one thing only, namely, how he can do most harm to the souls of men.

§ 3. Ðonne moton ða hyrdas beon swiðe wácore 7 geornlice clypiende ðe wið ðone ðeodscaðan folce sceal[1] scyldan: ðæt synda[n][2] bisceopas 7 mæssepreostas ðe godcunde heorda bewarian 7 bewerian sceolan mid wislicum laran, þæt se wodfreca werewulf to swiðe ne slite ne to feola abíte of godcundre heorde.

§ 4. And se ðe ofærhogie þæt he Godes bodan hlyste, hæbbe him gemǽne þæt wið God sylfne.

Á sy Godes nama écelice gebletsod 7 lof him 7 wuldor 7 wurðmynt symble æfre to worulde! Amen[3].

II CANUTE

Ðis is ðonne[4] seo woruldcunde gerædnysse ðe ic wille, mid minan witenan ræde, þæt man healde ofer eall Englaland.

1. Þæt is ðonne æryst, þæt ic wylle[5] þæt man rihte lage up arǽre 7 æghwylce unlage georne afylle, þæt man awéodige 7 awyrtwalie æghwylc unriht, swa man geornost mæge, of [ð]issum[6] earde 7 arǽre up Godes riht.

§ 1. 7 héonon forð lǽte manna gehwylcne, ge earmne ge eadigne, folcrihtes weorðe[7] 7 him man rihte domas deme.

2. 7 we læráð þæt[8], þeah hwa agylte 7 hine sylfne deope forwyrce, ðonne gefadie[9] man ða[4] steore, swa hit for Gode sy gebeorhlic 7 for worulde aberendlic.

2a. 7 geðence swiðe georne se ðe domes geweald áge hwæs he sylf gyrnne[10], ðonne he ðus cweðe: "Et dimitte nobis debita nostra sicut et nos dimittimus[11]."

---

[1] sceolon G; -an A, Ld.   [2] syndas B.

[3] Á—Amen. Not in A; written in the margin in later handwriting in G, Ld.

[4] Om. G.   [5] And witena gerædnes is þæt man D.   [6] di. B.

[7] f. wurðe beon D with the rest of the clause omitted.

[8] And witena gerædnes is þæt D.   [9] medemige D.

[10] hwæt he æt us sylf gyrne D.

[11] G adds:—þæt is on Englisc: 7 forgyf us Drihten ure gyltas swa we forgyfað þam ðe wið us agyltað.

§ 3. Therefore the shepherds whose duty it is to guard the people against this spoiler, namely, the bishops and priests whose duty it is to protect and provide for the safety of the divine flocks with wise precepts, must be very active, and keep earnestly crying out, in order to prevent this ravening wolf[1] from inflicting excessive injury and from making very frequent depredations upon the divine flock.

§ 4[1]. And he who disdains to hearken to the messengers of God shall have to settle his case with God himself.
Ever be the name of God eternally blessed[2], and praise and glory and honour be to Him for ever and ever. Amen.

II CANUTE

This is further the secular ordinance[1] which, by the advice of my councillors[2], I desire should be observed over all England.

1[1]. The first provision is, that I desire that justice be promoted and every injustice zealously suppressed, that every illegality be rooted up and eradicated from this land with the utmost diligence, and the law of God[2] promoted.

§ 1[1]. And henceforth all men, both poor and rich, shall be regarded as entitled to the benefit of the law, and just decisions shall be pronounced on their behalf.

2[1]. And we enjoin that, even if anyone sins and commits grievous crime[2]. the punishment shall be ordered as shall be justifiable in the sight of God and acceptable in the eyes of men.

2a[1]. And he who has authority to give judgment shall consider very earnestly what he himself desires when he says thus: "And forgive us our trespasses as we forgive [them that trespass against us]."

§ 1. 7 we forbeodað[1] þæt man Cristene men for ealles to
lytlum huru to deaðe ne forráéde, ac elles geráéde man
friðlice steora folce to ðearfe 7 ne forspille man[2] for
ιytlum Godes handgeweorc 7 his agene ceap ðe he
deore[3] gebohte.

3. We beodað[4] þæt man Cristene men ealles to swiðe of eardan
ne sylle ne on hæðendóme huru ne bringe, ac beorgan man
georne[5], þæt man ða sawla ne forfáre ðe Crist mid his agenum
life gebohte.

4. 7 we beodað[6] þæt man eard georne clǽnsian aginne on
æghwylcum énde 7 manfulra dæda æghwár geswíce.

4a. Wiccean[7].
Gyf wiccan oððe wigeleres[8], morðwyrhtan oððe horcwéonan
ahwar on lande wurðon agytene, fyse hi man georne ut of
ðissan earde, oððe on earde forfare hi mid ealle, buton hi
geswican 7 ðe deoppor gebétan.

§ 1. We beodað[6] þæt wiðersacan 7 útlagan Godes 7 manna
of earde gewítan, buton hig gebúgan 7 ðe geornor
gebétan[9].

§ 2. 7 ðeofas 7 ðeodsceaðan to tíman forwurðan, buton hi
geswican.

5[10]. Be hæðenscipe.
We forbeodað eornostlice ælcne hæðenscipe.

§ 1[10]. Þæt[11] bið þæt man idol[12] weorðige, hæþne[13] godas 7
sunnan oððe monan, fyr oððe flod, wǽterwyllas oððe
stanas oððe æniges cynnes wudutréowa, oððe wicce-
cræft lufie, oððe morðweorc gefremme on ænige wisan,
oððe on blote[14] oððe on fyrhte, oððe swylcra gedwímera
ænig ðing dreoge.

---

[1] *beodað* G, A; *And witena gerædnes is þ.* D.   [2] Om. G, A, D.
[3] *deope* A, Ld.   [4] *forbeodað* A, Ld; *And witena* &c. D.
[5] *huru—georne* om. A, Ld.   [6] *And witena* &c. D.
[7] The rubrics are found only in B.
[8] *wigel* with *eres* added later on an erasure in B; *wigleras* G, A, D, Ld.
[9] *betan* A, Ld.   [10] Om. D.
[11] Added later in B; *hæðenscipe* G; *hædenscype* A, Ld.
[12] *deofolgyld* G; *idola* A, Ld.   [13] *þæt is þæt man weorðige h.* G, A, Ld.
[14] *hlotæ* A; *-e* Ld; cf. *sorte* Q.

§ 1[1]. And we forbid the practice of condemning Christian people to death for very trivial offences. On the contrary, merciful punishments[2] shall be determined upon for the public good, and the handiwork of God and the purchase which he made at a great price[3] shall not be destroyed for trivial offences.

3[1]. We forbid the all too prevalent practice[2] of selling Christian people out of the country[3], and especially of conveying them into heathen lands, but care shall be zealously taken that the souls which Christ bought with his own life be not destroyed.

4[1]. And we enjoin that the purification of the land in every part shall be diligently undertaken, and that evil deeds shall everywhere be put an end to.

4a[1]. Wizards.

If wizards or sorcerers[2], those who secretly compass death[3], or prostitutes be met with anywhere in the land, they shall be zealously driven out of this land or utterly destroyed in the land, unless they cease from their wickedness and make amends to the utmost of their ability[4].

§ 1[1]. We enjoin that apostates and those who are cast out from the fellowship of God[2] and of men shall depart from the land, unless they submit and make amends to the utmost of their ability.

§ 2. And thieves and robbers[1] shall forthwith be made an end of, unless they desist.

5. Concerning heathen practices.

We earnestly forbid all heathen practices.

§ 1[1]. Namely, the worship of idols, heathen gods[2], and the sun or the moon, fire or water, springs or stones or any kind of forest trees, or indulgence in witchcraft, or the compassing of death in any way, either by sacrifice[3] or by divination[4] or by the practice of any such delusions.

6. Mannslagan 7 mánswaran, hádbrecan 7 áewbrecan gebugan 7 gebetan oððe of cyððan mid synnan gewitan.

7. Licceteras[1] 7 leogeras, ryperas 7 hreaferas Godes graman habban, buton hig geswican 7 ðe deoppor gebetan.

§ 1. 7 se ðe eard wylle rihtlice clænsian 7 unriht alecgan 7 rihtwisnysse lufian, ðonne mot he georne ðyllices steoran 7 ðyllic ascunian[2].

8. Feos bote.
Uton eac ealle ymbe friðes bote 7 ymbe feos bóte smeagian swiðe georne: swa ymbe friðes bote swa ðam bondan sy selost 7 ðam ðeofan sy laðost, 7 swa ymbe feos bóte, þæt an mynet gange ofer ealle ðas ðéode butan ælcon fal[s]e[3]; 7 þæt nan man ne forsace.

§ 1. 7 se ðe ofer ðis fals wyrce ðolie ðara handa ðe he þæt fals mid worhte, 7 he hí mid nanum ðingum ne bycge, ne mid golde ne mid seolfre.

§ 2. 7 gyf man[4] ðone refan[5] téo, þæt he be his hléafe þæt fals worhte, ladie hine mid ðryfealdre lade, 7 gyf seo lád ðonne byrste, habbe ðone ilcan dóm ðe se ðe þæt fals worhte.

9. Geméta 7 gewihta rihte man georne 7 ælces unrihtes [heonan forð][6] geswíce.

10. 7 burhbota 7 brycgbota[7] 7 scipforðunga[8] aginne man georne 7 fyrdunga eac swá, á ðonne ðearf sy for mænelicre[9] neode.

11. 7 smeage man georne[10] on æghwylce wísan, hu man fyrmæst mæge ráed aredian ðeode to ðearfe 7 rihtne Cristendóm swiðast aráeran 7 æghwylce unlage georne[11] afyllen.

[1] licceras A, Ld.   [2] At this point the extract in D ends.
[3] falfe B.   [4] q. m. þonne G, A. Ld.   [5] gerefan G, A, Ld.
[6] G, A, Ld; om. B, and inserted in cap. 10.
[7] br. heonan forð B.   [8] Later altered to ·fyrð. B.
[9] gemæn. G, Ld; gemen. A.   [10] symle G, A, Ld.
[11] geornost G, Ld; -nnod A.

6[1]. Murderers and perjurers[2], injurers of the clergy and adulterers[3] shall submit and make amends or depart with their sins from their native land.

7[1]. Hypocrites and liars, robbers and plunderers shall incur the wrath of God, unless they desist and make amends to the utmost.

§ 1. And he who desires to purify the land aright[1] and to suppress injustice and cherish righteousness must zealously prohibit and avoid such crimes.

8[1]. The reform of the coinage.

Let us all likewise very zealously take thought for the promotion of public security and the improvement of the coinage—for the promotion of public security in such a way as shall be best for householders and worst for thieves[2], and for the improvement of the coinage in such a way that there shall be one currency free from all adulteration throughout this land; and no-one shall refuse it.

§ 1. And he who henceforth coins false money shall forfeit the hand[1] with which he made the false money, and he shall not redeem it in any way, either with gold or with silver.

§ 2[1]. And if the reeve is accused of having granted his permission to the man who coined false money[2], he shall clear himself by the triple oath of exculpation[3], and if it fails, he shall have the same sentence as the man who has coined the false money.

9[1]. Measures and weights shall be diligently corrected, and an end put to all unjust practices.

10[1]. And henceforth the repair of fortifications and bridges, and the preparation of ships and the equipment of military forces likewise shall be diligently undertaken for the common need, whenever the occasion arises.

11[1]. And thought shall diligently be taken in every way how best to determine what is advisable for the public good, and how best to promote true Christianity and diligently suppress every injustice.

§ 1. Forðam þurh þæt hit sceal on earde godian to ahte, þæt man unriht alecge 7 rihtwisnysse lufie for Gode 7 for worulde. Amen[1].

12. Ðis syndon ða gerihta ðe se cyning ah ofer ealle men on Wessexan, þæt is mundbryce 7 hamsocne, forstal[2] 7 fyrdwite[3], buton hwǽne he[4] furðor gemæðian[5] wylle[6].

13. Utlaga.

Se ðe útlages weorc gewyrce wealde se cyng ðæs friðes.

§ 1. 7 gyf he bócland habbe, sy þæt forworht ðam cynge to hánde, sy ðæs mannes man ðe he sy.

§ 2. 7 lóchwá ðone fleman féde oððe feormie, gylde fif pund ðam cýnge, butan he hine geladige þæt he hine flema nyste.

14. 7 on Myrcean he ah, ealswa her beforan gewriten is, ofer ealle men.

15. 7 on Dena lage hé ah fihtwite 7 fyrdwita, griðbryce 7 hamsocne, butan he hwǽne[7] furðor gemæðrian wylle.

15a. 7 gyf hwá ðonne[8] friðleasan man healde oððe feormie[9], bete swa hit[10] lagu wǽs.

§ 1. 7 se ðe unlage rǽre oððe undóm gedeme héonan forð, for lædðe oððe for feohfange, beo se wið ðone cyng hundtwelftig scill'[11] scyldig on Engla láge, buton he míd aðe cyðan durre, þæt he hít na rihtor ne cuðe, 7 ðolie áá his þegenscipes, butan he híne æt ðam cýng gebycge[12], swa he him geðafian wylle.

---

[1] Om. A, Ld.   [2] forsteal 7 flymena fyrmðe G.
[3] fyrdigce A, for which Liebermann, in view of Q's reading fyrdunga, suggests the emendation fyrdinge.
[4] he hwæne ðe G; he hw. A, Ld.   [5] gemæðrian G, Ld; mæðrian A.
[6] G adds: 7 he him ðæs weorðscipes geunne.   [7] he hw. ðe G.
[8] þæne G.   [9] o. flyman f. G.   [10] b. þæt s. h. ær G, A, Ld.
[11] w. þonne cyninge his weores sc. A, Ld.   [12] eft gebicge G.

§ 1. For it is only by the suppression of injustice and the love of righteousness, in matters both religious and secular, that any improvement shall be obtained in the condition of the country. Amen.

12. These are the dues[1] to which the king is entitled from all men in Wessex, namely, [the payments for] violation of his *mund*[2], and for attacks on people's houses, for assault[3] and for neglecting military service[4], unless he desires to show especial honour to anyone [by granting him these dues][5].

13. Outlawry.
If anyone does the deed of an outlaw[1], the king[2] alone shall have power to grant him security.

§ 1[1]. And if he has land held by title-deed, it shall be forfeited into the hands of the king without regard to the question whose vassal he is.

§ 2[1]. And whoever feeds or harbours the fugitive shall pay £5[2] to the king, unless he clear himself by a declaration that he did not know[3] that he was a fugitive.

14. And in Mercia he is entitled to all the dues described above, from all men.

15[1]. And in the Danelaw he has the receipt of fines for fighting[2], neglect of military service, breach of the peace and attacks upon people's houses, unless he desires specially to honour anyone [by granting him these dues].

15a. And therefore if anyone maintains or harbours an outlawed man[1], he shall make amends in accordance with the established law[2].

§ 1[1]. And he who henceforth promotes injustice or pronounces unjust judgments[2], as the result of malice or bribery, shall forfeit 120 shillings[3] to the king, in districts under English law, unless he is prepared to declare on oath that he did not know how to give a more just verdict[4], and he shall lose for ever his rank as a thegn, unless he redeem it from the king, provided the latter is willing to allow him to do so.

§ 1*a*. 7 on Dena laga lahslites scyldig, buton he híne[1] geladige,
　　þæt he na bet ne cuðe.

　§ 2. 7 se ðe rihte lage 7 riht dóm[2] forsace, beo se scyldig wið
　　ðone ðe hit age, swa wið cyng hundtwelftig scill', swa
　　wið eorl syxtig scill', swa wið hundred xxx[3] scill', swa
　　wið ælc ðára, gyf hit swa geweorðeð, on Engla lage.

　§ 3. 7 se ðe on Dena lage rihte lage wyrde, gylde hé lahslíte.

16.　7 se ðe oðerne mid wó forsecgan wille, þæt he aðer oððe feo
　　oððe freoma[4] ðe wyrse si, gyf ðonne se oðer þæt geunsoðian
　　mæge þæt hím　man on secgan wolde, sy he his tungan
　　scyldig, buton he him[5] mid his wére forgylde.

17.　Ne geséce nan man ðonne[6] cyng, buton he ne mote beon
　　nanes rihtes wurðe innan his hundrede.

　§ 1. Sece man his hundred.
　　Séce man hundredes gemót be wíte, ealswa hit riht[1]
　　is to secanne.

18.　7 habbe man ðreowa[7] burhgemot 7 twá[8] scirgemot be wíte,
　　ealswa hit riht is[9], buton hit oftor neod[10] sy.

　§ 1. 7 þær beo on ðære scire bisceop 7 se ealdorman 7 þær
　　ægðer tæcan ge Godes riht ge woruldriht.

19.　Be nááme.
　　7 ne nime nan man nane[11] náme ne inne scire ne ut of scire,
　　ær man hæbbe [þriwa on hundrede his][12] rihtes gebeden.

　§ 1. Gyf he æt ðam ðriddan cyrre nan riht næbbe, ðonne
　　fare he feorðan siðe[13] to scirgemote 7 seo scir him sette
　　ðone feorðan andagan.

　§ 2. And gyf se[14] ðonne byrste, nime ðonne leafe ge heonan
　　ge ðeonan þæt he mote hæntan æfter [h]is[15] agan[16].

---

[1] Om. G.
[2] *rihtne dom* G, A, Ld; Liebermann suggests the reading *rihtdom* in B.
[3] G, A, Ld; xx B.　　　　　　　　[4] *freme* G; *feorme* A; *feorh* Ld.
[5] *hine* G, A, Ld.　　　　　　　[6] *ðone* G, Ld.
[7] *þriwa on geare* (·*a*) G, A, Ld.　　　　　　[8] *tuwa* G.
[9] *be w.—riht is.* Only in B and probably carried over from the preceding
clause.
[10] Om. G, A, Ld; added in B in 16th cent.　　　　　[11] Om. A.
[12] G, A, Ld; om. B.　　　　　　[13] *æt þam f. s.* A, Ld.
[14] *anddaga* added in 16th cent. in B.　　　　[15] *is* B.
[16] *agenan* G, A, Ld.

§ 1*a*. And in the Danelaw he shall forfeit *lahslit*[1], unless he clear himself, asserting that he did not know any better verdict.

§ 2[1]. And he who refuses [to observe] just laws and just judgments shall forfeit, in districts under English law, [a fine] to the party who is entitled thereto—either 120 shillings to the king, or 60 shillings to the earl, or 30 shillings to the hundred[2], or to all of them, if they are all concerned.

§ 3. And he who violates justice in the Danelaw shall pay *lahslit*.

16[1]. And if a man seeks to accuse another man falsely in such a way as to injure him in property or reputation[2], and if the latter can refute the accusation brought against him, the first shall forfeit his tongue, unless he redeem himself with his wergeld.

17[1]. And no-one shall appeal to the king, unless he fails to obtain justice within his hundred.

§ 1[1]. Everyone shall attend his hundred [court].
Everyone shall attend the hundred court, under pain of fine[2], whenever he is required by law to attend it.

18[1]. And the borough court shall be held three times and the shire court twice, in accordance with the law[2], under pain of fine, unless need arises for more frequent meetings.

§ 1[1]. And the bishop of the diocese and the ealdorman shall attend, and they shall direct the administration of both ecclesiastical and secular law.

19[1]. Concerning distraint of property.
And no-one shall make distraint[2] of property either within the shire[3] or outside it, until he has appealed for justice [three times in the hundred court].

§ 1. If on the third occasion he does not obtain justice, he shall go on the fourth occasion to the shire court, and the shire court shall appoint a day when he shall issue his summons for the fourth time.

§ 2. And if this summons fails, he shall get leave, either from the one court or the other[1], to take his own measures for the recovery of his property.

20. Þæt ælc mon beo on teoðunge.

We wyllað þæt ælc freoman beo on hundrede 7 on teoðunge gebroht, ðe lade wyrðe beon wylle oððe weres wyrðe, gyf hine hwa afylle[1], ofer[2] twelfwintre; oþþe he ne beo[3] æniges freorihtes[4] wyrðe, sy he heorðfæst, sy hé folgere—þæt ælc sy on hundre[d][5] 7 on borh[6] gebroht 7 gehealde se borh híne 7 gelæde to ælcon gerihte[7].

§ 1. Manig stræc man wyle, gyf he mæg 7 mot, werian his man, swa hwæðer swa him ðincð þæt he hine yð[8] awerian mæge—swá for frigne swá for ðeowne—ac we nyllað geðafian þæt unriht.

21. Be ðeofan.

We[9] wyllað þæt ælc man ofer twelfwintre sylle þone[10] að, þæt he nyle ðeof beon ne ðeofes gewita.

22. 7 sy ælc getreowe man ðe tihtbysi nære 7 naðer ne burste ne að ne ordal innan hundrede[11] anfealde lade wyrðe.

§ 1. And ungetreowan men ceose man anfealdne að on þreom hundredan 7 þreofealdne að[12] swa wíde swa hit to ðære byrig hyre, oððe gá to ordale[13].

§ 1a. Ofga mán anfealde láde mid anfealde foraðe 7 ðrifealde lade[14] mid ðrifealdan foraðe.

§ 2. 7 gyf ðegen hæbbe getreowe man to foraðe for híne þæt swa sy; gyf he næbbe, ofga sylf his spæce.

§ 3. 7 ne beo[15] ænig forað forgyfen.

---

[1] teon wylle G; fylle A. [2] o. þæt he byð G. [3] b. syððan G.
[4] freo added in 16th cent. in B. [5] hundre B.
[6] borge G, A; borghe Ld. [7] rihte G, A, Ld. [8] Om. A, Ld.
[9] Ac we G; 7 we A. [10] þonne (ð-) A, Ld. [11] i. his h. A, Ld.
[12] on þr. h...að. Added in margin of B in 16th cent. [13] þam o. G, A, Ld.
[14] mid anf....lade om. A, Ld. [15] ne b. æfre G, A, Ld.

20[1]. Every man shall be in a tithing.

It is our desire that every freeman, over twelve years of age, who desires to have the right of exculpation and of being atoned for by the payment of his wergeld, if he is slain[2], shall be brought within a hundred and a tithing[3]; otherwise he shall not be entitled to any of the rights of a freeman, whether he has an establishment of his own or is in the service of another—everyone shall be brought within a hundred and under surety, and his surety shall hold and bring him to the performance of every legal duty.

§ 1. Many self-assertive[1] men seek, if they can and may, to protect their men[2] in whichever way it seems to them that they can do so the more easily—namely, by representing them either as freemen or slaves—but we will not permit this injustice.

21. Concerning thieves.

It is our desire that everyone, over twelve years of age, shall take an oath that he will not be a thief or a thief's accomplice.

22. And every trustworthy man, who has never earned a bad reputation[1] and who has never failed[2] either in oath or in ordeal, shall be entitled to clear himself within the hundred[3] by the simple oath of exculpation[4].

§ 1. And for an untrustworthy man compurgators for the simple oath shall be selected[1] within three hundreds, and for the triple oath, throughout the district under the jurisdiction of the borough-court; otherwise he shall go to the ordeal.

§ 1a. In cases where a simple oath of exculpation is involved, the case shall be begun with a simple oath of accusation[1], but where a triple oath of exculpation is involved, it shall be begun with a triple oath of accusation[2].

§ 2. And if a thegn has a trustworthy man to give his oath of accusation for him, he may be allowed to make use of him; if he has not, he must begin his case in person.

§ 3. And there shall be no remission with regard to any oath of accusation[1].

23. Ne beo ænig man æniges teames wyrþe, buton he habbe treowe gewitnysse[1] hwanon him cóme þæt him mon æt befehð.

§ 1. 7 gecyðe seo gewitnysse[2] þæt on Godes helde 7 on his[3] hlafordes, þæt heo him on soðre gewitnysse si, swa heo hit eagum ofersæh 7 earum oferhyrdon, þæt he hit mid rihte begeate.

24. 7 nan man nan ðing ne bycge oter teower peninga weorð, ne libbende ne licgende, buton mon habbe getreowe gewitnysse feower manna, sy hit binnan byrig, sy hit up[4] on lande.

§ 1. 7 gyf hit mon ðonne gefó[5] 7 he ðyllice gewitnysse næbbe, ne beo ðær nan team, ac gyfe man ðam agen-frigean his agen 7 þæt æftergyld 7 þæt wite ðam ðe hit áge.

§ 2. 7 gyf he witnysse[6] habbe, swa we ær cwædon[7], ðonne tyma hit man ðriwa; æt þam feorðam cyrre áhnige hit oððe agyfe ðam ðe hit age.

§ 3. And us ne ðincð na[8] riht þæt ænig man ahnian scule, ðær gewitnysse bið 7 man[9] gec[n]awan[10] cán, þæt þær brygde biþ; þæt nan man hit nah to geahnianne raðost ðinga ær syx monðum ðe[11] hit forstolen wæs.

25. 7 se ðe tyhtbysig sy 7 folce ungetreowe 7 ðas gemot forbuga ðríwa, ðonne sceawie[12] man of ðam feorðan gemote ða ðe him to ridan, 7 finde ðone[13] gyt borh, gyf he mæge.

25a. Gyf he ðonne ne mæge, gewylde man hine swa hwæðer swa man mæge, swa cwicne swa deadne, 7 nimen eall þæt he ah[14].

[1] getrywe witnesse (wittenesse) G, A, Ld.
[2] hwanon him come wrongly repeated in B after gewit.   [3] Om. G, A, Ld.
[4] In 16th cent. changed to upp in B.   [5] befo G, A, Ld.
[6] gewitnesse G; -witnysse A.
[7] s. w. her beforan cw. G; swa hær b. cw. is A, Ld.
[8] Changed in 16th cent. to nan.
[9] 7 man...biþ. Added in the margin in 16th cent. in B.
[10] gecra. B.   [11] æfter ðam þe G, A, Ld.   [12] scepiye A, Ld.
[13] þonne G, Ld.   [14] ahte G; age A, Ld.

23. And no man shall be entitled to vouch to warranty[1], unless he has trustworthy witnesses [to declare] whence he acquired the stock which is attached in his possession.

§ 1. And the witnesses, as they wish to obtain the favour of God and of their lord, shall declare that, in bearing testimony on his behalf to the effect that he acquired it legally, they are speaking the truth[1], in accordance with what they saw with their eyes and heard with their ears.

24. And no-one shall buy anything over four pence in value, either livestock or other property[1], unless he have four men as trustworthy witnesses, whether [the purchase be made] within a town or in the open country[2].

§ 1. If, however, any property is attached, and he [who is in possession of it] has no such witnesses, no vouching to warranty shall be allowed, but the property shall be given up to its rightful owner and also the supplementary payment[1], and the fine to the party who is entitled thereto.

§ 2. And if he has witnesses in accordance with what we have declared above, vouching to warranty shall take place three times. On the fourth occasion he shall prove his claim[1] to it or give it back to its rightful owner.

§ 3. But we regard it as unjust that anyone should claim ownership in a case where there is evidence by which it can be recognised that fraud is involved; so that no-one ought to claim ownership of it in less than six months at least from the time when it was stolen.

25[1]. And if anyone who is of bad reputation and unworthy of public confidence fails to attend the court-meetings three times, men shall be chosen from the fourth meeting who shall ride to him, and he may then still find a surety, if he can.

25a. If, however, he cannot [do so], they shall seize him as they can, either alive or dead, and they shall take all that he has.

§ 1. ⁊ gylde man ðam teonde his ceapgyld ⁊ fó se hlaford
elles to healfum ⁊ to healfum þæt hundred.

§ 2. ⁊ gyf aðor oððe mæg oððe fremde man[1] ða ráde forsace,
gylde ðam cynge hundtwelfti[2] scill'.

26. Be ðeofan.
⁊ gesece se ebǽra ðeof þæt he sece[3], oððe se ðe on hlafordsearwe gemet sy, þæt hi næfre feorh ne gesecan.

§ 1. ⁊ se ðe ofer ðis stalie, sece þæt he sece, þæt he næfre
þæt feorh ne[4] séce æt openre ðyfðe.

27. ⁊ se on gemote mid wiðertihtlan hine sylfne oððe his man[5]
werie, hæbbe eall þæt forspecen ⁊ geandwyrde ðam oðrum,
swa hundrede riht ðynce.

28. ⁊ þæt nan man nænne man underfó[6] na leng ðonne iii niht,
buton híne se befæste ðe[7] he ær folgade.

§ 1. ⁊ nan man his men fram him ne tǽce, ær hé clǽne sy
æt[1] ælcere spǽce ðe he ær beclypad wæs.

29. ⁊ gyf hwá ðeof gemete ⁊ hine his ðances aweg lǽte buton
réame, gebete be ðæs ðeofes wére oððe hine mid fullum aðe[8]
geladige, þæt he him mid nan facn nyste.

§ 1. ⁊ gyf hwa ream gehyre ⁊ hine forsitte, gylde ðæs
cynges oferhyrnysse oððe hine be fullan geladige.

30. Swyðe ungetreowe.
⁊ gyf hwylc man sy swa ungetreowe ðam hundrede ⁊ swa
tihtbysig ⁊ hine[9] ðreo men ætgædere téon, ðonne ne beo
ðær nan oðer, buton ðæt hé ga to ðam ðrifealdan ordale.

---

[1] Om. G, A.
[2] cxx G, Ld; *hundtwentig* A.
[3] *þæt þæt he gesece* G, A, Ld.
[4] From *gesecan* to *ne* om. A.
[5] Changed in 16th cent. to *mann* B.
[6] *ne u.* G, A, Ld.
[7] *buton he (se) h. b. se ðe* A, Ld.
[8] Beside this in the margin Ld has *al. lade.*
[9] *h. þonne* G, A, Ld.

§ 1. And they shall pay to the accuser the value of his goods, and the lord shall take half of what remains and the hundred half.

§ 2. And if anyone, either kinsman or stranger, refuses to ride [against him], he shall pay the king 120 shillings.

26. Concerning thieves.
And the proved thief and he who has been discovered in treason against his lord, whatever sanctuary he seeks, shall never be able to save his life.

§ 1. And he who steals after this—if the case is one of open theft—shall never save his life, whatever sanctuary he seeks.

27. And he who in Court tries to protect either himself or one of his men by bringing a countercharge[1] shall have wasted his words, and shall meet the charge brought by his opponent in such a way as the hundred court shall determine.

28. And no-one shall entertain any man for more than three days, unless he is committed to his charge by the man whom he has been serving[1].

§ 1[1]. And no-one shall dismiss one of his men from his service until he is quit of every accusation which has been brought against him.

29[1]. And if anyone comes upon a thief and of his own accord lets him escape without raising the hue and cry, he shall make compensation by the payment of the thief's wergeld, or clear himself with the full oath[2], [asserting] that he did not know him to be guilty of any crime.

§ 1. And if anyone hears the hue and cry and neglects it, he shall pay the fine for insubordination to the king, or clear himself by the full oath.

30. Thoroughly untrustworthy men.
If anyone has forfeited the confidence of the hundred[1], and has charges brought against him to such an extent that[2] he is accused by three men at once, no other course shall be open to him but to go to the triple ordeal.

§ 1. Gyf se hlaford ðonne secge þæt him naðor ne burste ne að ne ordal sypðan þæt gemot wæs on Winceastre, níme se hlaford him twegen getrywe men to innan ðam hundrede, and swerian þæt him næfre að ne burste ne ordal ne ðeófgyld ne gulde—buton hé ðone[1] gerefan hæbbe þe þæs wurþe si[2] ðe þæt don mæge.

§ 2. Gyf se að ðonne forðcume, ceose se man ðe ðær betyhtlod sy swa hwæðer swa[3] he wylle, swa anfeald ordal swa pundes wurðne að innan ðrim hundrede, ofer xxx peninga.

§ 3. Be ordale.

7 gyf hi ðonne[4] að syllan ne durran, gange he to ðam ðrifealdan ordale.

§ 3a. 7 ofgá man þæt ðryfealde ordal ðus, nime fife 7 beo him[5] sylf syxta.

§ 3b. 7 gyf he ðonne ful wurðe, æt ðam forman cyrre bete ðam teonde twygylde 7 ðam hlaford his wér ðe his wites[6] wyrðe sy 7 sette getreowe borgas, þæt he ælces yfeles geswice[7].

§ 4. And æt ðam oðran cyrre ne sy ðær nan oþer bot, gyf[8] he ful wurðe, buton ðæt man ceorfe him ða handa oððe ða fét óf oððe ægðer, be ðam ðe seo dæd sy.

§ 5. 7 gyf h[e][9] ðonne gyt mare weorc geweorht hæbbe, ðonne do man ut his eagan 7 ceorfan of his nose 7 eáran 7 ða uferan lippan oððe hine héttian, swylc ðisra[10] swa man wyle, oððe[11] ðonne geráede ða ðe ðærto ræedan sceolon; swa man sceal[12] steoran 7 eac ðære saule beorgan.

§ 6. Gyf he ðonne ut leape 7 þæt ordal forbuge, gylde se borh ðam teonde his ceapgyld 7 ðam cynge his wer oððe ðam ðe his weres[13] wyrðe sy.

---

[1] þonne A.   [2] þe þ. w. si. Added in the margin in 16th cent. in B.
[3] swæðer he G, Ld; swa weðer he A.   [4] þone G, Ld.
[5] he G; om. A, Ld.   [6] þe þæs wyrðe A.   [7] eft g. G, A, Ld.
[8] gif G, A, Ld; buton gyf B.   [9] hit B, Ld.
[10] swa hwylc þyssa (þissa) G, A; -ce ðissa Ld.   [11] w. o. om. G, A.
[12] sceal written above in 16th cent. in B; mæg G, A, Ld.
[13] wites G, A, Ld.

§ 1. If, however, his lord asserts that he has failed neither in oath nor in ordeal since the assembly was held at Winchester[1], he (the lord) shall choose two trustworthy men within the hundred—unless he have a reeve who is qualified to discharge this duty—and they shall swear that he has never failed in oath or in ordeal or been convicted of stealing.

§ 2[1]. If the oath is forthcoming, the man who is accused there shall choose whichever he will—either the simple ordeal or an oath equivalent to a pound in value, [supported by compurgators found] within the three hundreds, [in the case of an object] over 30 pence in value.

§ 3. Concerning the ordeal.

If they dare not give the oath, he (the accused) shall go to the triple ordeal.

§ 3a. And a case which involves the triple ordeal shall be opened as follows: five [compurgators] shall be selected by the accuser and he himself shall make a sixth.

§ 3b[1]. And if then he (the accused) is proved guilty, on the first occasion he shall pay double value to the accuser and his wergeld to the lord who is entitled to receive his fine, and he shall appoint trustworthy sureties, that henceforth he will desist from all wrong-doing.

§ 4[1]. And on the second occasion, if he is proved guilty, there shall be no compensation possible to him but to have his hands or his feet cut off or both, according to the nature of the offence.

§ 5. And if he has wrought still greater crime, he shall have his eyes put out and his nose and ears and upper lip cut off or his scalp removed[1], whichever of these penalties is desired or determined upon by those with whom rests the decision of the case; and thus punishment shall be inflicted, while, at the same time, the soul is preserved from injury.

§ 6[1]. If, however, he escapes and avoids the ordeal, his surety shall pay the value of his goods to the plaintiff and the wergeld of the accused to the king or to the man who is entitled to receive his wergeld.

§ 7. And gyf mon ðone[1] laford teo, þæt he be his ræde ut
léope 7 ær unriht worhte, nime him fif getreowe men[2]
tó 7 beo him sylf sixta 7 ladige hine ðæs.

§ 8. Gyf seo lád [forðcume, beo he þæs weres wyrðe.

§ 9. 7 gif heo][3] forð ne cume, fo se cyng to þam wére 7 beo
seo þeof utlah wið eal folc.

31. Be hiredmonnum.
7 hæbbe ælc laford his hiredmen on his agenum borhge[4].

31a. 7 gyf hine man æniges ðinges téo, andswarie innan ðam
hundrede ðær he on beclypod béo, swa hit lagu[5] séo.

§ 1. 7 gyf he betyhtlod weorðe 7 he ut ætleape[6], gylde se
hlaford ðæs mannes wér ðam cynge.

§ 1a. 7 gyf hi[7] ðone laford teon[8], þæt he be his ræde ut leope,
ladige hine mid fif ðegnum 7 beo him sylf syxta.

§ 2. [Gyf him seo lad berste, gylde þam cingce his were][3]
7 beo se man utlah wið ðone cyng[9].

32. 7 gyf þeo[w]man[10] æt ðam ordale ful wurðe, mearcie [man][3]
hine ðonne[2] æt ðam forman cyrre.

§ 1. 7 æt ðam oðran cyrran ne sy ðær nan bot[11] buton þæt
heafod.

33. Be ungetreowum mannum.
Gyf hwylc man sy ðe eallum folce ungetrywe sy, fare ðæs
cynges geréfa to 7 gebringe hine under borge, þæt híne man
to rihte lǽde ðam ðe him on specan.

§ 1. Gyf he ðonne borh næbbe, slea hine man 7 on fulan
lecge.

§ 1a. 7 gyf híne hwá forstande[12], beo hig begen anes rihtes
wyrðe.

§ 2. 7 se ðe ðis forsitte 7 hit geforðian nylle, swa ure[13] cwide
is, sylle ðam cynge hundtwelftig scill'.

[1] þonne A, Ld.   [2] Om. G, A, Ld.   [3] G, A, Ld; om. B.
[4] Written above in 12th cent. in B.   [5] rihtlagu (-a) G, A, Ld.
[6] oðhleape G, Ld; hleape A.
[7] man G, A, Ld; hi written on an erasure in B.
[8] n added later to earlier teo in B.   [9] w. ð. c. Not in G, A, Ld.
[10] G, Ld; ðeofman B, A.   [11] n. oðer b. G.
[12] forene f. G; fora f. A, Ld.   [13] u. ealra (eallre) G, A, Ld.

§ 7. And if the lord is accused of advising the man who had done wrong to escape, he shall choose five trustworthy men, and shall himself make a sixth, and shall clear himself of the accusation.

§ 8. If he succeeds in clearing himself, he shall be entitled to the wergeld.

§ 9. And if he fails, the king shall take the wergeld, and the thief shall be treated as an outlaw by the whole nation.

31. Concerning the men belonging to a household.
And every lord shall be personally responsible as surety for the men of his own household.

31a. And if any accusation is brought against one of them, he shall answer [it], in accordance with the law, within the hundred in which he is accused.

§ 1[1]. And if he is accused and escapes, the lord shall pay his (the man's) wergeld to the king.

§ 1a. And if the lord is accused of advising him to escape, he shall clear himself with [the help of] five thegns, himself making a sixth.

§ 2. [And if he fails to clear himself, he shall pay his (own) wergeld to the king], and the man shall be an outlaw towards the king[1].

32. And if a slave[1] is found guilty at the ordeal, he shall be branded on the first occasion.

§ 1. And on the second occasion he shall not be able to make any amends except by his head.

33[1]. Concerning untrustworthy men.
If there is anyone who is regarded with suspicion by the general public, the king's reeve shall go and place him under surety so that he may be brought to do justice to those who have made charges against him.

§ 1. If he has no surety, he shall be slain and buried in unconsecrated ground.

§1a. And if anyone interposes in his defence, they shall both incur the same punishment.

§ 2. And he who ignores this and will not further what we have all determined upon shall pay 120 shillings to the king.

34. 7 stande betwyx burgum an laga æt ladunge.

35. Be freondleasan.

Gyf freondleas man oððe feorran cuman swa geswencad
wurðe ðurh freondlæste þæt he borh næbbe, æt frumtyhtlan
ðonne gebugé he hengene 7 ðær gebide, oð þæt he ga to Godes
ordale 7 gefáre ðær þæt he mæge.

§ 1. Witodlice, se ðe freondleasan 7 feorran cumenan wyrsan
dóm demeð ðonne his geferan, he derað him sylfum.

36. Be mænan aðe.

Gyf hwa mæne að on haligdome swerie 7 he oferstǽled
weorðe, ðolie ðara hánda oððe healfes weres, 7 ðæt sy
gemæne hlaforde 7 bisceope.

§ 1. 7 ne beo ðanon forþ aðes wyrðe, buton he for God ðe
deoppor gebete 7 him borh finde, þæt he æfre eft
swylces geswice.

37. Be leasre gewitnesse.

And gyf hwa on leasre gewitnysse openlice stande 7 he
oferstæled wurðe, ne stande his gewitnysse syððan for naht[1],
ac gylde ðam cynge oððe landrican[2] be halsfange.

38. Nis on ænigne[3] timan unriht alyfad, 7 ðeah man sceal freols-
tídan[4] 7 on freolsstowan geornlicost bebyrgan[5].

§ 1. 7 a swa man bið mihtigra oððe maran hades, swa sceal
hé deoppor for Gode 7 for worulde unriht gebetan.

§ 2. 7 godcunde bote sece man georne[6] 7 symble[7] be
boctale[8], 7 woruldbote[9] sece man be woruldlage.

[1] aht G.   [2] l. þe his socne ahe G.   [3] nanre Ld.
[4] freolst. 7 fæstentidan G.   [5] beorgan G, A, Ld.
[6] symle g. G, A, Ld.   [7] 7 s. om. G, A, Ld.
[8] boctæcinge G.   [9] woruldcunde bote G; for w. b. A, Ld.

34. And the various boroughs shall have one common law with regard to exculpation.

35. Concerning the friendless.

If a friendless man or one come from afar is so utterly destitute of friends as not to be able to produce a surety, on the first occasion that he is accused he shall go to prison, and wait there until he goes to God's ordeal where he shall experience whatever he can.

§ 1. Verily, he who pronounces a more severe judgment upon one who is friendless or come from afar than upon one of his own acquaintances injures himself.

36[1]. Concerning perjury.

If anyone swears a false oath on the relics and is convicted, he shall lose his hand[2] or half his wergeld which shall be divided between the lord and the bishop.

§ 1. And henceforth[1] he shall not be entitled to swear an oath, unless he makes amends to the best of his ability before God, and finds surety that ever afterwards he will desist from such [perjury].

37[1]. Concerning false witness.

And if anyone has given testimony which is manifestly false, and is convicted thereof, his testimony henceforth shall be valueless, and he shall pay to the king or to the lord of the manor a sum equivalent to his *healsfang*[2].

38[1]. Lawlessness is not permitted at any time, yet at sacred seasons and in sacred places special care must be taken to prevent it.

§ 1[1]. And in all cases, the greater a man is and the higher his rank, the more stringent shall be the amends which he shall be required to make to God and to men for lawless behaviour.

§ 2[1]. And ecclesiastical amends shall always be diligently exacted in accordance with the directions contained in the canon law, and secular amends in accordance with secular law.

39. Gif hwa preost ofslea.

Gyf hwa weofodðegen afylle, sy he utlaga wið God 7 wið men, buton he ðurh wrecsið ðe deoppor gebete 7 eac wið ða mægða, oððe ladige[1] mid werlade.

§ 1. 7 binnon xxx nihta aginne þa[2] bote ægðer ge wið God ge wið men be eallum ðam ðe he age.

40. Gyf man gehadodne man[2] oððe ælðeodigne man[2] ðurh ænig ðingc forræde æt feo oððe æt feore, ðonne sceal him se[2] kingc beon for mæg 7 for mundboran, buton he elles oðerne[3] hæbbe.

§ 1. 7 beton[4] ðam kyninge swa hit gebyrige, oððe he ða dæde wrece swyðe deope.

§ 2. Cristenum kyninge gebyrað swyðe rihte þæt he Godes æbylðe wrece swyðe deope, be ðam ðe seo dæd sy.

41. Be gehadedum mannum.

Gyf weofodðegen manslaga wyrðe oððon[5] elles to swiðe mánweorc gewyrce, ðonne ðolie he ægðer ge hades ge éðles, 7 wrécnige swa wíde swa se[2] papa him scrife 7 dædbete georne.

§ 1. 7 gyf he ladian wylle, ladie hine[6] mid ðryfealdan.

§ 2. 7 buton he binnon xxx nihta bote agynne wið God 7 wið men, ðonne sy he utlaga.

42. Ðæt man gehadodne man [ne][7] bende ne beate.

Gyf hwa gehadodne man bende oððan[5] beate oððon[5] swyðe bismærige[8], bete wið hine swa[9] hit riht sy, 7 ðam[2] bisceope weofodbote be ðæs[2] hades mæðe, 7 ðam[2] laforde oððe þam[2] kynincge be fullan mundbryce, oððe geladige hine sylfne[10] mid fulre lade.

---

[1] geladige hine G, A, Ld.   [2] Om. G, A.   [3] o. hlaford G.
[4] bete man G, A, Ld.   [5] Altered in 16th cent. to oððe.
[6] .N. ladige A; hine in B added later on an erasure; om. G.
[7] Om. in B.   [8] gebysmrige G, A, Ld.   [9] swa swa G, A, Ld.
[10] h. s. written in the margin in 16th cent. in B; sylfne om. G, A.

39. If anyone slay a priest.

If anyone slays a minister of the altar, he shall be both excommunicated and outlawed, unless he make amends to the best of his ability by pilgrimage[1], and likewise by [the payment of compensation] to the kin [of the slain man], or else he shall clear himself by an oath equal in value to his wergeld.

§ 1. And he shall begin to make amends both to God and men within 30 days[1], under pain of forfeiting all that he possesses.

40[1]. If an attempt is made to deprive in any wise a man in orders or a stranger of either his goods or his life, the king shall act as his kinsman and protector, unless he has some other.

§ 1[1]. And such compensation as is fitting shall be paid to the king, or he shall avenge the deed to the uttermost.

§ 2[1]. It is the duty most incumbent upon a Christian king that he should avenge to the uttermost offences against God, in accordance with the nature of the deed.

41[1]. Concerning men in holy orders.

If a minister of the altar[2] commits homicide or perpetrates any other great crime, he shall be deprived of his ecclesiastical office and banished, and shall travel as a pilgrim as far as the Pope appoints for him, and zealously make amends.

§ 1. And if he seeks to clear himself, he shall do so by the triple mode of proof.

§ 2. And unless he begins to make amends both to God and men within 30 days, he shall be outlawed.

42[1]. A man in holy orders shall not be bound or beaten.

If anyone binds or beats or deeply insults a man in holy orders, he shall make amends towards him in accordance with the law, and shall pay the fine due to the bishop for sacrilege[2], in accordance with the rank [of the injured man], and to his lord or to the king the full fine for breach of his *mund*, or he shall clear himself by the full process of exculpation.

43. Gyf gehadod man hine forwyrce mid deaðscylde, gewylde
man hine 7 healde to ðæs[1] bisceopes dome, be ðam ðe seo
dæd sy.

44. Gyf deaðscyldig man scriftspréce gyrne, ne wyrne him nan[1]
man næfre[2].

§ 1. 7 gyf him man[3] wyrne, gebete þæt wið ðone[4] kyninge
mid hundtwentig scyllinga oððe geladige hine—nime
v men[5] 7 beo him[6] sylf vɪ-ta.

45. Gyf man wealdan mæge, ne dyde man næfre[7] on Sunnandæges freolse ǽnigne forworhtne man, buton he fleo oððe
feohte, ac wylde man hine[8] 7 healde þæt se freolsdæg agan sy.

§ 1. Be haligdæiges freolse.
Gyf frigman freolsdæge wyrce, ðonne gebete he[1] þæt
mid his healsfange, 7 huru wið God bete hit georne, swa
swa him man tæce.

§ 2. Ðeowman, gyf he[9] wyrce, ðolie his hyde oððon hydgyldes, be ðam ðe seo dæd sy.

§ 3. Gyf laford his ðeowan freolsdæge nyde to weorce, ðolie
ðæs ðeowan 7 beo he syððan folcfrig; 7 gylde lahslit se
laford mid Denum, wite mid Englum, bi ðam þe seo
dæd sy; oððe geladie hine.

46. Be festene.
Gyf friman riht[10] fæsten abrece, gylde lahslit mid Denum,
wite mid Englum, be ðam ðe[10] seo deed sy.

§ 1. Yfel bið hit[1] þæt man fæstentide[11] ær mæle éte, 7 gyt
hit[1] bið[1] wyrse þæt man mid flæscmete hine sylfne[10]
gefyle.

§ 2. Gyf hit ðeowman gedó, ðolie his hyde oððe hydgyldes[12],
be ðam ðe seo dæd sy.

¹ Om. G, A, Ld.   ² æfre G, A, Ld.   ³ hwa G, A, Ld.
⁴ Om. A, Ld.   ⁵ Om. G, A.   ⁶ Om. G, A; he Ld.
⁷ æfre G, A.   ⁸ m. h. om. G, A.   ⁹ Om. G.
¹⁰ Written above in 16th cent. in B.   ¹¹ rihtf. G.
¹² o. h. om. A, Ld.

43[1]. If a man in holy orders places his life in jeopardy by committing a capital crime, he shall be arrested, and his case shall be reserved for the bishop's decision, according to the nature of the deed.

44[1]. If a condemned man desires confession, it shall never be refused him.

§ 1. And if anyone refuses it to him, he shall make amends for it to the king by the payment of 120 shillings, or he shall clear himself. He shall select five men and be himself a sixth.

45[1]. If it can be so contrived, no condemned man shall ever be put to death during the Sunday festival, unless he flees or fights, but he shall be arrested and kept in custody until the festival is over.

§ 1[1]. Concerning the Sunday festival.

If a freeman works during a church festival, he shall make amends for doing so by the payment of his *healsfang*, and especially he shall zealously make amends to God, according to the directions given him.

§ 2[1]. If a slave works, he shall undergo the lash or pay the fine in lieu thereof, according to the nature of the offence.

§ 3[1]. If a lord compels his slave to work during a church festival, he shall lose the slave, who shall henceforth obtain the rights of a freeman, and the lord shall pay *lahslit* in a Danish district and a fine in an English one, according to the nature of the offence, or else he shall clear himself.

46[1]. Concerning fasts.

If a freeman breaks a legally ordained fast, he shall pay *lahslit* in a Danish district, a fine in an English one, according to the nature of the offence.

§ 1. It is wrong for anyone during a fast to eat before the appointed time, and it is still worse for anyone to defile himself with flesh.

§ 2[1]. If a slave does so, he shall undergo the lash or pay the fine in lieu thereof, in accordance with the nature of the deed.

47. Gyf hwa opendlice lencgtenbryce gewyrce ðurh feohtlac
oððe ðurh wiflac oððe ðurh reaflac oððe ðurh ænige healice
misdæde, sy þæt twibote[1], swa eac[2] on heahfreolse, be ðam
ðe seo dæd sy.

§ 1. And gyf man ætsace, ladige hine[3] mid ðryfealdre lade.

48. Gif hwa forwyrne godcunde gerihte.

Gyf hwa godcundra rihta[4] mid wige forwyrne, gylde lahslit
mid Denum 7[5] fulwite mid Englum, oððe geladige hine—
nime xɪ men[5] 7 beo him[5] seolf twelfta.

§ 1. Gyf he man wundige, gebete þæt 7 gylde fulwite ðam
hlaforde 7 æt ðam[5] bisceope þa handa alyse oððon
híg forlete[6].

§ 2. Gyf he man afylle, beo he utlage 7 his hænte mid
hearme ælc ðara ðe riht wylle.

§ 3. Gyf he gewyrce þæt man hine afylle ðurh þæt ðe he
ongean riht geanbyrde, gif mann þæt gesoðian mage[7],
licge he[5] ǽgylde.

49. Gif hwá hadbryce gewyrce, gebete þæt be ðæs[3] hades mæðe,
swa be were swa be wite swa be lahslite swa be ealre are.

50. Be æwbryce.

Gif hwa æwbryce gewyrce, gebete þæt be ðam þe seo dæd sy.

§ 1. Yfel æwbryce bið þæt eawfeste m[a]n[8] wið emtige[hine][9]
forlicge, 7 mycele wyrse wið oðres æwe oððe wið gehadode.

51. Be siblegere.

Gyf hwa sibleger gewyrce, gebete þæt be sibbe mæðe, swa
be were swa be wite swa be ealra æhta.

---

[1] *twybete* G, A, Ld.　　　　[2] Om. G, A; written above the line in B.
[3] Om. G, A.　　[4] *gerihta* G, A, Ld.　　　[5] Om. G, A, Ld.
[6] *alæte* G, A, Ld.　　[7] *þ. gesoðige* G, A, Ld.　　[8] G, A, Ld; *men* B.
[9] Om. G, A, Ld; written above the line in 16th cent. in B.

47[1]. If anyone openly causes a breach of the fast of Lent by fighting or by intercourse with women or by robbery or by any great misdeed, he shall pay double compensation[2], in accordance with the nature of the offence, just as he must do during a high festival.

§ 1. And if anyone denies [the charge], he shall clear himself by the triple process of exculpation.

48[1]. If anyone refuses to render ecclesiastical dues.

If anyone resists by force the payment of ecclesiastical dues, he shall pay *lahslit* in a Danish district, and the full fine[2] in an English one, or he shall clear himself: he shall select 11 men and shall himself make a twelfth.

§ 1[1]. If he wounds anyone, he shall make amends for doing so, and shall pay the full fine to the lord and redeem his hands[2] from the bishop or lose them.

§ 2[1]. If he kills a man, he shall be outlawed, and he shall be pursued with hostility[2] by all those who wish to promote law and order.

§ 3[1]. If he so acts as to bring about his own death by setting himself against the law, no compensation shall be paid for him, if this can be proved.

49. If anyone injures one of the clergy[1], he shall make amends according to the rank of the person injured, either by the payment of [his] wergeld or a fine or *lahslit*, or by the forfeiture of all his property.

50. Concerning adultery.

If anyone commits adultery[1], he shall make amends according to the nature of the offence.

§ 1. It is wicked adultery for a pious man to commit fornication with an unmarried woman, and much worse [for him to do so] with the wife of another man or with any woman who has taken religious vows.

51[1]. Concerning incest.

If anyone commits incest, he shall make amends according to the degree of relationship [between them], either by the payment of wergeld or of a fine, or by the forfeiture of all his possessions.

§ 1. Ne byð na gelic þæt man wið swustor gehæme 7 þes þe[1] hit bið[2] feor sibbe.

52. Be wydewan.

Gyf hwa wuduwan nydnæme, gebete þæt be his[3] were.

§ 1. Mæden.

Gyf hwa mæden nydnæme, gebete þæt be his[3] were.

53. Ðæt nan wif heo ne forlicgge.

Gyf be cwicum ceorle wif hig be oðrum were forlicge, 7 hit open wyrðe, gewyrðe heo to woruldsceame syððan hyre sylfre, 7 hæbbe se rihtwere eall þæt heo age[4], 7 heo ðonne[3] ðolie ægðer ge nosu ge ða earan[5].

§ 1. And gyf hit tihtla beo 7 lad forbersta, ðonne wealde se[3] bisceop 7 stiðlice deme.

54. Gyf wiffæst wer[6] hine forlicge be his agenre wylne, ðolie ðære 7 bete for hine sylfne wiþ Godd[7] [7][8] wið men.

§ 1. And se ðe habbe rihtwif 7 eac cefese, ne do him nan preost nan ðære rihte[9] ðe man Cristenum men don sceal, ær he geswice 7 swa deope gebete swa him se[3] bisceop tæce, 7 æfre swilces geswice.

55. Ælðeodige men, gif hig heora hemed rihtan nellað, [driue hi man of][10] lande mid heora æhtan 7 on[3] synnan gewitan.

56. Open morð.

Gif open morð weorðe ðæt man amyrred[11] sy, agyue man magum[12] [þone banan][10].

§ 1. 7 gif hit tihtle sy 7 æt lade mistide, deme se bisceop.

[1] þ. þ. om. G, A, Ld.   [2] wære G, A, Ld.   [3] Om. G, A, Ld.
[4] ahte G, A, Ld.   [5] þolige nasa (-e) 7 earena G, A.
[6] G, A, Ld; were B.
[7] w. G. G, A, Ld; added in the margin in 16th cent. in B.
[8] G, A, Ld; om. B.   [9] þæra (þara, ðara) gerihta G, A, Ld.
[10] Written in the margin in 16th cent. in B; om. G, A, Ld.
[11] amyrdred (-drede) A, Ld.   [12] þam (þara, ðara), m. G, A, Ld.

§ 1. The cases are not alike if incest is committed with a sister or with a distant relation.

52[1]. Concerning widows.

If anyone does violence to a widow, he shall make amends by the payment of his wergeld.

§ 1. Maidens.

If anyone does violence to a maiden he shall make amends by the payment of his wergeld.

53. No woman shall commit adultery.

If, while her husband is still alive, a woman commits adultery with another man and it is discovered, she shall bring disgrace upon herself, and her lawful husband shall have all that she possesses, and she shall then lose both her nose and her ears.

§ 1. And if a charge is brought and the attempt to refute it fails, the decision shall then rest with the bishop[1], and his judgment shall be strict.

54[1]. If a married man commits adultery with his own slave, he shall lose her and make amends for himself both to God and to men.

§ 1[1]. And if anyone has a lawful wife and also a concubine, no priest shall perform for him any of the offices which must be performed for a Christian man, until he desists and makes amends as thoroughly as the bishop shall direct him, and ever afterwards desists from such [evildoing].

55[1]. Foreigners, if they will not regularise their unions, shall be driven from the land with their possessions, and shall depart in sin.

56. Murder which is discovered.

If anyone dies by violence and it becomes evident that it is a case of murder[1], the murderer shall be given up to the kinsmen [of the slain man].

§ 1. And if the accusation[1] is brought and the attempt [of the accused] to clear himself fails, the bishop[2] shall pronounce judgment.

57. Lafordes syrwunge.

Gyf hwa embe kinincg syrwe oððe ymbe[1] his[1] hlaford, sy
he his feores scyldig 7 ealles ðæs ðe he age, buton he ga to
ðryfealdan ordale [7 þær clæne wyrþ][2].

58. Be borhbryce.

Gif hwa kynincges borh abrece, gebete þæt mid v pundum.

§ 1. Gyf hwa arcebisceopes borh brece oððe æðelinges,
gebete þæt mid ðrym pundum.

§ 2. Gyf hwa leodbisceopes oððe ealdormannes borh[3] abrece,
gebete[4] mid twam pundum.

59. Be ðam þe on cynincges hirde feohteð.

Gyf hwa on kynincges hirede gefeohte, ðolie ðæs liues, buton
him se kynincg geárian wylle.

60. Be ðam þæt man oðerne bewepnað.

Gyf man æt unlagum man bewepnie, forgylde hine be his[1]
healsfange, 7 gyf man hine gebinde, forgildon hine[5] be
healfan were.

61. Griðbryce.

Gyf hwa on fyrde griðbryce fulwyrce, ðolie liues oððon
weregyldes.

§ 1. Gyf he samwyrce[6], bete be ðam ðe seo dæd sy[7].

62. Hamsocne.

Gyf hwa hamsocne gewyrce, gebete ðæt mid v pundum
ðam kynincge on Engla lage[8], [7 on Dena][9] lage swa hit ær
stod.

§ 1. 7 gyf hine man ðær afylle[10], licge ægylde.

63. Reaflac.

Gyf hwa reaflac gewyrce, agyue 7 forgylde 7 beo his weres
scyldig wið ðone kinincg[11].

---

[1] Om. G, A, Ld.   [2] Written in the margin in 16th cent. in B;
om. G, A, Ld.   [3] burg A.   [4] g. þæt G, A, Ld.
[5] forgilde be G, A, Ld.   [6] ran wyrce Ld.   [7] G adds ·N·.
[8] 7 on Cent æt hamsocne v þam cingce 7 þreo þam arcebisceope G.
[9] Written above the line in 16th cent. in B.   [10] alecge A, Ld.
[11] oððe wið þone þe his socne age G.

57[1]. Of plotting against a lord.

If anyone plots against the king or against his own lord, he shall forfeit his life and all that he possesses, unless he goes to the triple ordeal and there proves himself innocent.

58[1]. Concerning the violation of protection.

If anyone violates the king's protection, he shall pay £5 as compensation.

§ 1. If anyone violates the protection of an archbishop or of a member of the royal family[1], he shall pay £3 as compensation.

§ 2. If anyone violates the protection of the bishop of a diocese or of an ealdorman, he shall pay £2 as compensation.

59[1]. Concerning those who fight at the king's Court.

If anyone fights at the king's Court[2], he shall lose his life, unless the king is willing to pardon him.

60. Concerning the case of one man disarming another.

If one man unjustly disarms another, he shall compensate him[1] by the payment of a sum equivalent to his *healsfang*, and if he binds him[2], he shall compensate him by the payment of a sum equivalent to half his wergeld.

61. Breach of the peace.

If anyone is guilty of a capital deed of violence[1] while serving in the army, he shall lose his life or his wergeld.

§ 1. If he is guilty of a minor deed of violence[1], he shall make amends according to the nature of the deed.

62[1]. Attacks upon men's houses.

If a man makes forcible entry into another man's house, he shall pay £5 to the king as compensation for so doing in districts under English law[2], and in the Danelaw the amount fixed by existing regulations.

§ 1[1]. And if he is slain in such a case, no compensation shall be paid for his death.

63. Robbery.

If anyone is guilty of robbery, he shall restore [the stolen goods], and pay the injured man as much again[1], and forfeit his wergeld to the king[2].

64. Husbryce.

Husbryce 7 bærnet 7 open ðyfð 7 æbere morþ 7 hlafordswice æfter woroldlage is botleas.

65. Burhbote.

Gyf hwa buruhbote oððe brygcebote[1] oððe fyrdfare forsitte, gebete mid hundtwentigum[2] scill' ðam kyncge on Engle lage, 7 on Dena lage swa hit ær stod, oððe geladige hine, (7)[3] namige man him xiiii 7 begyte xi[4].

§ 1. To cyricbote sceal eall[5] folc fylstan mid rihte.

66. Be Godes flyman.

Gyf hwa Godes flyman hæbbe on unriht, agyfe hine mid[6] rihte 7 forgylde ðam ðe hit gebyrige, 7 gylde ðam kynincge[7] be[8] wergilde.

§ 1. Gyf hwa amansodne[9] man oððon utlagene hæbbe 7 healde, plihte him sylfum 7 ealre his are.

67. Gyf hwa wille georne fram unrihte to rihte gecyrran[10], mildsige man him[11] for Godes ege, swa man betst mæge[12], ðam men swyðe georne.

68. And uton don, swa us ðearf is, helpan æfre[13] ðam raðost ðe helpes behofoð[14]; [þonne nime[15] we þæs lean þær us leofast byð][16].

§ 1. Be unstrangan.

Forðam a man sceal ðam unstrangan men for Godes lufan 7 for[11] his[3] ege liðelicor deman 7 scrifan ðonne ðam strangan;

§ 1a. forðamðe we magon witan fulgeorne, þæt se unmaga 7 se mage ne mæg[17] gelice[18] mycele[19] byrðene aberan[20], ne se unhala ðam halan gelice.

---

[1] The earlier reading bryceb. has been altered later to brygceb. in B.
[2] cxx G; hundtwe(l)ftigum A, Ld.   [3] Om. G, A.
[4] þærtó added in the margin in 16th cent. in B; om. G, A, Ld.
[5] G, A, Ld; written in the margin in 16th cent. in B.   [6] to G, A, Ld.
[7] cyninge ·N· A.   [8] be his w. G.
[9] Altered later to amansumodne in B.
[10] gecirran (-y-) eft to r. G, A, Ld.   [11] Om. G, A, Ld.
[12] m. ðam men B, with ð. m. crossed out.   [13] áá G, A, Ld.
[14] h. betst (best) behofað (be ofað A) G A Ld.   [15] lese A, Ld.
[16] G, A, Ld; om. B.
[17] Forþampe ne mæg se unmaga þam magan, w. witon fullgeorne. gelice G; f. n. m., we witan f., se u. þ. m. A, Ld.
[18] The rest of the sentence is missing in both A, Ld.   [19] Om. G.
[20] ahebban G.

64[1]. Assaults upon houses.

According to secular law assaults upon houses[2], arson[3], theft which cannot be disproved, murder which cannot be denied and treachery towards a man's lord[4] are crimes for which no compensation can be paid[5].

65. The repair of fortifications.

If anyone neglects the repair of fortifications or of bridges or military service[1], he shall pay 120 shillings as compensation to the king in districts under English law, and in the Danelaw the amount fixed by existing regulations; or he shall clear himself—[the court] shall nominate 14 compurgators for him and he shall obtain the support of 11 of them.

§ 1. The whole nation, in accordance with the law, shall assist in the repair of churches[1].

66. Concerning excommunicated persons.

If anyone unlawfully maintains an excommunicated person, he shall deliver him up in accordance with the law, and pay compensation to him to whom it belongs, and to the king a sum equivalent to his wergeld.

§ 1[1]. If anyone keeps and maintains an excommunicated man or an outlaw, it shall be at the risk of losing his life and all his property.

67. If anyone zealously desires to turn from lawlessness to observance of the law, as great mercy as possible shall be shown to him, with the utmost readiness, through the fear of God.

68[1]. And let us, as our duty is, ever render help with the utmost speed to those who require help; [then shall we receive the reward for so doing where we most desire it].

§ 1[1]. Concerning the weak.

For the fear of God and out of reverence to him, greater leniency shall always be shown in passing judgment and in imposing penance upon the weak than [in doing so] upon the strong.

§ 1a. Because we may know full well that the weak and the strong cannot bear an equally heavy burden, nor can the sick man bear one equal to that borne by him who is sound.

§ 1*b*. 7 þi we sculon medemian 7 gescadelice todælan ylde 7 geogoðe, [welige 7 wædle, frige 7 þeowe]¹, hale 7 unhale.

§ 1*c*. And æðer man sceal, ge on godcundan scriftum ge on woruldcundan dome, ðas ðincg tosceadan.

§ 2. Eac on gemeanre² dæde ðonne man bið nydwyrhta, ðonne bið se man³ ðe bet wyrðe gebeorges, ðe he for neode dyde þæt þæt he dyde.

§ 3. And gyf hwa ungewealdes hwæt⁴ gedeð, ne byð þæt eallunga⁵ gelíc ðam⁶ ðe hit gewealdes deð⁷.

69. Ðis is ðonne se lihtincg ðe ic wylle eallon folce gebeorgan, ðe hig ær ðyson mid gedrehte wæron ealles to swyðe.

§ 1. Ðæt is ðonne ærost, þæt ic bebeode eallum minan gerefan þæt hig on minon agenan rihtlice⁸ tilian 7 me mid ðam feormian, 7 þæt him nan man ne ðearf to feormfultume nan ðincg syllan, butan he sylf wille.

§ 2. And gyf hwá æfter ðam⁴ wite crauian [wille]⁹, beo he his weres scyldig wið ðone cyningc.

70. Be hergeate.

Gyf of ðysum life man¹⁰ gewíte cwydeleas, sy hit ðurh his gymelyste, sy hyt ðurh færlicne deaþ, ðonne ne teo se laford nan mare on his æhte butan his rihtan heregeate.

§ 1. Ac beo be his dihte seo æht gescyft swyðe rihte wife 7 cildan 7 neahmagon, ælcon be ðære mæðe ðe him to gebyrige.

71. And beon ða herigeata swa gefundene¹¹ swa hit mæðlic sy.

71*a*. Eorles.

Eorles swa ðærto byrie, þæt syndon eahta hors, IIII gesadelode 7 IIII unsadolede, 7 IIII helmas 7 IIII byrnan 7 VIII spera 7 swa¹² fela scylda 7 IIII swyrd 7 twa hund mancus goldes.

---

¹ *w.* 7 *w. f.* 7 *þ.* written in 16th cent. on an erasure in B; *welan* 7 *w. freot* 7 *þeowet* (-*æt*) G, A, Ld.
² *mænigre* (*man.*) G, A; *manige* Ld.   ³ Om. G, A.   ⁴ Om. A, Ld.
⁵ *eallumga* B; -*unga na* G; *eallum na* A, Ld.   ⁶ Om. G, A, Ld.
⁷ *gewurþe* G; *geded* A, Ld.   ⁸ *a. me r.* G.
⁹ Om. B; *crafige* G, A, Ld.   ¹⁰ *And gif hwa cw.* &c. G, A, Ld.
¹¹ *swa fundene* G; om. A, Ld.   ¹² *callswa* G, A, Ld.

§ 1*b*. And therefore we must make due allowance and carefully distinguish between age and youth, wealth and poverty, freemen and slaves, the sound and the sick.

§ 1*c*. And discrimination with regard to these circumstances must be shown both in [imposing] ecclesiastical amends and in [passing] secular judgment.

§ 2. Likewise, in many cases of evil-doing, when a man is an involuntary agent, he is more entitled to clemency because he acted as he did from compulsion.

§ 3. And if anyone does anything unintentionally, the case is entirely different from that of one who acts deliberately.

69. Now this is the mitigation by means of which I desire to protect the general public in cases where, until now, they have been far too greatly oppressed.

§ 1[1]. The first provision is: I command all my reeves to provide for me in accordance with the law from my own property and support me thereby, and [declare] that no man need give them anything as purveyance, unless he himself is willing to do so.

§ 2[1]. And if anyone [of my reeves] shall demand[2] a fine [in such a case], he shall forfeit his wergeld to the king.

70. Concerning heriots[1].

If a man departs from this life intestate, whether through negligence or through sudden death, his lord shall take no more from his property than his legal heriot.

§ 1. But, according to his direction, the property shall be very strictly divided among his wife and children and near kinsmen, each according to the share which belongs to him.

71. Heriots shall be fixed with due regard to the rank of the person for whom they are paid.

71*a*. An earl's heriot.

The heriot of an earl, as is fitting, shall be eight horses, four saddled and four unsaddled, and four helmets and four byrnies and eight spears and as many shields and four swords and 200 mancuses of gold.

§ 1. Kyncges ðeines.

And syððan kyncges ðægnes[1] heregeata[2] ðe him nyxste syndon—IIII hors, II gesadelode 7 twa ungesadelode, 7 II swyrd 7 IIII spera 7 ealswa[3] feola scylda 7 helm 7 byrnan 7 fiftig mancus goldes.

§ 2. Oðres ðeines.

And medemra ðegen—hors 7 his gerædan 7 his wepna oððe his healsfang on Westsæxan, 7 on Myrcen II pund, 7 on Eastengle II pund.

§ 3. And kyncges ðegnes heregeata inne mid Denum ðe his socne hæbbe—IIII pund.

§ 4. 7 gyf he to ðam kyncge furðor cyððe hæbbe—II hors, an gesadelod 7 oðer ungesadolod, 7 an swyrd 7 II spera 7 twegen scyldas 7 fiftig mancus goldes.

§ 5. 7 se ðe læsse habbe 7[4] læsse maga sy—II pund.

72. And ðær se bunda sæt uncwyd [his deig][5] 7 unbecrafod, sitte þæt wif 7 ða cild [on þam ylcan][6] unbesacen.

§ 1. And gyf se bunda, ær he dead wære, wære beclypad, ðonne andwyrde ða yrfnumen swa he sylf sceolde, ðeah he lif hæfde.

73. Be wydewan, þæt heo sitte XII monðas ceorlæs.

And sitte ælc wuduwe werleas twelf monað 7[7] ceose heo[7] syððan þæt heo sylf wille.

73a. 7 gyf heo ðonne[7] binnon ðæs[7] geares fæce wer geceose, ðonne ðolie heo ðære morgengeafe 7 ealre [þære][8] æhtan ðe he[o[9] þurh þone[7] ærran were heafde, 7 fon þa nyxtan frynd to þam lande[10] 7 to þam æhte[11] þæt heo ær hæfde.

§ 1. 7 si he his] weres scyldig wið ðone kyning oððe wið ðone ðe he hit[12] geunnen hæbbe.

---

[1] þegnas G; þegenas A.   [2] Om. G, A.   [3] swa G, A, Ld.
[4] l. h. 7 om. G, A.
[5] Om. G, A, Ld; written in the margin in 16th cent. in B.
[6] G, A, Ld; om. B.   [7] Om. G, A, Ld.
[8] Written above in 16th cent. in B.
[9] o þurh…he his. Written in the margin in 16th cent. in B.
[10] landan G.   [11] þan æhtan (ch.) G, A, Ld.   [12] his socne G.

§ 1. The heriot of a king's thegn.

And further, the heriots of king's thegns who stand in immediate relation to him[1] shall be four horses, two saddled and two unsaddled, and two swords and four spears and as many shields and helmets and byrnies and 50 mancuses of gold.

§ 2. The heriot of another thegn.

And the heriot of ordinary[1] thegns shall be a horse and its trappings and his weapons or his *healsfang* in Wessex, and in Mercia £2, and in East Anglia £2.

§ 3. And among the Danes the heriot of a king's thegn who possesses rights of jurisdiction shall be £4.

§ 4. And if he stands in a more intimate relationship to the king[1], it shall be two horses, one saddled and the other unsaddled, and one sword and two spears and two shields and 50 mancuses of gold.

§ 5. And for the man who is inferior in wealth[1] and position the heriot shall be £2.

72[1]. And when a householder has dwelt all his time free from claims and charges, his wife and children shall dwell [on the same property] unmolested by litigation.

§ 1. And if the householder had been cited before his death, then his heirs shall answer the charge, as he himself would have done, had he been alive.

73[1]. Concerning widows, that they remain for a year without a husband.

And every widow shall remain twelve months without a husband, and she shall afterwards choose what she herself desires.

73*a*[1]. And if then, within the space of the year, she chooses a husband, she shall lose her morning-gift and all the property which she had from her first husband, and his nearest relatives shall take the land and the property which she had held.

§ 1. And he (the second husband) shall forfeit his wergeld to the king or to the lord to whom it has been granted.

§ 2. 7 ðeah heo neadnumen wyrðe, ðolie ðæra æhta, buton heo fram ðam ceorle wille eft ham ongean 7 næfre eft his [no]¹ wyrðe.

§ 3. And ne hadige man næfre² wuduwan to hrædlice.

§ 4. 7 gelæste ælc wuduwe ða heregeata binnon twelf monðum, buton hyre ær to onhagie, witeleas.

74. And ne nyde³ man næfre⁴ naðor ne wif ne mæden to ðam þe hire sylfre mislicige, ne wið sceatte ne sylle, buton he hwæt agenes ðances gyfan wylle.

75. Be ðam þæt man his spere to oðres mannes dure sette.
And ic læte riht⁵, ðeah hwá his agen⁴ spere sette to oðres mannes huses duru 7 he ðiderin ærende hæbbe, oððon gyf mon oðer wépn gedreohlice lecge ðær [hi]⁶ stille mihton beon, gyf hi moston, 7 hwilc man ðonne þæt wepn gelæcce 7 he⁴ hwylcne hearm ðærmid gewyrce, ðonne is⁷ þæt riht, þæt se ðe ðonne⁸ hearm geworhte, þæt se ðone hearm eac⁹ gebete.

§ 1. And se ðe þæt wepn age, hine geladige, gyf he durre, ðæt hit næfre næs naðer ne his gewill ne his geweald ne his ræd ne his gewitnes; ðonne is þæt Godes riht, þæt he¹⁰ beo clæne.

§ 2. And wite se oðer þe þæt weorc geworhte, þæt he hit bete, swa swa lagu tæce¹¹.

76. Be forstolene æhta.
Gyf hwa¹² forstolen ðinge ham to his coton bringe 7 he arefned¹³ wyrðe, riht is⁷ þæt he hæbbe þæt he æftereode.

§ 1. 7 buton hit under ðæs wifes cæglocan gebroht wære, sy heo clæne.

¹ Written above in 16th cent. in B; *ne* G, A, Ld.   ² *æfre* G, A.
³ *nime* A.   ⁴ Om. G, A, Ld.
⁵ *nelle* B, with *l. r.* written above it in 16th cent.; *ic l. r.* G; *ic wille* A, Ld.
⁶ Written in the margin in 16th cent. B.   ⁷ *his* B.   ⁸ *þone* G, Ld.
⁹ Om. G.   ¹⁰ *heo* B.   ¹¹ *lagan* (later changed to *laga*) *tæcean* G.
¹² *hwylc* (*hwilc*) *man* G, A, Ld.
¹³ *arasod* G, A, Ld; Liebermann suggests the emendation *arefsed* for B.

§ 2[1]. And although she has been married by force, she shall lose her possessions, unless she is willing to leave the man and return home and never afterwards be his.

§ 3. And no widow shall be too hastily consecrated as a nun.

§ 4. And every widow shall pay the heriots within twelve months without incurring a fine, if it has not been convenient for her to pay earlier.

74[1]. And no woman or maiden shall ever be forced to marry a man whom she dislikes, nor shall she be given for money, except the suitor desires of his own freewill to give something.

75. Concerning the case of a man setting his spear at another man's door.
And I hold it right that if anyone sets his spear at the door of another man's house, he himself having an errand inside, or if anyone carefully lays any other weapons in a place where they might remain quietly, if they were allowed to, and if anyone then seizes the weapon and works mischief with it, the law shall be, that he who wrought the mischief shall likewise pay compensation for it.

§ 1. And he who owns the weapon shall clear himself, if he dare, asserting that the mischief was done without his desire or authority or advice or cognisance; then according to the law of God he shall be clear [of any charge of complicity].

§ 2. And the other who wrought the mischief shall see to it that he pays compensation for it, according as the law directs.

76[1]. Concerning stolen goods.
If anyone carries stolen goods home to his cottage and is detected[2], the law is that he (the owner) shall have what he has tracked.

§ 1[1]. And unless the goods had been put under the wife's lock and key, she shall be clear [of any charge of complicity].

§ 1a. Ac ðara cægan heo sceal weardian, þæt is hire heddernes cæge[1] 7 hyre cyste cæge[2] [7 hire tægan][3]; gyf hit under ðyssa ænigum gebroht byð, ðone[4] bið heo scyldig.

§ 1b. And ne mæg nan wif hire bundan forbeodan þæt he ne mote into his cotan gelegian[5] þæt þæt he wille.

§ 2. Hit wæs ær ðysson þæt þæt cild ðe læg on ðam[6] cradole, þeah hit næfre metes ne abite, þæt ða gytseras lætan ealswa[7] scyldigne 7 hit gewittig wære.

§ 3. Ac ic hit forbeode heonon forð eornostlice 7 eac swyðe manega[8] ðincg[2] ðe Gode syndon swyðe[9] laðe.

77. Be ðam þe flihð fram his laforde.

And ðe man ðe fleo[10] fram his hlaforde oððe fram his geferan for his yrhðe, sy hit on scypfyrde, sy hit on landfyrde, ðolie he[2] ealles ðæs ðe he age 7 his agenes feores, 7 fo se hlaford to ðam æhton 7 to his lande ðe he him ær sealde. [§ 1. 7 gyf he bocland hæbbe, ga þæt þam cingce to handa.][11]

78. Be ðam ðe toforan his laforde fealleð.

And se man ðe on fyrdunge[12] ætforan his hlaforde fealle, sy hit innon lande, sy hit ut[2] of lande, beon ða heregeata forgyfene, 7 fon ða yrfenuman to lande 7 to æhte 7 scyften hit swiðe rihte.

79. And se ðe land gewerod hæbbe on scypfyrde 7 on landfyrde[13] be[14] scire gewitnysse[15], habbe he unbesaken on dæge 7 æfter dæge to syllanne 7 to gyfane ðam ðe him leofost sy.

80. Be huntnaðe.

And ic wylle þæt ælc man sy his huntnoðes wyrðe on wuda 7 on felda on his agenan.

§ 1. 7 forgá ælc man minne huntnoð lochwar ic hit gefriðod wille habban [on minon agenan][16], be fullan wite.

---

[1] h. hordern 7 G, A, Ld.　　　　　　　　　[2] Om. G, A, Ld.
[3] Written in the margin in 16th cent. in B; 7 hyre tege (tyge) G, A; tyge Ld, with in the margin al. teah.
[4] Cf. cap. 25; þonne G, A, Ld.
[5] Altered later to gelogian which is also G's reading; gelaðyan A.
[6] Om. G, A.　　　　　　　　　　[7] efen G, A, Ld.
[8] 7 swylce (swilce) manege (manage, manige) G, A, Ld.
[9] Om. A, Ld.　　　　　　　　　[10] ætfleo G, A; ·flea Ld.
[11] G, A, Ld; om. B.　　　　　　　[12] on þam f. G, A; æt ð. f. Ld.
[13] o. sc. 7 on l. Only in B.　　　　[14] on G.
[15] G adds: 7 se nolde oððe ne mihte þe hit ær ahte.
[16] on m. ag. written above in 16th cent. in B; om. G, A, Ld.

§ 1*a*. But it is her duty to guard the keys of the following— her storeroom and her chest and her cupboard[1]. If the goods have been put in any of these, she shall be held guilty.

§ 1*b*[1]. But no wife can forbid her husband to deposit anything that he desires in his cottage.

§ 2[1]. It has been the custom up till now for grasping persons to treat a child which lay in the cradle, even though it had never tasted food, as being as guilty as though it were fully intelligent.

§ 3. But I strictly forbid such a thing henceforth, and likewise very many things which are hateful to God.

77[1]. Concerning the man who deserts his lord.
And the man who, through cowardice, deserts his lord or his comrades on an expedition, either by sea or by land[2], shall lose all that he possesses and his own life, and the lord shall take back the property and the land which he had given him.

[§ 1[1]. And if he has land held by title-deed it shall pass into the king's hands.]

78. Concerning the man who falls before his lord.
And the heriots of the man who falls before his lord during a campaign, whether within the country or abroad[1], shall be remitted, and the heirs shall succeed to his land and his property and make a very just division of the same.

79. And he who, with the cognisance of the shire, has performed the services demanded from a landowner[1] on expeditions either by sea or by land shall hold [his land] unmolested by litigation during his life, and at his death shall have the right of disposing of it or giving it to whomsoever he prefers.

80. Concerning hunting.
And it is my will that every man shall be entitled to hunt in the woods and fields on his own property.

§ 1. But everyone, under pain of incurring the full penalty, shall avoid hunting on my preserves, wherever they may be[1].

81. 7 dryncelean 7 hlafordes rihtgyfu stande æfre unawended.

82. And ic wille þæt ælc man beo griðes wyrðe to gemote 7 fram gemote, buton he æbere ðeof beo.

83. Se ðe ðas lage wyrde ðe se kyninge hæfð nu ða[1] eallum mannum forgyfen, seo he Denisc sy he[2] Engli[s]c[3], beo he his weres scyldig wið ðone kyninge.

   § 1. And gyf he hit eft wyrde, gylde twywa his were.

   § 2. And gyf he ðonne swa dyrstig sy þæt he hi[4] ðridde siðe abrece[5], ðolige ealles ðæs ðe he age.

84. Nu bidde ic georne 7 on Godes naman beode manna gehwylcne, þæt he inweardre[6] heortan gebuga to his Drihtene, 7 oft 7 gelome smeage[7] hwæt him sy to donne 7 hwæt to forganne.

   § 1. Eallum us is mycel ðearf þæt we God lufian 7 Godes lage fylian[8] 7 godcundan lareowan[9] geor[n]lice[10] hyran[11].

   § 1a. Forðam hig us sceolan lædan forð æt ðam dome, ðonne God demeð manna gewilcum be ærran gehwyrhtum.

   § 2. And geselig byð se hyrde ðe ðonne ða heorde into Godes rice 7 to heofenlicre myrðe bliðe mot lædan for ærran[12] gewyrhtan.

   § 2a. And wel ðære heorde ðe gefolgað ðam hyrde ðe hig deoflum ætwenað 7 Gode hig gestreonað.

   § 3. Uton ðonne ealle anmodre heortan georne urum Drihtene cweman mid rihte 7 heononforð mid rihte[13] symble scyldan us georne wið ðone hatan bryne ðe weallað on helle.

   § 4. And do nu eac lareowas 7 godcunde bydelas swa swa riht is 7 ealra manna ðearf is: bodian gelome godcunde ðearfe.

   § 4a. And ælc ðe gescead wite, hlyste him georne 7 godcunde lare gewha on geðance healde swyðe fæste him sylfum to ðearfe.

---

[1] Om. A, Ld.   [2] D. oððe E. G.   [3] Englic B.
[4] hit G; om. A, Ld.   [5] wyrde G, A, Ld.   [6] inweardlice A, Ld.
[7] sm. swyðe (swiðe) georne G, A, Ld.   [8] fylgean G, A, Ld.
[9] lar. 7 g. B.   [10] georl. B.   [11] A repeats: 7 Godes lage fylgean.
[12] G, A; his ærran B.   [13] m. r. om. G, A, Ld.

81¹. And there shall never be any interference with bargains successfully concluded² or with the legal gifts made by a lord.

82. And it is my will that every man shall be entitled to protection in going to and from assemblies, unless he be a notorious thief.

83¹. He who violates the law which the king has now granted to all men, whether he be a Dane or an Englishman, shall forfeit his wergeld to the king.

§ 1. And if he violates it again, he shall pay his wergeld twice over.

§ 2. And if he is so presumptuous as to break it a third time, he shall lose all that he possesses.

84¹. Now I earnestly entreat all men and command them, in the name of God, to submit in their inmost hearts to their lord, and often and frequently consider what they ought to do and what they ought to forgo.

§ 1. There is great need for us all to love God and to follow God's law, and zealously to obey our spiritual teachers.

§ 1a. For it is their duty to lead us forth to the judgment where God shall judge each man according to the works which he has wrought.

§ 2¹. And blessed is the shepherd who then may gladly lead his flock into the kingdom of God and to the joy of Heaven, because of the works which they have wrought.

§ 2a. And well is it for the flock which follows the shepherd who delivers them from devils and wins them for God.

§ 3¹. Let us all then, with humble heart, be zealous in pleasing our Lord aright, and henceforth, by doing what is right, always zealously guard ourselves from 'the hot fire which surges in hell.

§ 4¹. And likewise teachers and spiritual messengers shall do what is right and for the well-being of all men: they shall frequently inculcate spiritual duties.

§ 4a. And everyone who has discernment shall earnestly give heed to them, and everyone for his own well-being shall keep fast in his mind their spiritual instruction.

§ 4*b*. And[1] manna gehwylc to weorðunga his Drihtene do to gode þæt[2] he mæge wordes 7 weorces[3] 7 dæde[4] glædlice æfre; ðonne byð us eallum God[5] þe gearwera.

§ 5. A[a][6]sy Godes nama ecelice gebletsod, 7 lof him 7 wuldor 7 wyrðmynt æfre[7] to worulde. Amen[8].

§ 6. God ælmihtig us eallum gemiltsie swa his willa sy[9]. Amen.

---

[1] 7 *á* G; *and ha* A.   [2] *þæs þe* A, Ld.
[3] 7 *w.* om. G, A, Ld.   [4] 7 *d.* 7 B.
[5] *Godes milts (miltsa)* G, A, Ld.   [6] *á* G, A; *aá* Ld; *ac* B.
[7] *symle (symble)* æ. G, A, Ld.   [8] Om. G, A, Ld.
[9] *s. his milda w. sig* 7 *gehealde us æfre on ecnesse! Si hit swa!* G.

§ 4*b*. And every man, for the honour of his Lord, shall always gladly do his utmost by word and by work and by deed[1] for the furtherance of what is good; then shall God be the more ready [to help us].

§ 5[1]. May the name of God be eternally blessed, and to Him be praise and glory and honour for ever and ever. Amen.

§ 6. God Almighty have mercy upon us all, as His will may be. Amen.